Letters from World War II

Grant's Story

Grant Henderson was born in on December 21, 1924 to parents of modest means. He was from a family of three boys. Grant being the oldest next was Doug who enlisted in the air force and his youngest brother Peter was in high school at this time. Grant, a highly intelligent man, lived all his life in Edmonton. His mother was a mere 19 years older than him and his father was a World War 1 vet who had been injured in action.

These letters were written during the time that he was away from North America until his return, June of 1944 till November of 1945. The majority of these letters were all written to his mother with a few written to his two younger brothers.

Grant Henderson is my father. Until recently I was not aware of the letters home although I have all my life been familiar with his serving in World War II. . He has related amusing stories and the war has left an undeniable mark on his life. He has always had what I thought were unreasonable fears from his experiences in the war. These fears are not relayed in his letters to his mother.

I will introduce some of the people that Grant talks about in his letter. Grant was a volunteer and refers to those who were drafted as zombies. He refers to Ma. Ma was Grant's grandmother. Two other people he talks about are Junior and Bud. They are actually his uncles, Ma's sons that were very close in age to Grant.

In one of his letters, he talks about the opportunity for university that was offered to veterans of the Second World

War. Although he seems excited about the opportunity at the time, Grant never went to university. The firm that he had been employed with prior to the war held his job and offered it to him on his return.

The statements in these letters may seem that they are made by someone who is wise beyond his years and yet there are also comments made that bring you back to the fact that Grant was nineteen and twenty when these letters were written.

Acknowledgements

I would like to thank my mother Rose, for giving me this idea. I would also like to thank Ruth, for proofing the many pages of typing and Chris for writing the conclusion. Most of all I would like to thank my father Grant for sharing these letters with me and allowing me to create this book.

Contents

Dear Mom:-

Well, lady, at long last I can settle down and write. As you know by my wire (I hope) I got here safe and sound. It was a quiet journey and nothing of any importance happened. I wasn't seasick or anything like that. On board, however, I bought 500 cigarettes and a cigar package of Edgeworth pipe tobacco – all for 4 [illegible] so I have enough to smoke for some time to come. I also got 10 packages of razor blades and a few bars of soap so I'm fairly well fixed for a while anyway. So far our food [illegible] got pretty well fed and can buy [illegible] in the canteen so I wouldn't bother to send any food along. I am making a pay assignment of 15 days pay to you [illegible] at all. I don't think a lot of [illegible] England's beer. [illegible] Britain has it all [illegible]. I didn't touch that 20 dollar bill you and dad gave me until yesterday when I turned in my [illegible] to get changed to English money. I turned in 24 bucks and got 5 pounds [illegible] shillings which is quite a chunk of dough. [illegible] I thought was very funny [illegible]. Did you know that? Well my address is name & number, [illegible] Canadian Army, England. Would you let me know [illegible] if any, faster than ordinary mail? If it is I might as well write [illegible] letters to you on it. I'll mail another letter in a couple of days [illegible] ordinary mail so you can see what the difference is. I'm going to [illegible] [illegible] I mightn't get a chance to see him for quite some time – months probably. However I shall let him know that I'm here. (see flaps)

ARMED FORCES AIR LETTER

AIR MAIL

This letter must be posted in Armed Forces Postal channels. If posted in a Civil Post Office or pillar box, it will not be given air transmission.

TO: Mrs E.L. Henderson
7665 - 81 ave.
Edmonton Alberta
Canada

If anything is enclosed in this letter it will be sent by ordinary mail.

FROM: (Sender's full name and address)
[illegible]

Fold Here

[illegible]

July 1944

Dear Mom:

Well, lady, at long last I can settle down and write. As you know by my wire (I hope) I got here safe and sound. It was a quiet journey and nothing of any importance happened. I wasn't seasick or anything like that. On board, however, I bought 500 cigarettes and a dozen packages of Edgeworth pipe tobacco – all for 4 bucks. So I have enough to smoke for some time to come. I also got 10 packages of razor blades and a few bars of soap so I'm well fixed for a while anyway. So far as food goes we get pretty well fed and we can buy tarts etc in the canteen so I wouldn't bother to send any food along. I am making a pay assignment of 15 days pay to you – before the next few days are up. They apparently are eager for us to do so and so it is no trouble at all. I don't think a hell of a lot of England's beer. Tastes flat but they say you acquire a taste for it. Boy oh boy what a money system! No wonder there's a metal shortage, Britain has it all tied up in her coins. I didn't touch that 20 dollar bill you and dad gave me until yesterday when I turned in my wealth to get changed to English money. I turned in 24 bucks and got 5 pounds & 5 shillings roughly which is quite a chunk of dough. One thing I saw in Quebec I thought was very funny was that the French tricolor flew on all flag poles instead of the Union Jack. Did you know that? Well my address is name & Number M8827 #1 C.I.R.V. Canadian Army, England. Would you let me know if this is much if any faster than ordinary mail? If it is I might as well write most of my letters to you on it. I'll mail another letter in a couple of days via ordinary mail so you can see what the difference is. I'm going to drop a line or two to Junior right away but now that I'm here I realize that I mightn't get a chance to see him for quite some time – months probably, however I shall let him know that I'm here.

How is Doug coming along? Okay I hope. Send me his address and I'll drop him a line. Is about time I wrote to him. My friend Ed Hobson is with me no more. He is at a different place. That's the sad part about the army, you get to know a person pretty well, then one goes one way, the other the other way, oh well such is life. I can't complain, though as most of the rest of my chums are with me.

Well England is a beautiful place. Most of it, at least what I've seen looks like a big park. But like parks it's nice to visit but not to live in. England is for the English and Canada for me! But I am sure looking forward to a leave so I can look at it at my leisure. Well sweetheart, that is all for now. I'll write soon.

Loads of Love

Grant.

July 1 Saturday

Dear Mom —

Hello lady, its me again! Well how is every little thing? About the same as usual, I suppose.

I'm doing ok myself, and it finally looks as though I may get a course. This course is something that I had never thought about but I imagine its ok. It's a [illegible] week course in either [illegible] [illegible]. Don't ask me what its all about because I really don't know. [illegible] Yesterday [illegible] of us were asked if we wanted it and [illegible] [illegible]

[illegible]

ARMED FORCES AIR LETTER

AIR MAIL

This letter must be posted in Armed Forces Postal channels. If posted in a Civil Post Office or pillar box, it will not be given air transmission.

TO: Mrs C.R. Henderson
[illegible]
Edmonton, Alberta
Canada.

Fold Here

CPC 11
10. P.&S. 1443

If anything is enclosed in this letter it will be sent by ordinary mail.

FROM:
(Sender's full name and address)
[illegible]

Fold Here

[illegible]

July 1, 1944

Dear Mom:

Hello lady, it's me again! Well, how is every little thing? About the same as usual, I suppose.

I'm doing o.k. myself and it finally looks as though I may get a course. This course is something that I had never thought about but I imagine its o.k. It's a 10 week course in either infantry or Driver operator signals. Don't ask me what is all about because I really don't know however if I can get the Driver ops course there's trades pay attached to it from 25 cents to 75 cents a day. I know it has something to do with wireless code etc but that's about all. Yesterday 8 or 9 of us were asked if we wanted it and the Lieut. said we would be leaving in about a week or may 2 weeks. However I'm not counting too many chickens till I'm on the train headed south. It would be pretty soft going to a school again, wouldn't it?

Incidentally I'm living in a different place today. We moved from the depot to a unit yesterday afternoon. It was just a 2 or 3 mile walk. We are still in the same estate. I'm really in love with the country around here; in fact I hate the idea of leaving. It is a rather historic place, you know. Remember Robin Hood? He used to live in the forest I'm in now. I've seen old Friar Tucks abbey, Robin Hood's favorite tree etc. I've also been in a ballroom in the estate where all the kings for several hundred years past have danced. The "Sunken Gardens" in this place are the talk of the country. There are beautiful deer wandering about and big white swans in the brook. In the stream itself are 5 of 6 different kinds of fish.

The people are as friendly as can be but my God, what an accent!

The country in general is still not so pretty as Scotland, especially around Glasgow. Nothing could be prettier than the hills with all their heather. They say Ireland is the country where everything is so green but it couldn't be as green as the hills in Scotland. That's where I am going on my next leave.

I still haven't got any pay assigned to you but I'll get that straightened up on Monday without fail. I'm just drawing 1.40 a day darn it. I don't draw 1.50 until I've been in 6 months.

Just imagine nothing at all to do tomorrow! I am getting one of my uniforms pressed and I think I'll walk around the estate tomorrow and see as much as possible of it. For the first time since I got here I had a little time to spare so this morning I got a little bit of my washing done. In a few days I'll be completely organized with all my clothes cleaned and pressed etc.

Doug is 18 now eh? He is quite a man for his few years of life, isn't he? Not very many people have done so much as he has in such a short time.

How did Pete come along in school? Say hello for me.

I guess that all for now, lady. I'll write again on Tuesday or Wed. We get two of these forms a week so I think I'll send all my letters to you on them.

Loads of love

Grant

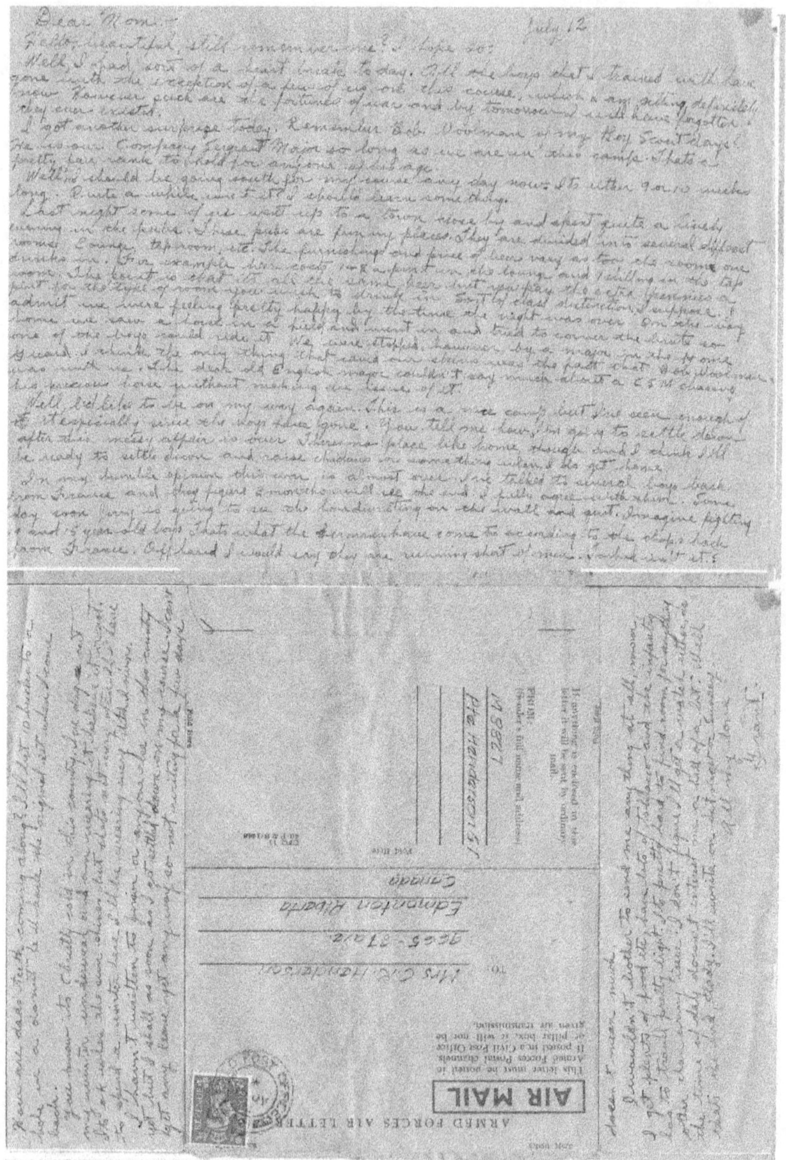

Dear Mom: — July 12

Hello beautiful, still remember me? I hope so.

Well, I had sort of a heart break today. All the boys that I trained with have gone with the exception of a few of us on this course, which I am getting definitely now. However such are the fortunes of war and by tomorrow I will have forgotten they ever existed.

I got another surprise today. Remember Bob Woolman of my Boy Scout days? He is our Company Sergeant Major so long as we are in this camp. That's a pretty big rank to hold for anyone of his age.

We should be going south for my course any day now. It's either 9 or 10 weeks long. Quite a while, isn't it? I should learn something.

Last night some of us went up to a town close by and spent quite a lively evening in the pubs. These pubs are funny places. They are divided into several different rooms, Lounge, taproom, etc. The furnishings and price of beers vary as to the rooms one drinks in. For example beer costs 1/- [illegible] a pint in the lounge and 1 shilling in the tap room. The beast is that it's all the same beer but you pay the extra pennies a pint for the type of room you wish to drink in. Sort of class distinction, I suppose. I admit we were feeling pretty happy by the time the night was over. On the way home we saw a horse in a field and went in and tried to corner the brute so one of the boys could ride it. We were stopped, however, by a major in the Home Guard. I think the only thing that saved our skins was the fact that Bob Woolman was with us. The dear old English major couldn't say much about a CSM chasing his precious horse without making an issue of it.

Well, I'd like to be on my way again. This is a nice camp but I've seen enough of it especially since the boys have gone. You tell me how I'm going to settle down after this messy affair is over. There's no place like home though and I think I'll be ready to settle down and raise chickens or something when I do get home.

In my humble opinion this war is almost over. I've talked to several boys back from France and they figure 2 months will see the end. I fully agree with them. Some day soon Jerry is going to see the handwriting on the wall and quit. Imagine fighting 14 and 15 year old boys. That's what the Germans have come to according to the chaps back from France. Offhand I would say they are running short of men. [illegible] isn't it?

How are dad's teeth coming along? I'll bet 10 bucks to a hole in a donut he'll have the original set when I come back.

You know it's Christly cold in this country. I've dug out my winter underwear and am wearing it [illegible]. It's ok when the sun shines but that's not very often. If I have to spend a winter here I'll be wearing every stitch I own.

I haven't written to [illegible] or anyone else in this country yet but I shall as soon as I get settled down on my course. I can't get any leave yet anyway so not writing for a few days doesn't mean much.

I wouldn't bother to send me anything at all, mom. I get plenty of food etc., have lots of tobacco and the infantry has to travel pretty light. It's pretty hard to find room for anything other than army issue. I don't figure I'll get a watch either, as the time of day doesn't interest me a hell of a lot. Well that's the lot, Lady. I'll write on [illegible] Sunday.

All my love

Grant

ARMED FORCES AIR LETTER

AIR MAIL

This letter must be posted in Armed Forces Postal channels. If posted in a Civil Post Office or pillar box, it will not be given air transmission.

TO: Mrs C.E. Henderson
9225-87 Ave.
Edmonton Alberta
Canada

If anything is enclosed in this letter it will be sent by ordinary mail.

FROM: (Sender's full name and address)
M58827
Pte Henderson G.T.

July 12, 1944

Dear Mom:

Hello, beautiful, still remember me? I hope so.

Well, I had sort of a heart break today. All the boys that I trained with have gone with the exception of a few o f us on this course, which I am getting definitely now. However such are the fortunes of war and by tomorrow I will have forgotten they ever existed.

I got another surprise today. Remember Bob Woolman of my Boy Scout days? He is our company Sergeant Major so long as we are in this camp. That's a pretty fair rank to hold for anyone of his age.

Last night some of us went up to a town close by and spent quite a lively evening in the pubs. These pubs are funny places. They are divided into several different rooms. Lounge, tap room etc. The furnishings and price of beer vary as to the room one drinks in. For example beer cost 1&3 in the lounge and one shilling in the tap room. The point is that it is all the same beer but you pay extra pennies a pint for the type of room you wish to drink in. Sort of a class distinction I suppose. I admit that we were feeling pretty happy by the time the night was over. On the way home we saw a horse in a field and went in and tried to corner the brute so one of the boys could ride it. We were stopped however, by a major in the Home Guard. I think the only thing that saved our skins was the fact that Bob Woolman was with us. The dear old English major couldn't say much about a CSM chasing his precious horse without making an issue of it.

Well I'd like to be on my way again. This is a nice camp but I've seen enough of it especially since the boys have gone. You tell me how I'm going to settle down after this messy affair is over. There is no place like home, though and I think I'll be ready to settle down and raise chickens or something when I do get home.

In my humble opinion this war is almost over. I've talked to several boys back from France and they figure 3 months will see the end. I fully agree with them. Someday soon Jerry is going to see the handwriting on the wall and quit. Imagine fighting 14 and 15 year old boys. That's what the Germans have come to according the chaps back from France. Offhand I would say they are running short of men. Too bad isn't It?

How are dad's teeth coming along? I'll bet 10 buckets to a hole in a donut he'll have the original set when I come back.

You know its Christly cold in this country. I've dug out my winter underwear and am wearing it, believe it or not. It's o.k. when the sun shines but that's not very often. If I have to spend a winter here, I'll be wearing every stitch that own.

I haven't written to Junior or anyone else in this country yet but I shall as soon as I get settled down on my course. I can't get any leave yet anyway so not writing for a few days doesn't mean much.

I wouldn't bother to send me anything at all, mom. I get plenty of food etc, have lots of tobacco and the infantry has to travel pretty light. It's pretty hard to find room for anything other than army issue. I don't figure I'll get a watch either, as the time of day doesn't interest me a hell of a lot. Well that's the end, lady. I'll write on Sat. night or Sunday.

All my love

Grant

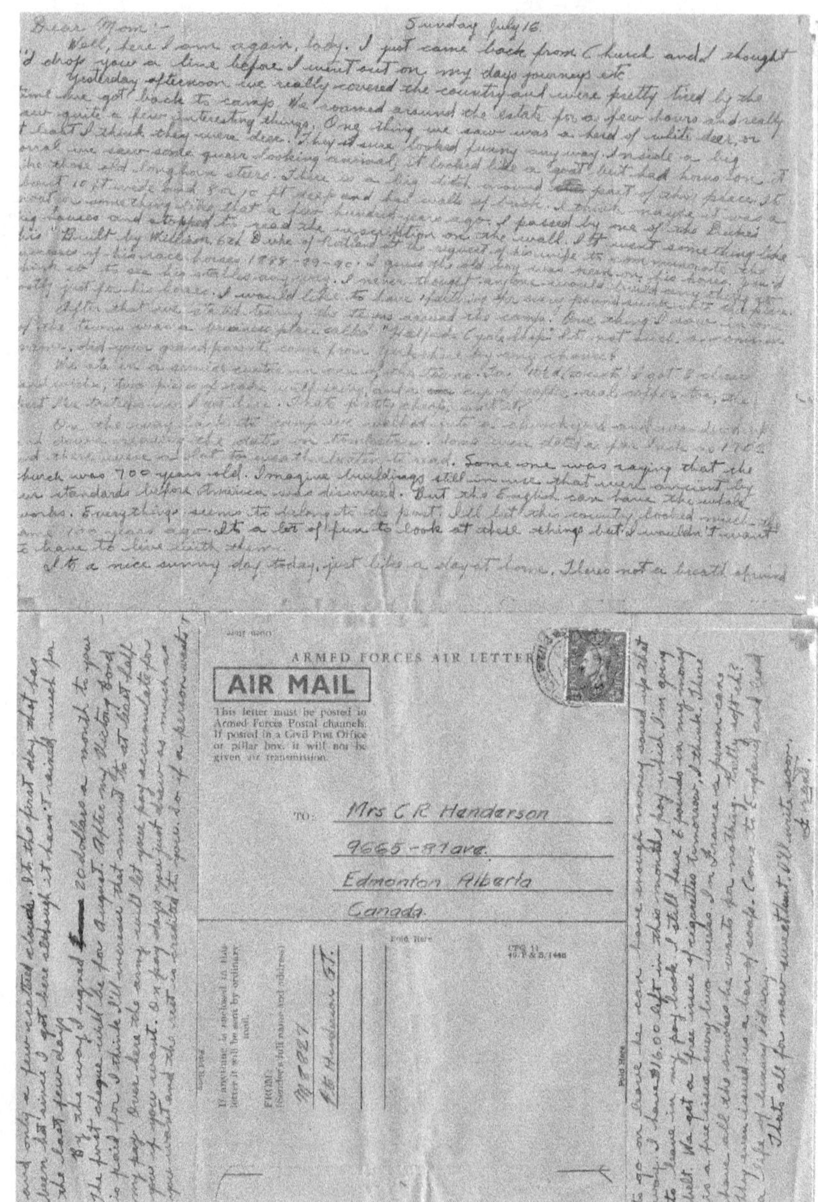

Dear Mom:– Sunday July 16.

Well, here I am again, lady. I just came back from Church and I thought I'd drop you a line before I went out on my days journeys etc.

Yesterday afternoon we really covered the country and were pretty tired by the time we got back to camp. We roamed around the estate for a few hours and really saw quite a few interesting things. One thing we saw was a herd of white deer, or at least I think they were deer. They sure looked funny anyway. Inside a big corral we saw some queer looking animal, it looked like a goat but had horns [illegible] like those old longhorn steers. There is a big ditch around part of this place. It [illegible] about 10 ft wide and 8 or 10 ft deep and has walls of brick. I think maybe it was a moat or something like that a few hundred years ago. I passed by one of the Dukes' [illegible] houses and stopped to read the inscription on the wall. It went something like this "Built by William, 6th Duke of Rutland at the request of his wife to [illegible] of his race horses 1888-89-90". I guess the old boy was [illegible] on his horses. [illegible] to see his stables anyway. I never thought anyone would build anything [illegible] just for his horses. I would like to have [illegible]

After that we started touring the towns around the camp. One thing I saw in one of the towns was a [illegible] place called "[illegible] Cycle Shop". [illegible] did your grandparents come from Yorkshire by any chance?

We ate in a [illegible] [illegible]

[illegible]

On the way back to camp we walked into a churchyard and [illegible] reading the dates on tombstones. Some were dated [illegible] and there were a lot too weather beaten to read. Some one was saying that the church was 700 years old. Imagine buildings still in use that were ancient by our standards before America was discovered. But the English can have the whole works. Everything seems to belong to the past. I'll bet this country looked much the same 100 years ago. It's a lot of fun to look at these things but I wouldn't want to have to live with them.

It's a nice sunny day today, just like a day at home. There's not a breath of wind

ARMED FORCES AIR LETTER

AIR MAIL

This letter must be posted in Armed Forces Postal channels. If posted in a Civil Post Office or pillar box, it will not be given air transmission.

TO: Mrs C R Handerson
9665-91 ave.
Edmonton Alberta
Canada.

If anything is enclosed in this letter it will be sent by ordinary mail.

FROM: (Sender's full name and address)

Sunday July 16, 1944

Dear Mom:

Well, here I am again, lady. I just came back from church and I thought I'd drop you a line before I went out on my days journeys etc.

Yesterday afternoon we really covered the country and were pretty tired by the time we got back to camp. We roamed around the estate for a few hours and really saw quite a few interesting things. One thing we saw was a herd of white deer or at least I think they were deer. They sure looked funny anyway. Inside a big corral we saw some queer looking animal, it looked like a goat but it had horns on it like those on long horn steers. There is a big ditch around part of this place. It's about 10 ft wide and 8 or 10 ft deep and has walls of brick. I think maybe it was a moat or something like that a few hundred years ago. I passed by one of the Dukes big houses and stopped to read the inscription on the wall. It went something like this "Built by William, 6th Duke of Portland at the request of his wife to commemorate the success of his race horses 1888-89-90" I guess the old boy was keen on his horses. You'd think so to see his stables anyway. I never thought anyone would build anything so costly just for his horses. I would like to have 1 farthing for every pound sunk into this place.

After that we started touring the towns around the camp. One thing I saw in one of the towns was a business place called "Halford Cycle Shops". It's not such a common name; did your grandparents come from Yorkshire by any chance?

We ate in a service centre in one of the towns. For 10 ½ p(20 cents) I got 3 cheese sandwiches, two pieces of cake with icing and a cup of coffee, real coffee too, the best I've tasted since I got here. That's pretty cheap, isn't it?

On the way back to camp we walked into a churchyard and wandered up and down reading the dates on tombstones. Some were dated as far back as 1702 and there were a lot too weather beaten to read. Someone was saying that the church was 700 years old. Imagine buildings still in use that were ancient by our standards before America was discovered. But the English can have the whole works. Everything seems to belong to the past. I'll bet this county looked much the same 100 years ago. It's a lot of fun to look at these things but I wouldn't want to have to live with them.

It's a nice sunny day today, just like a day at home. There's not a breath of wind and only a few scattered clouds. It's the first day that it has been hot since I got here although it hasn't rained much for the last few days.

By the way I signed 20 dollars a month to you. The first cheque will be for August. After my Victory Bond is paid for I think I'll increase that amount to at least half my pay. Over here the army will let your pay accumulate for you if you want. On pay days you just draw as much as you want and the rest is credited to you. So if a person wants to go on leave he can have enough money saved up that way. I have $16.00 left in this month's pay which I'm going to leave in my pay book. I still have 6 pounds in my money belt. We get a free issue of cigarettes tomorrow, I think. There is a *free issue every two weeks. In France a person can have all the smokes he wants for nothing. Pretty soft, eh?*

They even issue us a bar of soap. Come to England and lead a life of luxury, I'd say.

That's all for now sweetheart, I'll write soon.

Grant

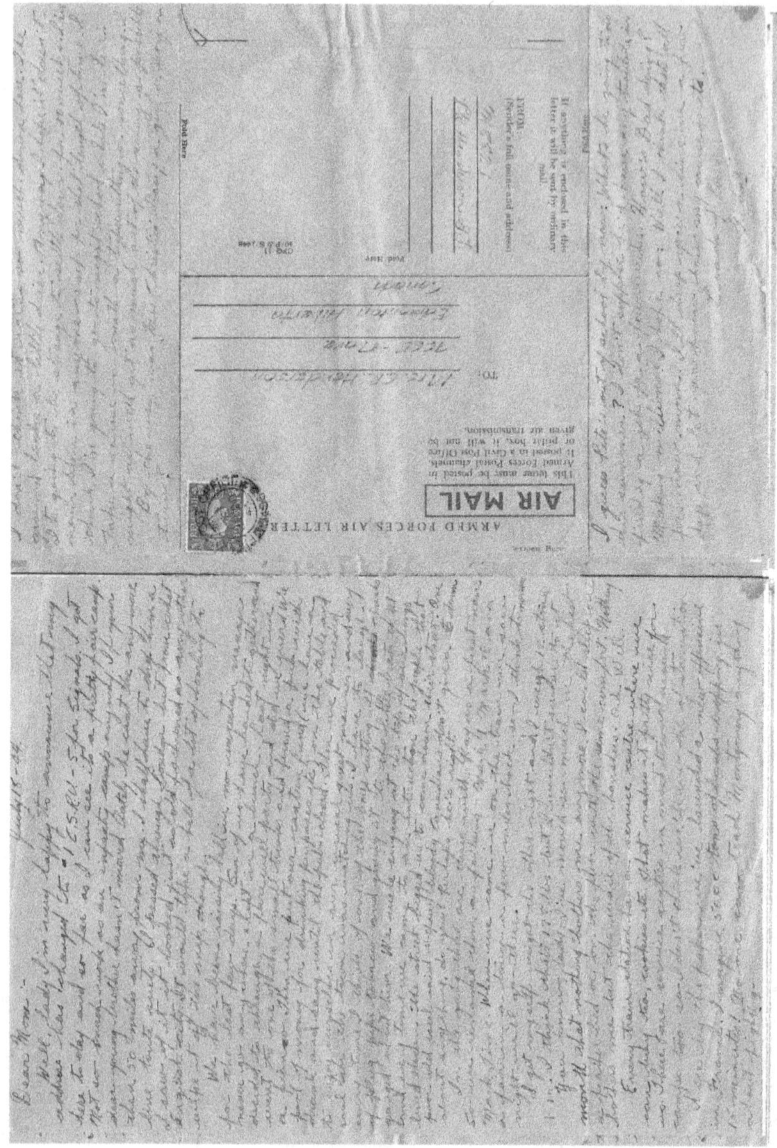

July 18, 1944

Dear Mom:

Well, lady I'm very happy to announce that my address has changed to C.S.R.V. – S for Signals. I got here today and so far as I can see it's a pretty fair camp, not so much work as an infantry camp anyway. If your dear young brother hasn't moved lately he can't be any more than 50 miles away from me. I shall have to drop him a line toute suite. I passed through London but from what I saw of it, it looked just as old fashioned as any other English city. It would take a hell of a lot of bombing to wipe it off the map though.

We have been raising hell in no uncertain manner for the last few days. Six of us have banded together and never go anywhere except in a bunch. Last night we decided to throw a farewell party and did we ever! We went to one of the small towns and found a pub with a piano. Then we put our canteen fund (we have a pool of money for drinking purposes etc) on the table and drank and drank until the pub closed. Then we proceeded to enjoy ourselves in our usual quiet manner and every soul in the town was watching us. I have to laugh every time I think of one of the boys cutting off chunks of plug pipe tobacco and giving it to the little brats that ganged about him. We were singing at the top of our lungs and every time we came to an intersection the people that lived down the street begged us to come down their street. One poor old soul said "You bloody Canadians don't give a dam about anything do you?" Perhaps he's right.

In the gang there are three with Ray as a first name so we renamed them as follows Mark I, Mark II and Mark time.

When we came in on the train we saw a fair in a town a few miles back, so I think tomorrow night we will go there.

I got myself weighed the other night and I weighed 12 stones plus 10. I think that is about 178 lbs but I wouldn't swear to it.

You know lady, I have moved so much in the first month that nothing bothers me anymore. I could sleep on a feather bed or on the floor with the same comfort. Nothing bothers me but the wail of the banishers. Oh well.

Every train station has a service centre where we can buy tea, cookies etc. That makes it pretty nice for us. There are service centres in most towns around camps too so I don't think we will ever die of starvation.

I see by the paper that we have launched a new offensive in France. Imagine 5000 tons of bombs dropping in 15 minutes! No one can teach Montgomery anything about fighting.

I don't think it rains so much down here. The ground looks a little drier. Anyways I hope it doesn't.

It's going to be strange to settle down for 10 weeks. I've never been in anyone camp for that length of time. I think I'm going to night school while I'm here. Take a course in math or typewriting or something. I might as well get as much out of the army as possible.

By the way, was Mrs. Christie's baby, a girl or boy or twins?

I guess Pete's out of school by now. What's he going to do this summer? I don't suppose he'd have any trouble in finding a job for a few weeks. How's Dad doing? Making millions? I hope so. Well I think that's all for now, mom. I'll drop you a line in a few days and let you know how my course is etc.

Loads of Love

Grant

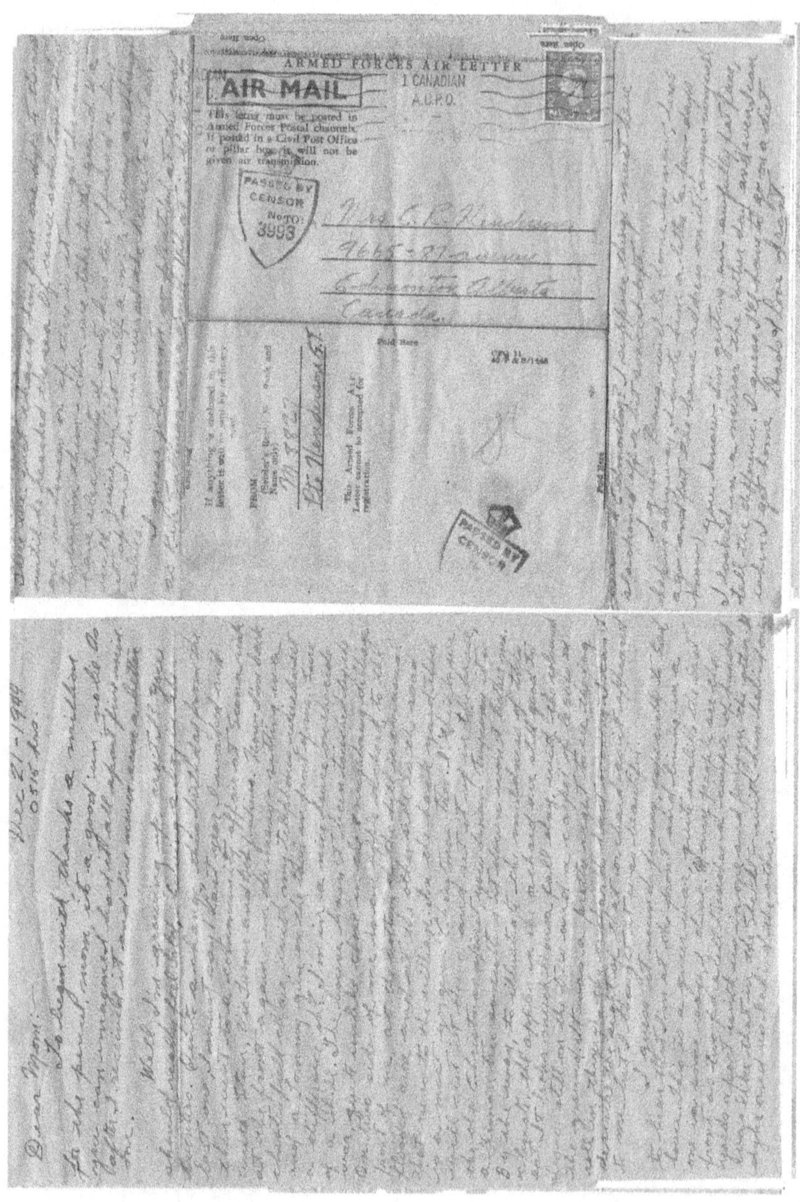

ARMED FORCES AIR LETTER

1 CANADIAN A.B.P.O.

AIR MAIL

This letter must be posted in Armed Forces Postal channels. If posted in a Civil Post Office or pillar box it will not be given air transmission.

PASSED BY CENSOR No. 3993

Mrs C. R. Henderson
9645-87 avenue
Edmonton Alberta
Canada.

Dec 21-1944

Dear Mom:

July 21, 44

Dear Mom:

Well, after 6 months of doing nothing mentally I am once again making my living by using my noggin. It looks as though all I should do for the next few weeks is study. I will not go so far as to say that I love it for I am very lonesome for the good old infantry. Perhaps that is hard to believe but I still say the infantry is the only branch of the service. However when this course is over I shall go back as an infantry signalman. The life here is very easy, much more comfortable than the camp I was in a previously. It's much warmer down here and is a little dusty but it's much more like good old Alberta Weather.

I feel like a school boy again, sitting in classes all day and wearing no equipment. I miss my rifle every so often. I always had it with me before and now it's sitting in the hut all by itself, poor thing. Oh well!

Last night we went and visited most of the local pubs. The best drinks I think are stout and pale ale. Pale ale taste a lot like good old Calgary Stock ale.

Well, what do you think of the situation in Germany? It looks pretty good doesn't it? I wouldn't be surprised to see a general revolt any day now. The Germans seem to be waking up. I would hate to be in the target area in that bombing raid in France yesterday. No one can teach our high priced help anything about offensive warfare now. It's a nice feeling to know that victory is just a matter of time now.

Something that you can send me, mom is a half pound of pipe tobacco. Old chum is the brand. There is no rush though as I have several weeks supply on hand.

Well, today marks the end of the 6th month in the army. I've sure seen a lot of new country in that time. I wonder what the next 6 months will bring. The first 3 are pretty well spoken for by this outfit and by then the war will be over.

Perhaps I shall get a week's leave and have a better look at Scotland. I would like to spend at least a week up there before I come home. How's Ma coming along? Have her dear boys been scaring the life out of her? I suppose so.

You should see our gang. It's made up of one truck driver, one farm hand, and one with B.A. at B.C. Union, one two year medical student, one accountant and me. What a collection of people doing the same thing now. Well I guess that all for now mom. I should have a little more news in a few days or at least something more interesting to write about.

Loads of Love

Grant

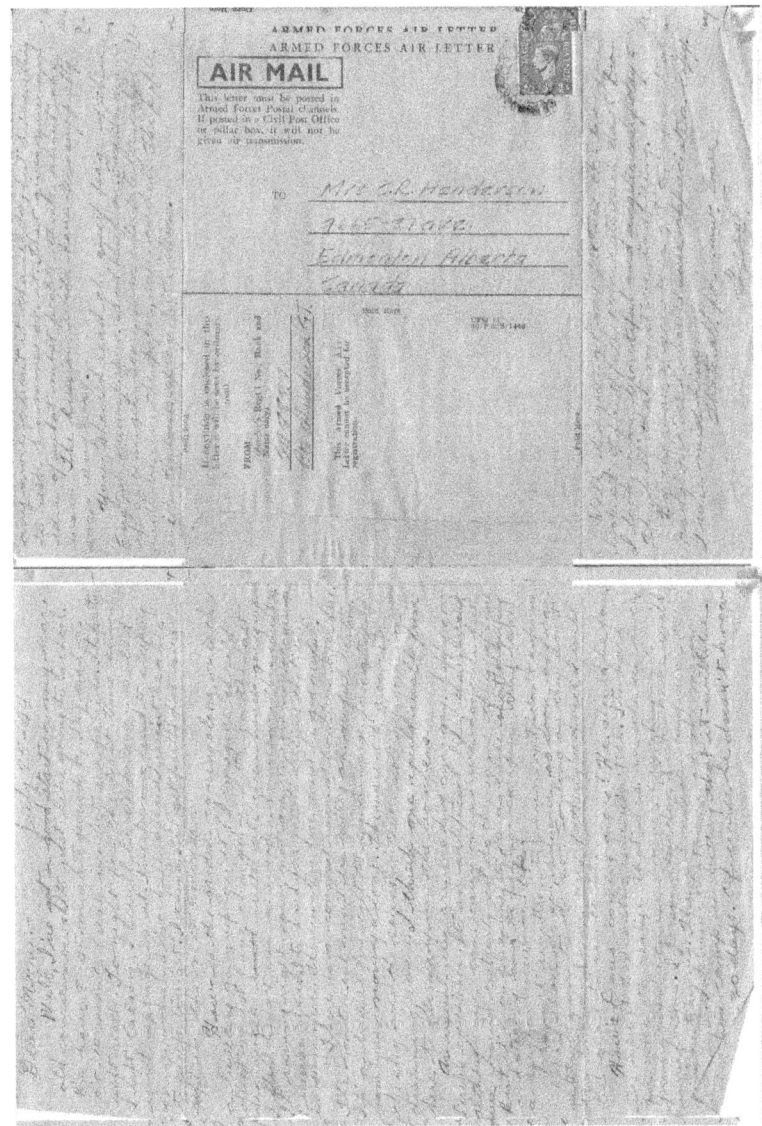

ARMED FORCES AIR LETTER

AIR MAIL

This letter must be posted in Armed Forces Postal channels. If posted in a Civil Post Office or pillar box, it will not be given air transmission.

TO Mrs C.R. Henderson
[illegible] Ave.
Edmonton Alberta
Canada

July 25, 1944

Dear Mom:

Well, I've got a good start on my dear old course now. It's just like going to school. We have 8 – 45 minute periods a day and a 5 or 10 minute break in between periods. It's pretty soft really. Tonight for the first time since I left Calgary, I will be sleeping in a bed with springs in it. I've become used to sleeping on wood and I'm half afraid I won't be able to sleep tonight. I think I'll get pretty fat and soft in the next 3 months.

How is the garden coming along, or is there a building going up on it? I image the old street must have changed a little in the last six weeks with all those houses going up. I still haven't seen a wooden house in this country. It's raining right now, not an uncommon occurrence I assure you. It's hard for me to believe that this is summer. The winter here must be God awful.

There is a constant roar of bombers over here. The continent must be getting an awful beating. It's a beautiful sight to see a large formation of bombers moving along. They seem to grow in the sky and the sound of their motors becomes a deafening roar. I think I could walk from here to Germany on the bombers.

As usual we are living our gay, happy go lucky existence. It's an artificial life though, although we can carry on as we do over here. But it is a pleasure to do as I like, short of killing and stealing and to feel so carefree. Why take a serious view of life?

I haven't written to junior yet, don't ask me why. I shall do so; however, as soon as I can settle down to do so. So long as they don't try to hand me any fatherly advice I will be glad to see them.

How's Doug coming along? He should be home in about 2 months, shouldn't he? It's hard for me to realize that he's in the air force, probably because I never saw him in uniform. I personally don't think he will finish training. The war looks very near to the end. I know that one of the majors in this camp is betting that it will be over in 30 days. Of course he doesn't know any more about it than I do, but he's willing to risk his money on it. That gives you an idea of what most people think about the war. The Russians will have Germany pretty soon anyways.

You should read the gossip page of these English newspapers. God help an Englishman if he ever gets home 10 minutes late for supper. It will be in the paper, sure as hell. The people evidently love spicy little items.

Well did you get my pictures o.k.? Do you look at it faithfully 10 minutes each day? Do I look more beautiful and angelic every day? Ah but that must be inspiring.

By the way, if you ever get a reprint of Doug's picture I would sure appreciate a copy. I sure miss him.

That's all for now, Love

Grant

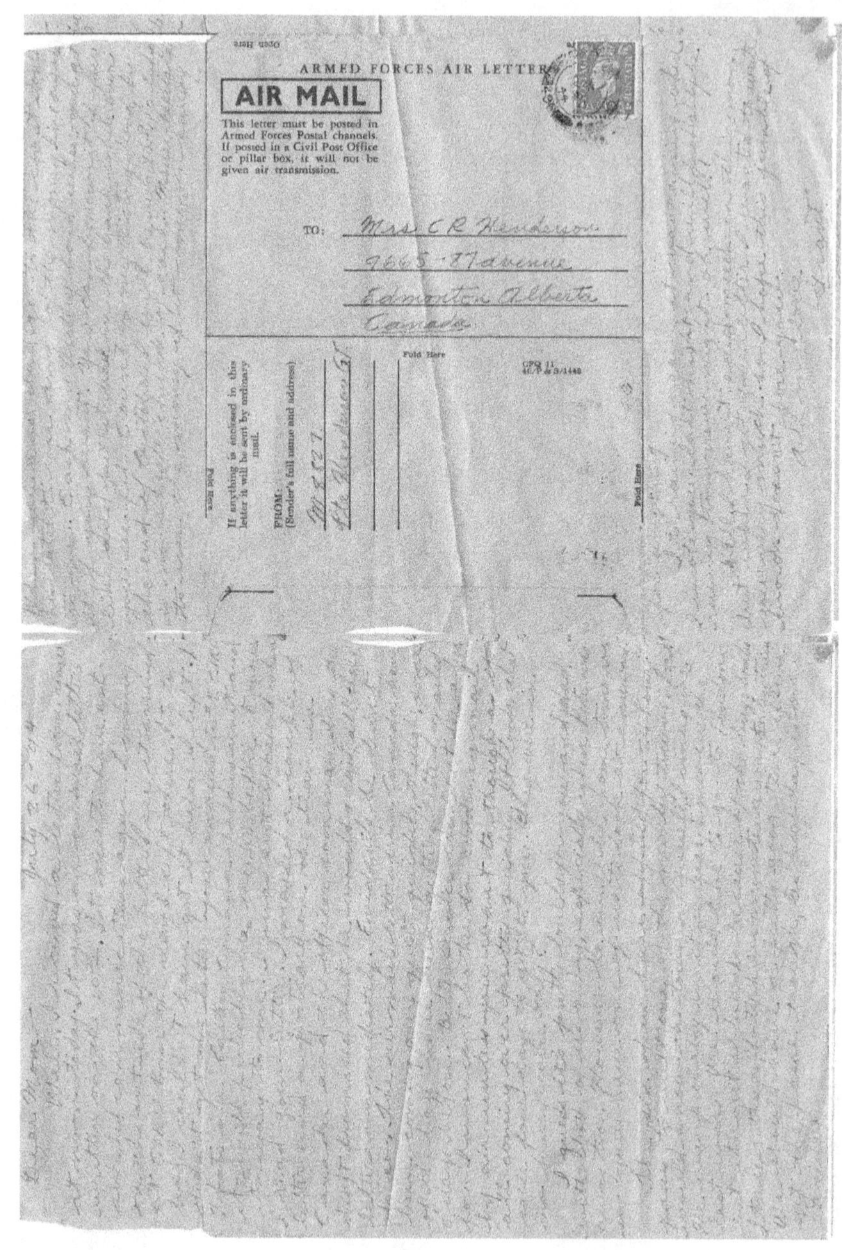

Open Here

ARMED FORCES AIR LETTER

AIR MAIL

This letter must be posted in Armed Forces Postal channels. If posted in a Civil Post Office or pillar box, it will not be given air transmission.

TO: Mrs C R Henderson
9665 - 87 avenue
Edmonton Alberta
Canada

Fold Here

If anything is enclosed in this letter it will be sent by ordinary mail.

FROM: (Sender's full name and address)

July 26, 1944

Dear Mom:

Well, I received a letter from you at noon today. It was an airmail letter written on the 10th. It's nice to have established communication again. Looking on the outside of the letter I see it arrived at CIRU Base the day I left there. It's too bad I couldn't have got it before I left. I didn't get the letter you mailed to #2 CIRU. That's an Eastern Canada holding unit and it will probably be weeks before it works its way to me! I was sort of peeved when I read your letter. I mailed a couple of letters and a postcard on the train in Canada and the officer commanding the draft promised that he would mail all those letters immediately. Evidently he didn't do so. The airmail letters from Canada have been coming over quite quickly, though some of the boys have been getting letters mailed 5 days before. Better service couldn't be asked for. I wouldn't bother to send my mail by air unless you want to, though as it's all coming over pretty quickly. It took that cable four days to get to you. They were in no hurry were they?

I guess it's pretty lonely for you and dad with both of us away, especially when Pete was away too. However he will be home tomorrow so you have one of us to look at anyway.

The six of us have applied for 24 hour passes to visit one of the nearby towns. Dad would know the town very well. I imagine he was probably in it several times in the last war. We would like to go to London but it's out of bounds because of the buzz bombs. We should have a pretty good time if we get the passes though, as payday is on Friday.

When you and dad go to the coast don't hesitate to use any of the money I've signed to you. Cash my victory bond when you get it if you want. You can borrow it if you like and put it back in the bank whenever you see fit. Counting my Victory bond by the end of October I will be worth $110 which is no small chunk of cash. Never hesitate to use the money if it comes in handy for anything.

It's raining again, it was raining when I wrote you last night and will probably be raining tomorrow night, oh well!

Well I haven't said much in this mom but when I got your letter I wanted to write you very much so I hope this jumble of words doesn't bore you.

All my love

Grant

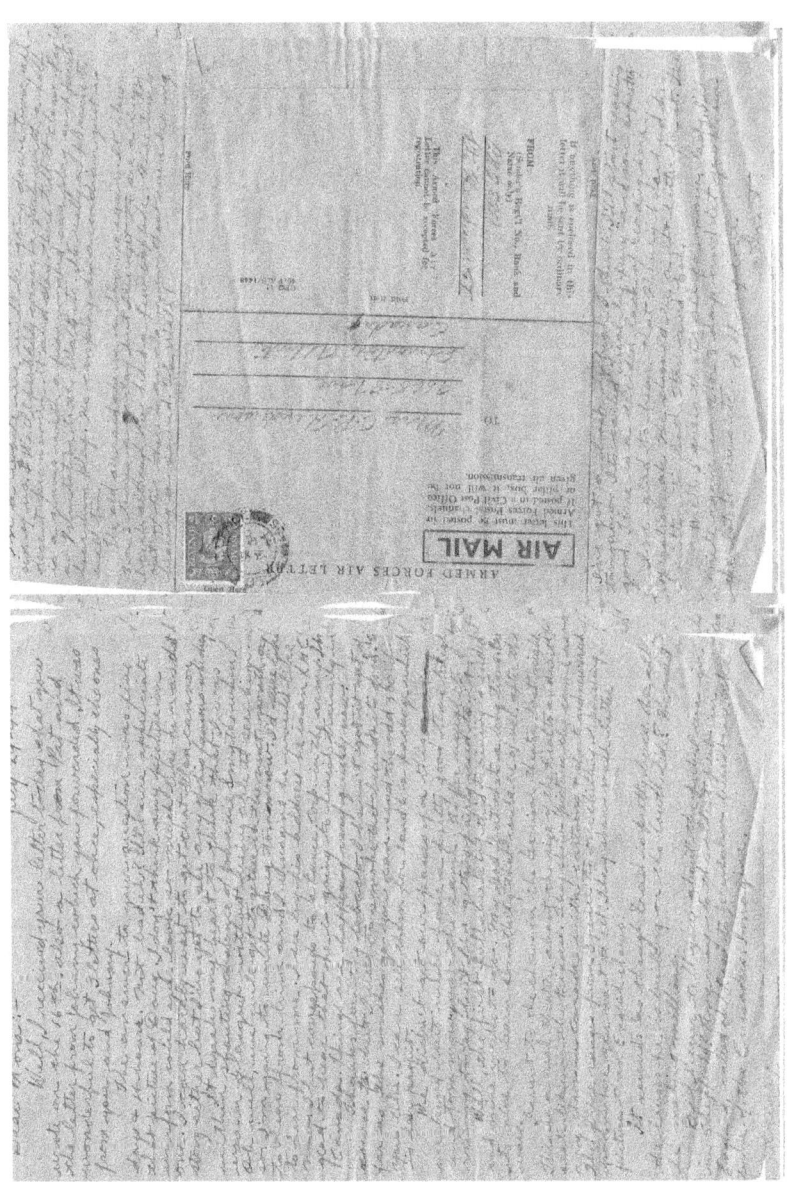

July 29, 1944

Dear Mom:

Well, I received your letter today that you wrote on the 16th, also a letter from Pat and the letter from Johnny which you forwarded. It was wonderful to get 3 letters at once, especially the ones from you and Johnny.

The answer to your question was five days & 16 hours. Not bad eh? I'll sure appreciate that picture of Doug. I don't think any picture in uniform could ever look so much like him as that one. I can hardly wait to get that Glen Cannon story either but I've yet to see any of his famous whiskey.

It breaks my heart to think that I was within shouting distance of Johnny Smyth when I was in Glasgow without being able to see him. Oh well, we will get together in the next month or so. I'm going to write Doug tomorrow. I'd sure like to hear from him and I imagine he would like to hear from me. I see by his address he is a LAC now. That corresponds to a Lance Corp. in the army. I'm glad to hear that he is going to finish training in Canada. Things are happening very quickly now.

Thanks for the tobacco. I haven't got it yet of course but I used to smoke that brand & it's good. So far as the smokes go you can send the odd 300 if you like. I can sell them for 1 and 6 a package which is a fair profit.

We didn't get our passes for this weekend but we'll have a pretty good time tonight and tomorrow just the same. As per usual it's raining today but I'm getting fairly used to it.

Well the first full week of this training is ended and nine weeks to go. My God but that a long time.
But it's nice to learn something that could be of use after the war.

I went to the show in the garrison theater last night. This is a real theater about the size of the Realto and with seats like in the Princess. They show pictures the same as any show in Canada with cartoons & shorts and newsreels. The price ranges from 3 pence to one shilling depending upon where you want to sit. They show much better pictures than English shows.

It sounds as though Dad is pretty busy. Are all the houses he is building on the Southside? He must be making millions.

Did I ever tell you about the pub I was in Sheffield? Anyway it's the oldest pub in England, called the road to Jerusalem built in the time of the Crusades. Imagine.

In a while we will be going down town, all six of us. We'll probably corner a pub with a half decent piano in it and stay there till it closes. Ray is a genus with a piano and can play such pieces as Invitation to the Waltz etc. It's really a pleasure to hear him play. He can play his accordion just as well too.

The old air raid alarm is blowing again. It blows 2 or 3 times a day but I've yet to see a buzz bomb though. I've heard a few explode. Nine times out of ten there is an alarm without even hearing a sound, oh well.

I've got a book which I think I'll start reading tomorrow. It's called Trial by Fury and sounds pretty good. There is a decided lack of reading here.

I'm glad to hear that Henry has had his operation o.k. He should be a lot better for it. I've written to both Stan and Bob.

Well I guess that's all for now, lady. I'll write you again in 2 or 3 days and let you know the latest news etc.

All my love

Grant.

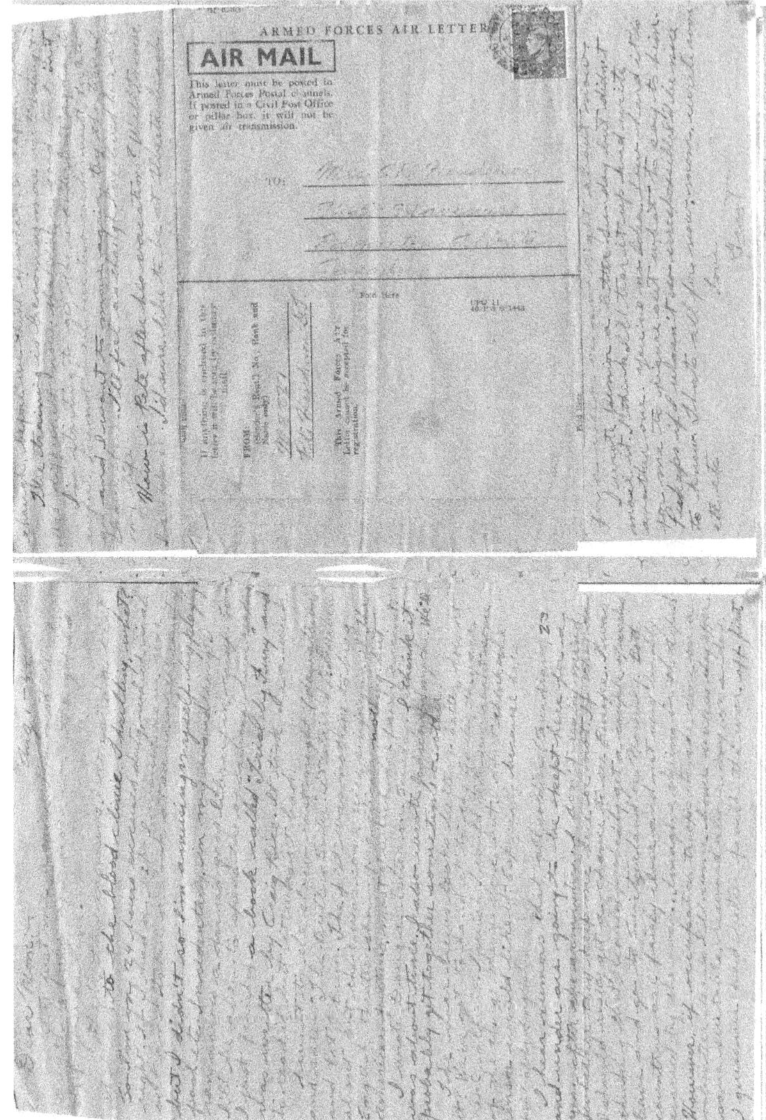

ARMED FORCES AIR LETTER

AIR MAIL

This letter must be posted in Armed Forces Postal channels. If posted in a Civil Post Office or pillar box, it will not be given air transmission.

TO:

Aug 1, 1944

Dear Mom:

It's just me again. I'm not doing anything this afternoon so I thought I'd drop you a line.

Well, this morning I donated a pint of blood to the blood clinic. Thrilling, what? So I'm on 24 hours of excused duty, which is all right. If I had a bike I would have gone out and taken a look at some of the country but I didn't so I'm amusing myself by playing pool etc. Incidentally in my in my wanderings I ran across a darn good library in the camp. So I'll be able to spend the occasional hour reading. I just finished a book called "Trial by Fury" that was written by Craig Rice. It took me a week to read it but it wasn't bad.

I went to the show last night (downtown) and saw "The Butlers Sister" It starred D. Durbin and Pat O'Brian. The plot was nothing to brag about but there was some nice singing in it. The English theatres show practically nothing but American pictures, most of which are fairly ancient.

I wrote Doug a letter on Sunday. I think it was about time. I also wrote Johnny Smyth. We'll probably get together sometime or other.

The news looks better and better, doesn't it? We've got to hand it to the Yanks, they are real soldiers. I wish I could tell you about some of the things they've done but I don't think the censor would like it. Especially because he's probably English.

I hear rumors that all soldiers (Canadians), 23 and under are going to be kept here for a year after armistice. I don't really mind whether they keep me here or not. If they do, I should really get a chance to see Europe. I was thinking that I could probably get a couple of weeks leave and go to Switzerland or Norway. Both countries are fairly close and not very badly scarred by the war. Imagine skiing in the Alps. However if occupation troops etc are done on a volunteer basis; I'll come home unless they offer some suitable reward above my 1.50 a day. I guess we had better finish the war off first though before we think of what is to happen after.

The training is becoming more interesting & less difficult now that I've a good start in it.

I'm starting to get the wanderlust again, it's awful, I've not been here two weeks with 8 or 9 to go and I want to move again. By the time I leave here I'll feel as though I've lived here all my life.

How is Pete after his vacation? Well tanned I suppose. I'd sure like to be at Alberta Beach for a week or so right about now.

I wrote Junior a letter Sunday but didn't mail it. I think I'll tear it up and write another one. You've no idea how hard it is for me to figure out what to say to him. Perhaps if I wasn't so irresponsible I'd be nice to know. That's all for now, mom, write soon, etc, etc,

Love Grant

ARMED FORCES AIR LETTER

AIR MAIL

This letter must be posted in Armed Forces Postal channels. If posted in a Civil Post Office or pillar box, it will not be given air transmission.

TO: Mrs E.R. Henderson
9665 - 87 avenue
Edmonton Alberta
Canada

Aug 4, 1944

Dear Mom:

Well, in the last 2 days I've had 3 letters from you. The first one was the one with Doug's picture, the Glen Cannon story etc. in it. Thanks a lot. The second one was written July 22. I'm sorry to hear that Don's brother is missing. I went to school with Art and knew him quite well. He's probably a prisoner, though; I think that most of the boys get out of the planes O.K. I hope Junior isn't too sick with pleurisy. I don't know much about it but I've met soldiers in Canada who have been sent from here to Canada because of it. I wouldn't tell Ma that, though. I'm going to drop Junior a line today.

The 3rd letter was the one you sent to 2CRIU. After reading the letter I must compliment you on your guessing the address. It was very close to being the right one. I don't see how you didn't get a letter from me by that time if Pat got one. I wrote you two letters on the train and mentioned my probable future address in one of them. I think the answer was that I gave Pat's letter to a little French Canadian kid to mail. I didn't trust him very far so I mailed a letter to you via a women running a store by the train stop. Either she didn't mail it or the army got it. Oh well. The letter got here quite quickly considering that it went to 3 dif RV's looking for me. Just a couple of days over a month.

So Henry didn't have a goiter after all! He better not let the army find out. Pat tells me his voice has changed. That would be annoying wouldn't it?

The weather has been glorious the past few days. The sky is practically cloudless and is about 65 or 70 above. Just right.

As you know, I gave a blood donation on Tuesday. In case you're interested my blood type according to their standards is Btype 3. It seems to be a fairly uncommon type. They give us different colour cards according to our type which we carry with us. The dates of all blood donations is marked in our pay book also our type.

Wed. night I was on guard duty and last night we went to a show down town. One of them was a cowboy show and the other picture was an English one but the girl in the show had a beautiful voice and sang quite a few nice songs.

It's past noon and there hasn't been an air raid alarm yet. Quite unusual I must say. I haven't seen any buzz bombs but I've heard them flying and have heard the explosions and felt the concussion. It seems, though, that whenever they fall around here they forget to sound the alarm and when they do sound an alarm no bombs fall. No one pays any attention to an alarm anyway so what's the odds?

I wrote a test yesterday & got 98% on it. Don't think I'm a genius though, if you ever wrote an army exam you'd know what I mean.

By the way, lady, when you get my V.Bond please cash it will you? I'd much rather have the money in the bank, but don't ask me why.

I see by this morning's paper that both the yanks and the Russians are advancing at a terrific pace. At the rate the Yanks are advancing they'll have a real chunk of France in a couple of weeks. The Germans are sure losing men at a terrific rate. I don't like the idea of us having to feed all those prisoners, though it's too costly.

That's all for now. I'll write on Sunday.

Love and Kisses

Grant

ARMED FORCES AIR LETTER

AIR MAIL

This letter must be posted in Armed Forces Postal channels. If posted in a Civil Post Office or pillar box, it will not be given air transmission.

TO: Mrs C R Henderson

If anything is enclosed in this letter it will be sent by ordinary mail.

FROM: (Sender's full name and address)

Aug 6, 1944

Dear Mom:

Well, the old air raid alarm just blew again. I actually saw a flying bomb on Friday night. I don't think they are much of a weapon, though.

The Yanks sure tore the Brest peninsula to pieces in a hurry, didn't they? It hardly seemed possible that such a supposedly well fortified place could be slashed to pieces in a few days. I'll bet the rest of France goes the same way. I see the Russians are in Prussia too. Soon the length of the war in Europe will be measured in days instead of weeks. What a celebration there will be when it folds up!

Well Friday night was a quiet one, just drank a few pints of beer, listened to Ray play the accordion for a while and then went to bed. Yesterday afternoon we went to another show and then had half a doz pints of stout, bought a bunch of fish and chips and went back to camp and played the old accordion again until bed time. This morning, I actually stayed in bed till 8:30. One of the boys bought me the morning paper and brought me a cup of tea so I read the paper and (with a stretch of imagination had breakfast in bed) some class eh?

I actually wrote Junior a letter and mailed it on Friday. I'm quite proud of myself.

It's another beautiful day, the kind that makes you glad to be alive. I think I'll go lay in the sun this afternoon and pick up a sun tan. We are thinking of going to church downtown tonight. It's not so much our religion but the beautiful choirs the English have.

You know lady; I'm beginning to wonder how I can ever get back to civilian life. Compared to this, civilian life is awfully monotonous, full of jealousy, gossip and God knows what. A person's own so called friends talk about him behind his back and a person spends 9 or 10 hours a day thinking of profit and loss and other dull things. Some uninformed people think that the army life is hard, especially the infantry, but they are so completely wrong it's laughable. We have real friends no troubles or care, all the necessities supplied us, spending money and actually a lot more free time than civilians. On top of that I think that Civilians worry a lot more about the war than we ever could. It's quite interesting to see the difference a few months of army life can make in a person. This becomes a lot healthier both mentally & physically.

I am getting quite excited at the thought that I might get a chance to get a good look at Europe on the army time after the war. What an opportunity!

Think of the high class so and so's who like to say they have been abroad. It costs them a small fortune but I will see it all for nothing, if I am lucky.

Well, it won't be long till the shooting season's open. I guess it will be a poor season, though, with the lack of shells etc. Oh well, there should be lots of shells on the market by next year.

I suppose Ross should be home on furlough this month. If you see him say hello for me. He was a good friend once but we've drifted apart so much it's doubtful if we can even pick up where we left off. Might though, never can tell. Well I guess that's all for now, mom, didn't have much to say but maybe something exciting will happen by the middle of the week.
Love Grant.

ARMED FORCES AIR LETTER

AIR MAIL

This letter must be posted in Armed Forces Postal channels. If posted in a Civil Post Office or pillar box, it will not be given air transmission.

TO: Mrs. C.R. Henderson
7665-57 ave
Edmonton, Alberta
Canada

Fold Here

Writ by hand

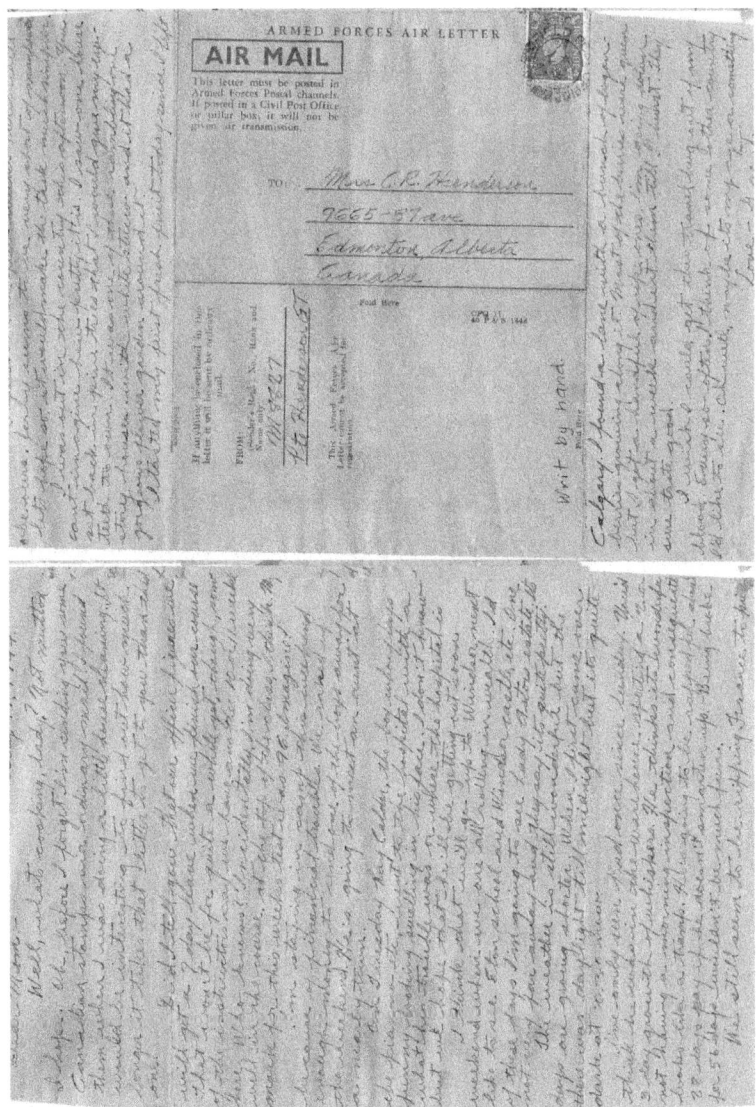

Aug 11, 1944

Dear Mom:

Well, what cooking, lady? Not mutton I hope. Oh before I forget I'm sending you some Canadian stamps via ordinary mail. I found them when I was doing a little house cleaning. It would be interesting to find out how much longer it takes that letter to get to you than this one.

Did I tell you that our officer figures we will get a 7 day leave when we finish our course? That won't be for quite a while yet, though, some of the instructors say we have another 10 or 11 weeks here. Who knows? Incidentally, I'm doing very well in the course. At the top of the class, I think. My mark for this week's test was 96. Imagine!

I'm staying in camp this weekend because of financial troubles. We raked up enough money to send one of the boys away for the weekend. He's going to meet an aunt at a nearby town.

On Tuesday Ray Calder, the boy who plays the piano etc went to the hospital with a funny looking swelling in his face. I don't know what his trouble was or where the hospital is but we hope that he'll be getting out soon.

I think that we'll go up to Windsor next weekend when we are all rolling in wealth. I'd like to see Eton school and Windsor castle, etc. One of these days I'm going to see Lady Astor's estate. It's not very far away and they say it's quite pretty.

The weather is still wonderful but the days are growing shorter. When I first came over there was day light till midnight but it's quite dark by 10:30 now.

I've only seen Bud once since Sunday. You'd think he was in the warehouse sporting a 2 or 3 day growth of whiskers. He thinks it's wonderful not having a morning inspection and consequently looks like a tramp. He's going to be rapped for about 28 days pay if he doesn't smarten up. Being broke for 56 days wouldn't be much fun.

We still seem to be ripping France to pieces don't we? I guess in a few weeks Paris will be ours. Jerry seems to be very short of manpower let's hope so, it would make the task much simpler.

I was out in the country this afternoon. You can't imagine how pretty it is. I saw one house set back in pine trees that I would give my eye teeth to own. It was one of these rambling one story houses with white stucco and it had a gorgeous flower garden around it.

I tasted my first fresh fruit today since I left Calgary. I found a lane with a bunch of Logan berries growing along it. Most of the berries were green but I got a handful of ripe ones. I'm going down in about a week and eat them till I burst. They sure taste good.

I wish I could get this travel bug out of my blood. Every so often I think of some other country I'd like to see. Oh well, maybe it's my age or something.

Love Grant.

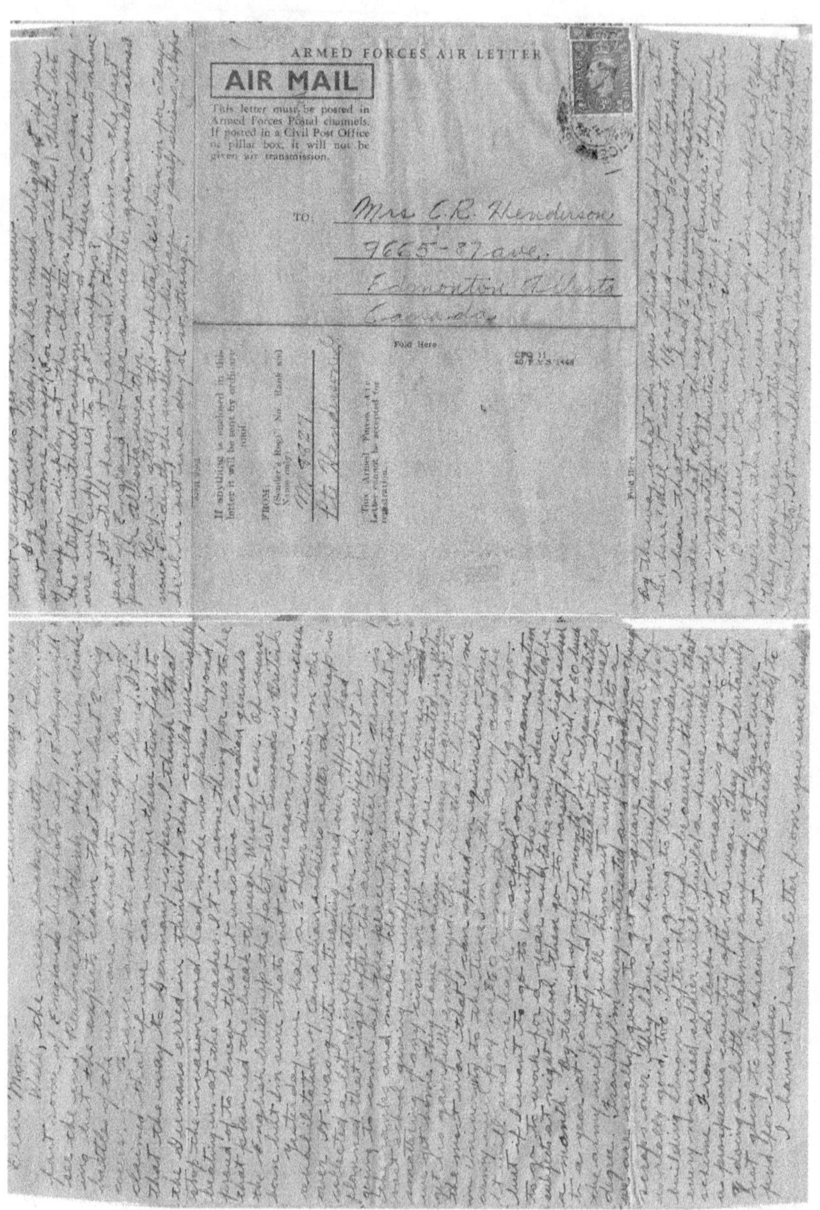

ARMED FORCES AIR LETTER

AIR MAIL

This letter must be posted in Armed Forces Postal channels. If posted in a Civil Post Office or pillar box, it will not be given air transmission.

TO: Mrs C.R. Henderson
7665-87 ave.
Edmonton Alberta
Canada

If anything is enclosed in this letter it will be sent by ordinary mail.

FROM: (Sender's Rank, No. and Name only)

This Armed Forces Air Letter cannot be accepted for registration.

Sunday Aug 13, 1944

Dear Mom:

Well, the news looks pretty rosy today. In fact some of England's big shots say 18 days will see the end. Personally I think they've been drinking but the experts claim that the last 2 big battles of the war are about to begin. One is of course in France and the other in Poland. It is claimed that if we can win these two fights that the way to Germany is open. I think that the Germans erred in thinking they could successfully stop the invasion and had made no plans beyond beating us at the beaches. It is something for us to be proud of to know that it was two Canadian Generals that planned the break through West of Cain. Of course the English build up the fact that Symonds is British born but I'm sure that's not the reason for his successes.

Yesterday we had a 2 hour discussion on the rehabilitation of Canadian soldiers after the scrap is over. It was quite interesting and our officer had collected a lot of information of the subject. It is planned that right after the armistice the army is going to comb all the peacetime instructors out of the ranks and make the whole army over here a vast school giving us unofficial refresher courses ona smattering of any civilian job we are interested in. When we get home they have various schemes figured out to get us gainfully employed. The one that interests me the most was that I can spend an equivalent time in University to the time in the army and the army will pay me $60 a month so long as I go. It will send me back to school on the same system but if I want to go to varsity the best idea would be to go to work for a year and take my nec .high school subject at night school then go to varsity for nil + 60 bucks a month. By the *end of next month I'm already entitled to a year at Varsity and if the student is doing well the army will not pull him out until he gets a degree. Frankly I'm interested and it looks as though we are really going to get a square deal after the scraps over. They have a home building scheme that is really good, too. There's going to be a wonderful building boom after the war because I think that every married soldier will build a house under the scheme. From the look of it Canada is going to be a prosperous country after the war. They are certainly not going to be thrown out in the streets and told to fend for ourselves.*

I haven't had a letter from you since Tuesday but I expect to get one tomorrow.

By the way , lady, I'd be much obliged if you sent me some soap (for myself, not clothes)There is lots of soap on display at the canteen but we can't buy the stuff without coupons and where in Christ's name are we supposed to get coupons?

It still hasn't rained. I think I'm in the best part of England so far as weather goes, would almost pass for Alberta weather.

Ray is still in the hospital, he's been in for 5 days now. Evidently the swelling in his face is fairly serious. I hope he'll be out in a day or so though.

By the way what do you think a head of lettuce costs over here? Well it costs 1/6 a head – about 35 cents, imagine! I hear that we've had 2 provincial elections. I wonder what King thought about Quebec? The French are ungrateful brutes aren't they? After all that our dear P.minster has done for them.

Believe it or not lady, I've only had 2 pints of beer in the last week. Awful isn't it? Ah me. They say beer is getting scarce in London but we still have lots. It would be the last straw if the beer ran out.

Love & Kisses

Grant.

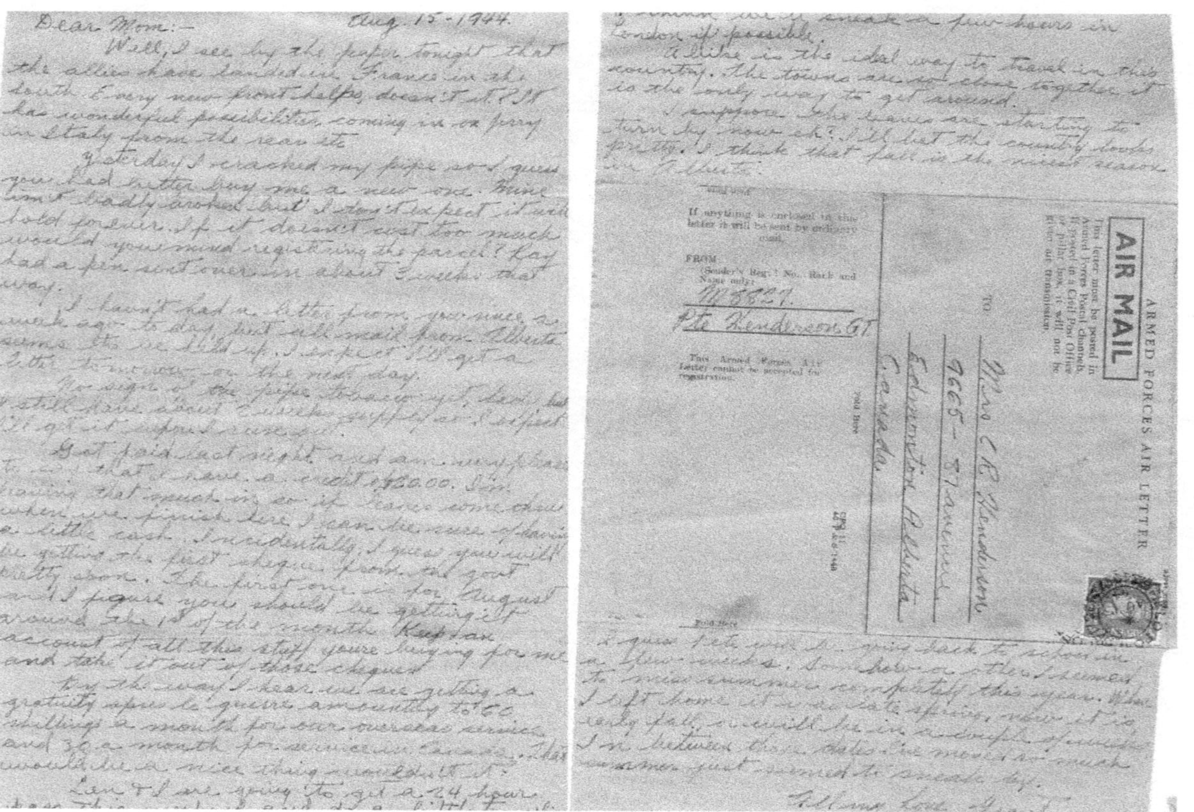

Dear Mom:— Aug. 15 - 1944.

Well, I see by the paper tonight that the allies have landed in France in the south. Every new front helps, doesn't it? It has wonderful possibilities coming in or [illegible] in Italy from the rear etc.

Yesterday I cracked my pipe so I guess you had better buy me a new one. Mine isn't badly cracked but I don't expect it will hold forever. If it doesn't cost too much would you mind registering the parcel? Kay had a pen sent over in about 3 weeks that way.

I haven't had a letter from you since a week ago to day but all mail from Alberta seems to be held up. I expect I'll get a letter tomorrow or the next day.

No sign of the pipe tobacco yet Mom but I still have about 2 weeks supply so I expect I'll get it before I run out.

Got paid last night and am very pleased to [illegible] that I have a credit of $20.00. I'm leaving that much in so if [illegible] come [illegible] when we finish here I can be sure of having a little cash. Incidentally, I guess you will be getting the first cheque from the govt pretty soon. The first one is for August and I figure you should be getting it around the 1st of the month. Keep an account of all this stuff you're buying for me and take it out of those cheques.

By the way I hear we are getting a gratuity of [illegible] amounting to 60 shillings a month for our overseas service and 30 a month for service in Canada. That would be a nice thing wouldn't it.

Len & I are going to get a 24 hour [illegible]

[illegible] sneak a few hours in London if possible.

A bike is the ideal way to travel in this country. The towns are so close together it is the only way to get around.

I suppose the leaves are starting to turn by now eh? I'll bet the country looks pretty. I think that fall is the nicest season in Alberta.

I guess Pete will be going back to school in a few weeks. Somehow or other I seemed to miss summer completely this year. When I left home it was late spring, now it is early fall. [illegible] I've been in a couple of weeks [illegible] between those dates I've moved so much summer just seemed to sneak by.

All my love [illegible]

ARMED FORCES AIR LETTER

AIR MAIL

This letter must be posted in Armed Forces Postal channels. If posted in a Civil Post Office or pillar box, it will not be given air transmission.

TO: Mrs C.R. Henderson
9665 - 87 avenue
Edmonton Alberta
Canada.

Fold Here

If anything is enclosed in this letter it will be sent by ordinary mail.

FROM
(Sender's Regt'l No., Rank and Name only)
M3827.
Pte Henderson GT.

This Armed Forces Air Letter cannot be accepted for registration.

Fold Here

Aug 15, 1944

Dear Mom:

Well, I see by the paper tonight that the allies have landed in France in the south. Every new front helps, doesn't it? It has wonderful possibilities coming in on Jerry in Italy from the rear etc.

Yesterday I cracked my pipe so I guess you had better buy me a new one. Mine isn't badly broken but I don't expect it will hold forever. If it doesn't cost too much would you mind registering the parcel? Ray had a pen sent over in about 3 weeks that way.

I haven't had a letter from you since a week ago today, but all the mail from Alberta seems to be held up, I expect I'll get a letter tomorrow or the next day.

No sign of the pipe tobacco yet, lady , but I still have about two weeks supply so I expect I'll get it before I run out.

Got paid last night and I'm very pleased to say that I have a credit of $20.00. I am leaving that much in so if leave comes thru when we finish here I can be sure of having a little cash. Incidentally, I guess you will be getting the first cheque from the govt pretty soon. The first one is for August and I figure you should be getting it around the 1st of the month. Keep an account of all the stuff you're buying for me and take it out of those cheques.

By the way, I hear we are getting a gratuity après le guere amounting to 60 shillings a month for our overseas service and 30 a month for service in Canada. That would be a nice thing wouldn't it?

Len & I are going to get a 24 hour pass this weekend and do a little travelling. I think we'll sneak a few hours in London if possible.

A bike is the ideal way to travel in this country. The towns are so close together it is the only way to get around.

I suppose the leaves are starting to turn by now eh? I'll bet the country looks pretty. I think that fall is the nicest season in Alberta.

I guess Pete will be going back to school in a few weeks. Somehow or other, I seemed to miss summer completely this year. When I left home it was late spring, now it's early fall, or it will be in a couple of weeks. In between those dates I've moved so much, summer just seemed to sneak by.

All my love

Grant

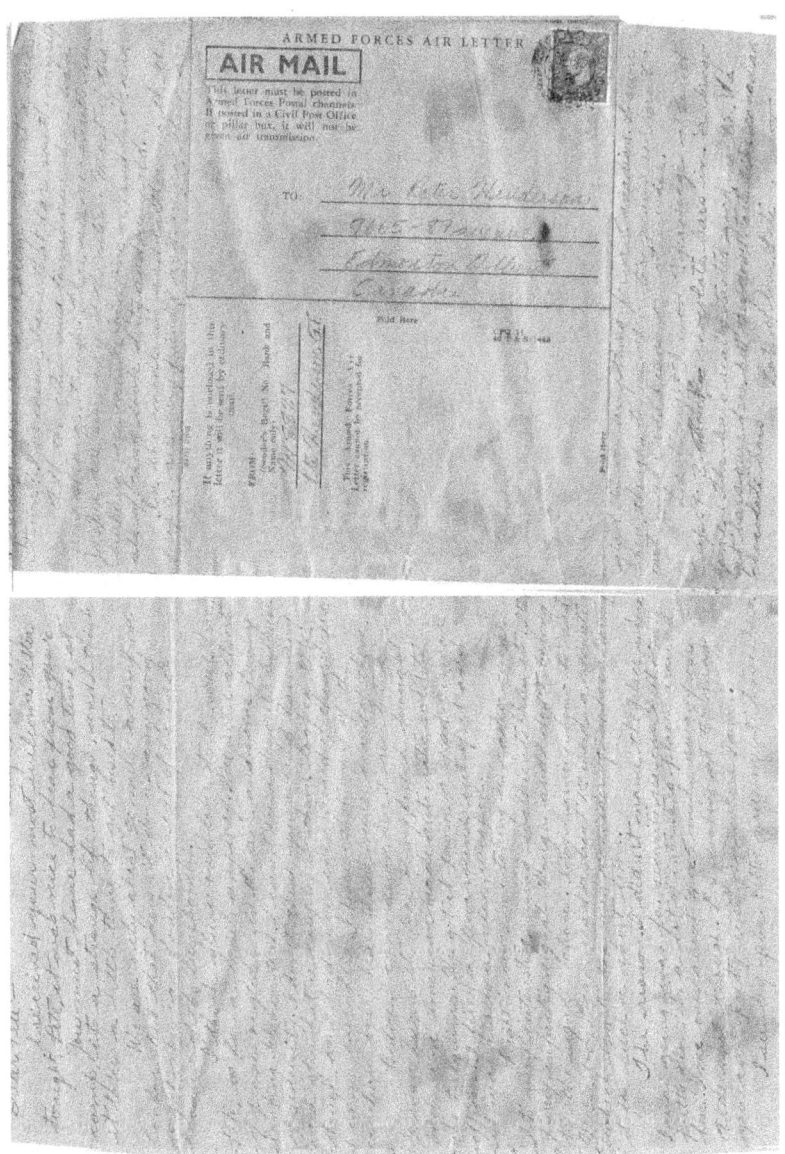

ARMED FORCES AIR LETTER

AIR MAIL

This letter must be posted in Armed Forces Postal channels. If posted in a Civil Post Office or pillar box, it will not be given air transmission.

TO:

Aug 17, 1944

Dear Pete:

I received your most welcome letter tonight, Pete; it was nice to hear from you.

You must have had a good time at camp, it's a strange life though and I think it takes a little time to get used to.

We are only about 30 miles away from London but that doesn't do us any good right now as London is out of bounds because of buzz bombs.

I think you would like to be over here Pete, for a while anyway. I've seen all sorts of planes and gliders in the air and some funny looking planes that I can't even describe because of security. I don't think you would have any idea of what a couple of them looked like though, as I had never even heard of them before I came over here. I know that most of the civilians over here have never heard of them.

Before I came down here I saw lots of German lugers etc. One of my friends brought back an American made automatic sold to the Belgian's. He got it from a dead German officer. I fired a few rounds out of it and it was a really a nice weapon.

Right now, I'm taking a radio course. It's very interesting using walkie talkies etc. It's purely infantry signals though and I don't belong to the signal choir. I'm learning how to read Morse too. I can read about 12 words a minute which isn't too bad considering I've been learning it for such a short time.

The reason I didn't name the place where I was going was for security reasons but I'm pretty close to a lot of interesting places around here. I'm only about 4 or 5 miles away from Aldershot though. By looking at the map you can pretty well see where I am.

I see by your letter you must have been pretty close to Lethbridge. Was it a nice town? I've never been that far south myself.

All the cities and towns over here look very strange though. There are no streets like Jasper Avenue in any of the cities. Most of the buildings are made of stone or / and brick and all of them look dirty and very old.

In the midlands land farther north the people are very friendly and any of them are glad to do anything for a Canadian. Down here they have seen too many soldiers to notice Canadians or otherwise.

Last night I won 2 packages of sweet cups & 2 chocolate bars in a bingo game. The bars really tasted good, no lie. We get bars over here but they don't taste like Canadian Chocolate bars.

Lot of Love Pete

Grant

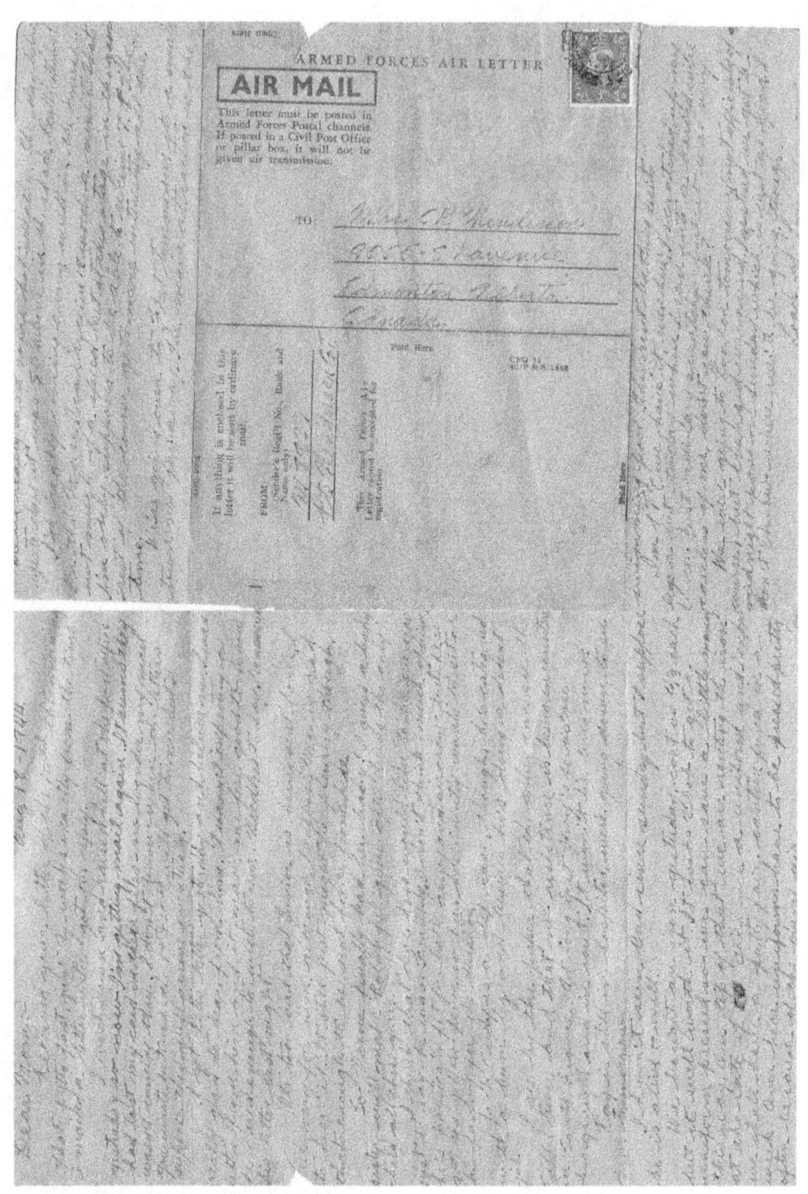

ARMED FORCES AIR LETTER

AIR MAIL

This letter must be posted in Armed Forces Postal channels. If posted in a Civil Post Office or pillar box, it will not be given air transmission.

TO:

Edmonton Alberta.

Canada.

Fold Here

If anything is enclosed in this letter it will be sent by ordinary mail.

FROM: (Sender's Regt'l No., Rank and Name only)

This Armed Forces Air Letter cannot be accepted for registration.

Fold Here

Aug 18, 1944

Dear Mom:

Received your letter of the 10th this morning. That's pretty fast, just 2 weeks exactly from the time I mailed a letter until I got the reply.

I went down and raised hell at the post office yesterday so now I'm getting mail again. It seems they had lost my card in their files – no wonder my mail wasn't coming thru. I don't know when the letters you wrote between the 1st & 10th will get to me but I suppose they will arrive eventually.

I got Pete's letter yesterday and believe me I was really glad to hear from him. I wasn't expecting a letter from him and it made me feel good to know he cared enough to write to me. Needless to say I answered his letter last night.

It's too bad that Junior is being sent home, I feel sorry for him, although I suppose Ma is glad to hear it. It still just might be pleurisy though, thats enough to be sent home from here.

So Verne finally had her baby! I guess a baby sister will make Bobby feel queer after being the only child all these years.

I think that dear Ross would like to be overseas just to say he was. Frankly, I don't think much of him, he's physically fit for both army and air crew but he's got the yellow fever so bad he evidently wants to sit on his fanny for the duration.

Jack Cardy is a dif. Case, though, he's categorized with a bum leg and besides he's doing a decent job.

I see by the paper that the allies can see the Eiffel tower and that no resistance is being encountered in South France. At long last Jerry's forces are disorganized and in rout. It won't be long now.

Ray is still in the hospital, were going down to see him tomorrow.

I haven't seen Bud since Sunday but I suppose he is alive & well.

We bought an iron yesterday, cost us 4/3 each but its' well worth it. It costs 2 bob to get a uniform pressed so we can save a little money this way. On top of that we are renting the iron at the rate of six pence a uniform and expect we shall have a pretty fair canteen fund in a week. Over here uniforms have to be pressed pretty often because of the damp air.

We've really had some hot weather. The day before yesterday it was 80 above in the shade. Really sticky!

I'm really coming along swell in the course. In the Morse I can receive 12 words a minute. That's not much of a speed but at this stage in the game I'm only supposed to be able to receive 7. The rest of the course gets more interesting all the time.

Were going over to Fleet tomorrow; it a small town not far away. The main attraction is the swimming pool. They rent bathing suits.

In PT (we have it, even here) I scratched up my legs a bit today when I ran into a barbed wire fence. Just ordinary scratches but it was very careless of me, don't you think?

We were going to London tomorrow. (Not officially of course) but changed our mind. Instead we got a midnight pass on Sunday which is just as good. I don't know where we'll be going though.

Loads of Love

Grant

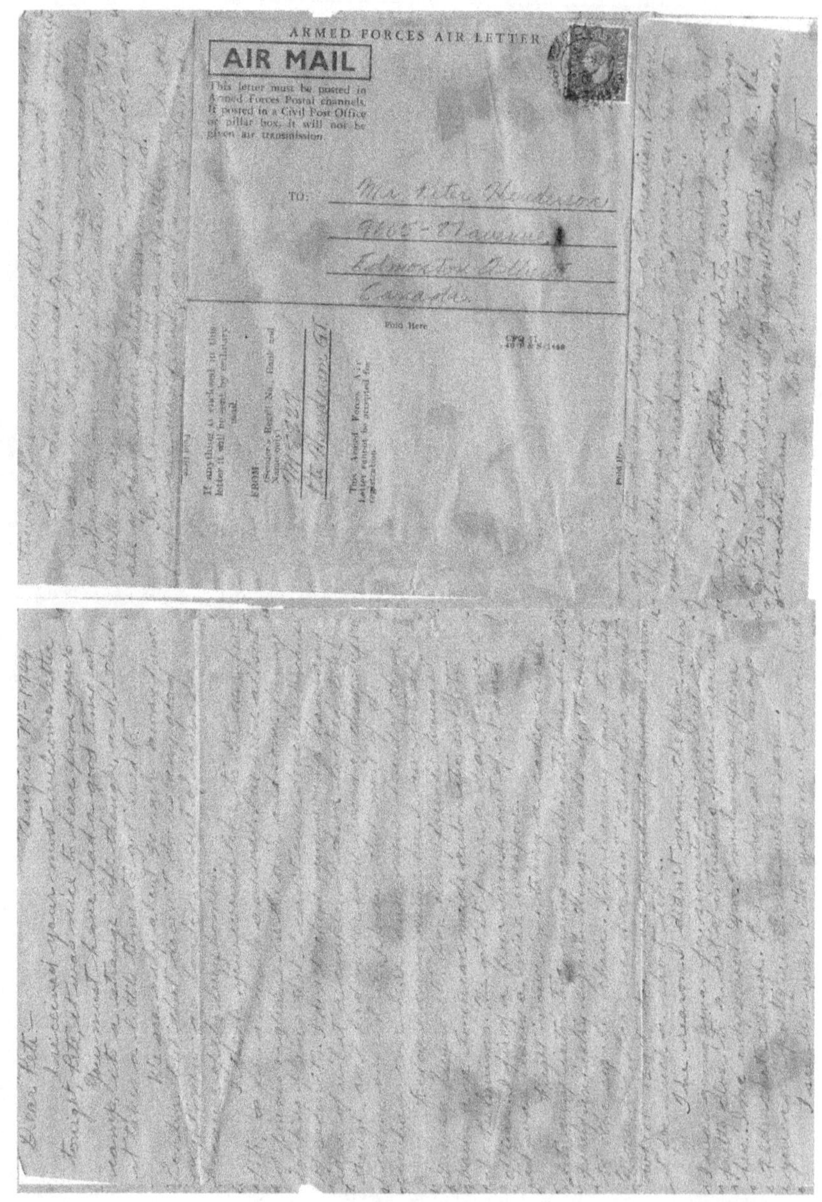
ARMED FORCES AIR LETTER
AIR MAIL
This letter must be posted in Armed Forces Postal channels. If posted in a Civil Post Office or pillar box, it will not be given air transmission.
TO:
Mr. Peter Henderson
Edmonton Alberta
Canada
Fold Here
If anything is enclosed in this letter it will be sent by ordinary mail.
FROM
This Armed Forces Air Letter cannot be accepted for registration.

Sunday Aug 20, 1944

Dear Mom:

Well, yesterday afternoon we went to the hospital and saw Ray. I was very pleased to see that he was almost better again. We found out what was wrong with him too. Something along the line of a boil had burst inside his cheek and then the next day or so his face had become so swollen that one eye was closed up and it was difficult for him to speak because of the swelling around his chin. When he was admitted to the hospital he was running a temp of 103. He sure got wonderful treatment. In the eleven days after he got into the hospital they gave him 47 shots of penicillin in the hip and it just ate the poison right up and dropped his temp in no time flat. Now all the swelling is gone except for one little lump about the size of a dime – they think they might lance that. The cost of the drug alone was 85 dollars a day. So if he had got that treatment in a civvy hospital it would have cost him over 1000 bucks counting doctors fees, hospital bills etc. They are sure doing some wonderful work in Canadian hospitals over here.

By the way, did you know that they don't use ether or chloroform to put you to sleep anymore? They just give a person a shot in the arm and the boys say that when they wake up they feel as though they feel as though they have just woke up from an ordinary sleep. It is very heartening to walk through a hospital over here. They are miles ahead of anything at home.

Yesterday we took 3 girls to the show. Don't worry; their ages were from 6 or so to about 10. It seems that kids can't go to shows over here unless they are convoyed by an adult. I felt quite domesticated etc when I wandered into the

theatre with one kid holding one of my hands and 2 on the other hand. Oh Well!
We were going to go to Winchester today, it's about 25 miles away but it's raining so we decided to stay around home.
I was reading about this gratuity scheme for us in the army paper. Do you realize that if I put 25 bucks in the old sock every month plus the 15 a month the govt gives me I'll be the best thing to a millionaire when the war is over? At least I'll have a little money to invest when I get home. I'm glad to hear that the zombies aren't included in the plan.

Well, the news looks brighter all the time, things are happening so quickly no one can keep up with the news. I'm willing to bet that in a month we'll be at the German border. With the Russians at the other border and with the combined air fleets something very interesting should happen to Germany. I personally figure they'll quit by the time the armies get to the border though.

One of the boys was a near casualty on Fri night. Ray Cullingme (one of the 3 Rays) was sleeping peacefully when the kid next to him had a nightmare and decided to strangle Ray. Believe me he almost succeeded too. Ray was well wrapped up in his blankets he couldn't do a damn thing. If we hadn't woke up, for another 60 sec. I think Ray would have been a goner. He was sure blue in the face and terrified when we freed him.

Love

Grant

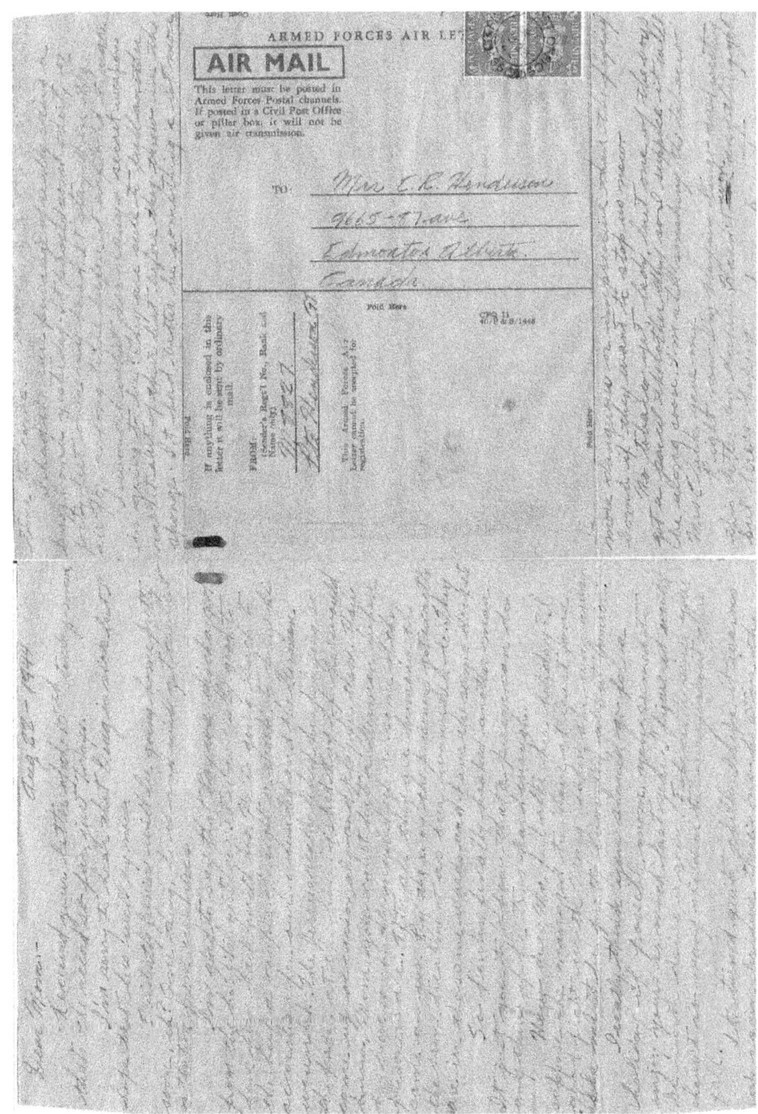

ARMED FORCES AIR LET

AIR MAIL

This letter must be posted in Armed Forces Postal channels. If posted in a Civil Post Office or pillar box, it will not be given air transmission.

TO: Mrs E. R. Henderson
9665-97 ave
Edmonton Alberta
Canada

Aug 22, 1944

Dear Mom:

Received you letter of the 15th today, mom that's the record so far, just 7 days.

I'm sorry to hear that Doug is sick but I hope that he's well by now.

Evidently Junior will be going home pretty soon, eh? One thing, he is and will get the best attention from our docs.

I'm glad to say that Ray was discharged from the hospital yesterday. It was really good to have him back with us. He is going back to the hosp. a couple of nights a week to play his accordion for our wounded and the German wounded. The Jerries really liked his playing so the padre at the hosp. asked Ray if he would come up occasionally and play for them. You know, Mom, you can't hate a German when he's been so badly mauled up as some of the prisoners are. After all they are humans the same as us. By the way the prisoners get exactly the same treatment as our wounded do. They are on the same wards and have the same docs etc.

So Pinky finally hooked another man. It just goes to show that a person can do anything if he tries hard enough.

How does Ma feel after her holiday? I suppose she managed to have at least one good fight with Marg when she was away. She must be pretty worried about Junior.

I really think you should go for a holiday if possible, mom, you seem to enjoy yours so much last year. I figure it would be worth doing again. Especially since you haven't so many children to worry about this fall.

Its' turned quite chilly. I hope it warms up again because there's no heat in the buildings and it won't be turned on for some time to come.

I had the rare privilege of really seeing a buzz bomb yesterday. It passed some thirty or forty feet over my head. It stayed in the air for a long time before it exploded though.

I wonder what Germany's secret weapon is going to be? They are sure to pull another rabbit out of their hat before they throw in the sponge. It had better be something a lot more dangerous or impressive then the flying bomb if they want to stop us now.

No tobacco yet, lady, but one of the boys got a parcel the other day so I suppose it will be along soon. I'm still smoking the tobacco Mrs. Clark gave me.

Right now I'm playing bingo and writing this letter by dashes. Haven't won anything yet but here's hoping.

Love Grant

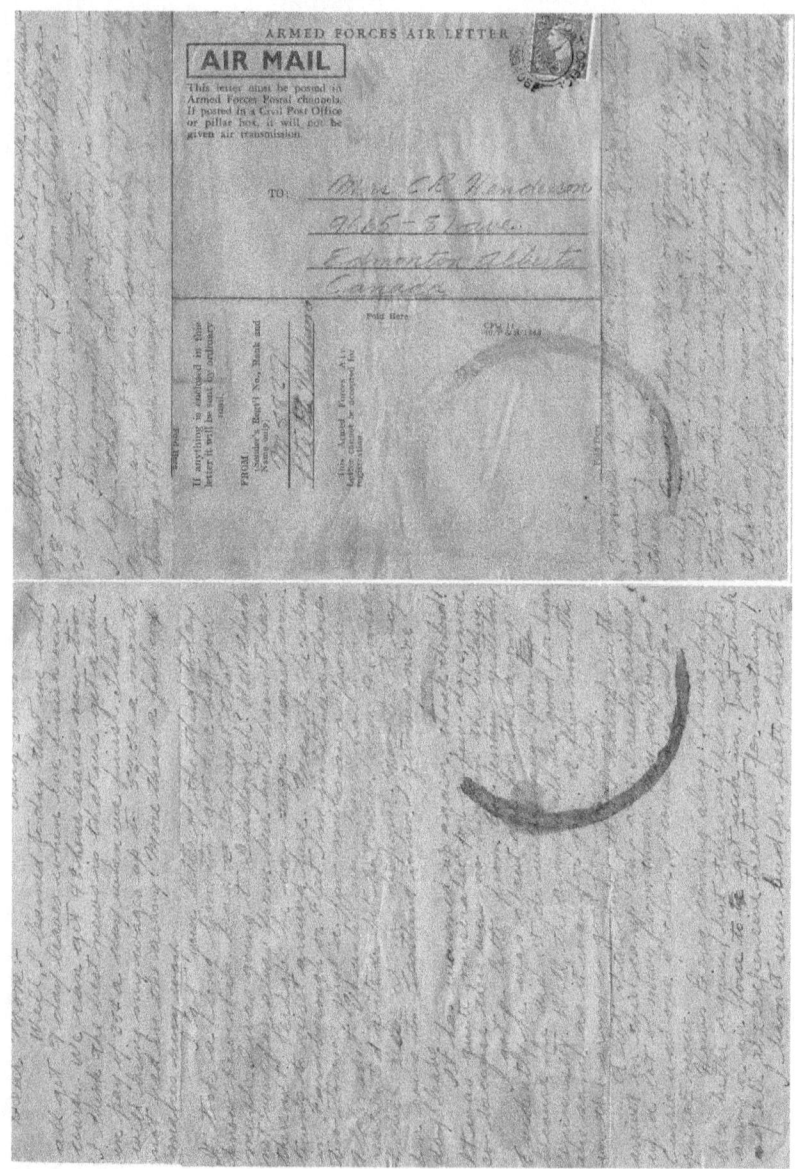

ARMED FORCES AIR LETTER

AIR MAIL

This letter must be posted in Armed Forces Postal channels. If posted in a Civil Post Office or pillar box, it will not be given air transmission.

TO: Mrs C.R. Henderson
Edmonton Alberta
Canada

Fold Here

If anything is enclosed in this letter it will be sent by ordinary mail.

FROM (Sender's Regt'l No., Rank and Name only)

This Armed Forces Air Letter cannot be accepted for registration.

Aug 25, 1944

Dear Mom:

Well, I learned today that we will all get 9 day leaves when we are finished our course. We can get 48 hour leaves now too. I think the best news is that we get a raise in pay of 25 cents a day when we finish. They will bring my wages to 52.50 a month not bad in the army. More than a full corp. makes anyway.

I got your letter of the third today. It took a long time to get here but you know how it is. Dad thought that maybe I was going to Guilford, eh? Well that's not very far away from here but I haven't been there yet. Perhaps he can suggest some towns to visit around here. Maybe he's been to Farnborough or Fleet. I'm in between those two towns, just a few miles away from Aldershot. Up until now travel had been restricted quite a bit but now I have the whole British Iles at my disposal. Needless to say I'm going to Scotland when I get my nine days leave.

It has warmed up again, thank the Lord! It was quite miserable for a few days, more so because there was no heat in the buildings.

I got a letter from Bob Jenkins yesterday. Evidently he was about due for the army because he didn't do well enough for University. Well, the army will be good for him the same as it was for me. A few months in the army is good for anybody.

A lot of boys that I trained with arrived in this camp this a.m. I really picked up a lot of news from them. My corporal at Currie was one of them of course he's just a private now.

How's Doug coming along? I sure hope he's better again, but there's no place like the army or air force to get sick in. Just think of all the expensive treatment for nothing!

I haven't seen Bud for pretty close to 2 weeks now but I guess he's o.k.

Monday's pay day! I think I'll draw a little extra money and apply for 48 this weekend. I haven't even had 24 for 10 weeks now oh well.

Four months from today is Christmas. I hope that by that time the war is over. Anyway it sure looks like it. I see by tonight's war map the Yanks are only 60 or 70 miles away from the Belgium border. I wonder if the Germans can stop us at their border?

Anyway dear old Montgomery figures it will be over before Nov 9. I wonder if they will try to force armistice on Nov 11? Stranger things have happened. Well I guess that's all for now, lady. I didn't have much to say but maybe something will happen in the next day or so.

All my love

Grant

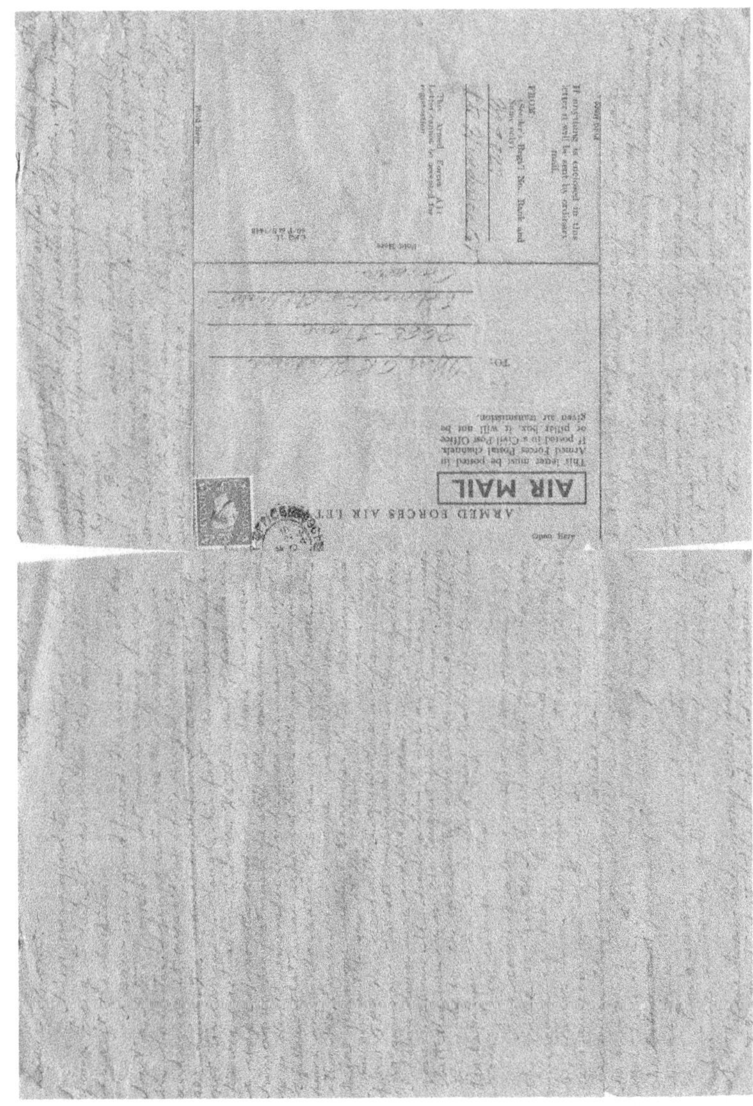

ARMED FORCES AIR LETTER

AIR MAIL

This letter must be posted in Armed Forces Postal channels. If posted in a Civil Post Office or pillar box, it will not be given air transmission.

TO:

Open Here

If anything is enclosed in this letter it will be sent by ordinary mail.

FROM (Sender's Regt'l No., Rank and Name only)

The Armed Forces Air Letter cannot be accepted for registration.

Fold Here

Aug 28, 1944

Dear Mom:

I'm very glad to say that I got a letter from Doug today. It was written the day after he left the hospital.

I saw a good friend Hennigar yesterday. I got a letter from him at noon saying he was in hospital. I found out where the hospital was and since it wasn't very far away, I went up to see him. He was wounded in France on 1st Aug. not too seriously though, his foot was smashed up & his leg fractured in 2 places. He'll be out of the hospital in a couple of months and on his way home because I imagine his foot will be stiff for some time. In case you don't remember who he was, he was one of the 2 fellows that I was supposed to see the first day I was home on embarkation. He lives in Grande Prairie. The other kid, Exner was his name was killed some time before Hennigar was hurt. Remember Watson the crazy kid I pointed out to you at the station when we came down from G.P. He's dead ditto. I guess there's no harm in telling you now that all my friends were in France before I came down here and I'm afraid that most of them are goners. Ah me. It's heartbreaking to me as you can imagine but they were in on the toughest job of the war. They paved the way for the spectacular advances being made now. Perhaps you can understand my dislike for Bud's kind now. But enough of that!

I am coming along swell on my course, all the more since I heard about the 25 cents a day increase in pay. But I'm afraid I'm going to be stuck here for months yet though. They haven't sent anyone out of here for a long time because they actually require so few of us. I'm beginning to think I'll be here for the rest of the war. From what the papers say I won't be finishing the course before the war is over.

Doug seems to have it pretty soft eh? From what he says he gets 48 every weekend. Boy oh boy.

You know lady money sure goes over here. I can't understand it. Thank the Lord tomorrow's pay day.

The weather's been beautiful for the past few days. Just like fall weather at home. You know when it's chilly in the morning and nice and hot by noon.

Had an apple yesterday, boy it was good! One of the boys has a cousin in London and she sent him some apples and plums. Unfortunately it took the parcel 2 weeks to get here so the plums were a bit spoiled. We were sort of figuring on making some wine out of them but we didn't have a recipe so, no sale.

I really had a laugh the other night. We wanted to play trick on a fellow and so we dismantled his bed when he was on leave and hid the pieces. He came in, in middle of the night and you can imagine his surprise when he found the bed was gone. It took quite a time to sink in his noodle that we were just having a little fun. Oh well!

How's Verna's baby. I'll bet it's cute.

That's all for now beautiful.

Love Grant

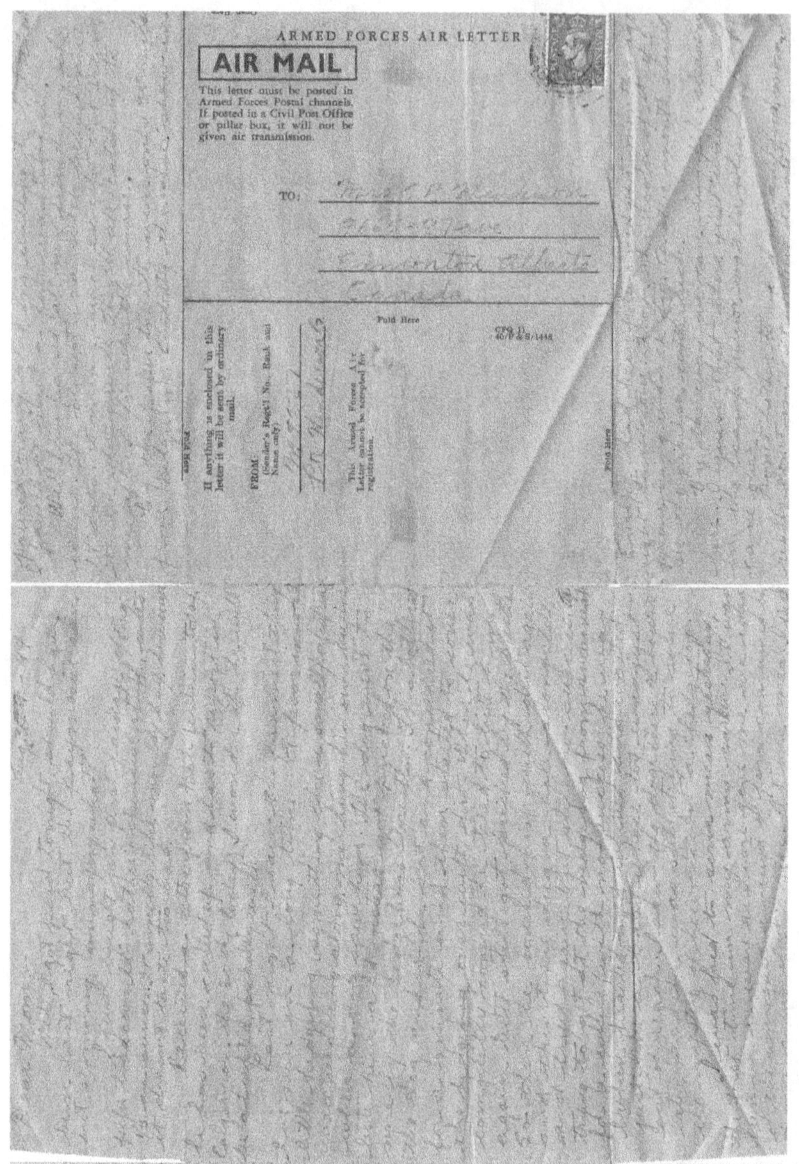

ARMED FORCES AIR LETTER

AIR MAIL

This letter must be posted in Armed Forces Postal channels. If posted in a Civil Post Office or pillar box, it will not be given air transmission.

TO:

Fold Here

CFQ D.
40/P & S/1448

Fold Here

If anything is enclosed in this letter it will be sent by ordinary mail.

FROM:
(Sender's Regt'l No., Rank and Name only)

This Armed Forces Air Letter cannot be accepted for registration.

Fold Here

Aug 30, 1944

Dear Mom:

Well, I got paid tonight, should have been last night but the paymaster ran out of money, annoying what?

I just bought my first package of Eng. pipe tobacco. It's rather expensive stuff, cost 1/3 an ounce. It smells like moldy hay, however it doesn't taste too bad.

Received a letter from Bob Jenkins today. He has been called up and has to report in Calgary on the 30th (today). I wonder if he will be accepted, probably will.

Last night I saw the funniest thing I've seen in a long time. A poor innocent little hedgehog (something like a small porcupine) was walking along minding his own business when a dog saw him. The dog went to bite him and instead got pricked on the nose by the hedgehog's bristles. This bothers the dog and so he sat and considered it for a minute and then started to cover the hedgehog over with dirt. When he was completely covered he tried to bite him again but still got pricked by the bristles. So then he covered him with dirt again and this time dug a hole alongside and tried again but still no success. After trying to get at the hedgehog from underneath for a while (with no success) he was broken hearted and whined and wailed. I was forced to serve meals yesterday, the first time in my army career. It was fun in a way and sure gave me an idea of the immense amount of food consumed by a camp of this size. At one meal I just poured gravy and I'm willing to bet that I poured at least a full washtub full.

Well I've passed all my friends in the course. The closest is a week behind me. It doesn't mean much except that I like to be doing well. They'll all catch up to me after I finish the course.

By the paper tonight we're only 35 mile from Belgium. Evidently the whole show in Europe had been planned out months ago right to victory. From the looks of it the planning was o.k. too. Another month should see the finish with luck.

By the way we can buy pipe cleaners here. I guess that there wasn't any in the camp Junior was in when he first came over.

Don't bother to send me any food mom. I really don't miss it. (Believe it or not)

Love Grant

ARMED FORCES AIR LETTER

AIR MAIL

This letter must be posted in Armed Forces Postal channels. If posted in a Civil Post Office or pillar box, it will not be given air transmission.

TO:

Fold Here

I guess the French towns that have

Sept 2, 1944

Dear Mom:

Received your letter of the 24th at noon today and am pleased to hear that my soap and the other stuff is on the way. Some of the boys have been getting parcels in as little as 3 weeks so here's hoping for a fast service. I was lucky enough to get some soap – enough to do me until the parcel arrives.

I'm sorry to hear that Verna is having so much trouble with her legs. I hope the condition clears up soon.

I guess the French towns that have been in the news for the past day or two will be familiar to Dad, Verdun, Arras etc. It was too bad you celebrated the fall of Paris a day or so too soon but it belongs to us now. I think it was a nice thing for the same Can. Regiment who were in Dieppe before to capture it this time, don't you? Everyone ever here seems to think we can expect an armistice any time now. Even Monty thinks it'll be over by October 1st. Very few fly bombs are coming over now so perhaps they will lift the ban on London for us!

Its' been raining (pouring) off and on since last night, rains for about 10 minutes and then stops for 10 and boy how it rains once it starts.

I was going up to see Hennigar today but I think I'll leave it till tomorrow in the hopes that it will stop raining. He's had four operations on his foot in the last week and evidently it's going to be almost as good as new before he gets out. He likes this new idea of a shot in the arm to put a person to sleep. You should see some of the fellows waking up, it's just as though they were drunk. They sing and giggle and act crazy as hell, it's really laughable.

I just finished my washing for the week – 2 towels, 4 pairs of socks, a shirt and a suit of underwear. I always feel pretty proud of myself when I get it finished.

As soon as we have supper, I think we will go up town, rain or no rain. After all it is Sat. and we have to do something. Or don't you think so?

I never hear from Junior, mom, but probably he's' been pretty sick and not in the mood to write. I think he'll be home pretty soon now because they're trying to clear the hospitals for causalities.

Someday next week I'm going up to have my eyes tested again. I think my eyes are much stronger so I might as well have new specs if I need them. That's the beauty about the army; costs never enter into any kind of med. Treatment.

I borrowed a pipe from Ray Calder until my new one arrives, thank the Lord for that. It's too bad I couldn't go and get my tonsils out or something because the Red Cross gives all that stuff to patients.

Still no tobacco, lady but it surely must come this week, those damn tobacco companies are slower that the second coming of Christ! Oh well, English tobacco is better than none. Well I guess that's it for now, lady.

Love and Kisses Grant

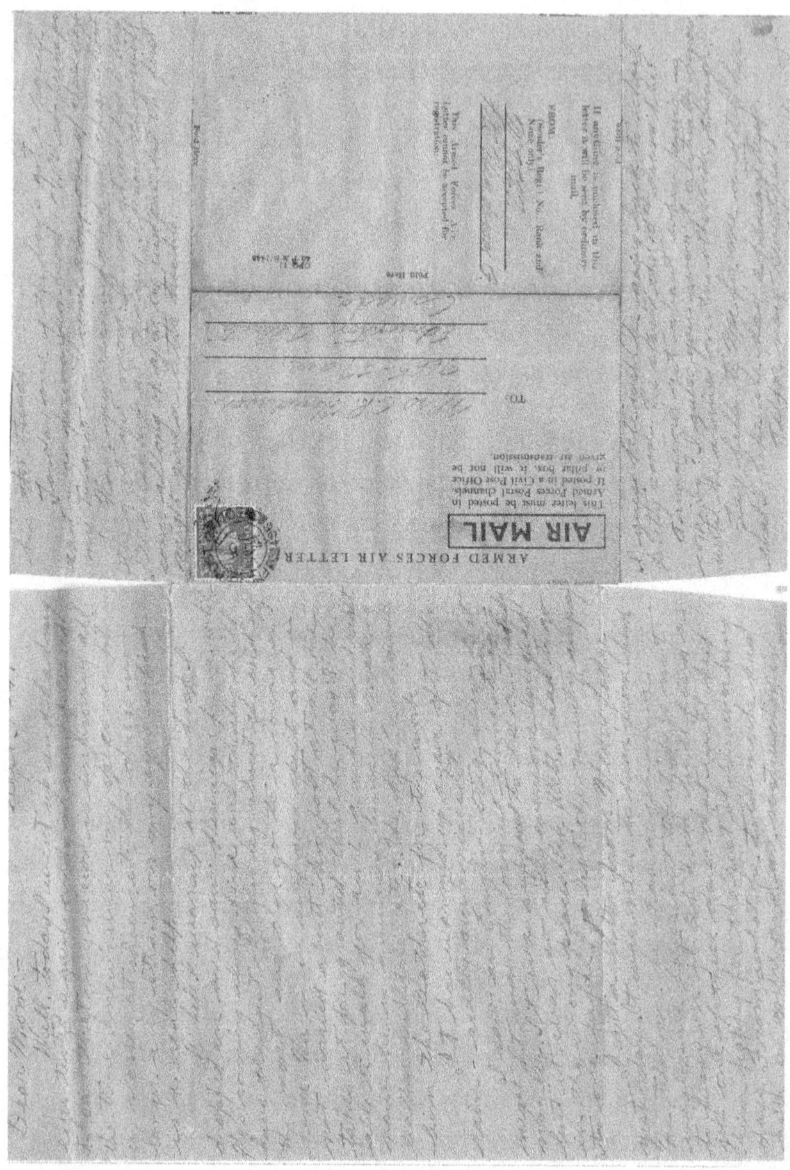

ARMED FORCES AIR LETTER

AIR MAIL

This letter must be posted in Armed Forces Postal channels. If posted in a Civil Post Office or pillar box, it will not be given air transmission.

TO:

Sept 5, 1944

Dear Mom:

Well, today I went up and had my eyes tested again and I'm very pleased to say that my vision is improving all the time. I never wear my specs except in classes, at shows, etc. but there is no longer any strain on my eyes which is a real help.

While I was up at the hosp. I dropped in and saw Hennigar for a while. He's coming along fine and thinks he'll have the cast off his leg about the end of the month and then go to a convalescent home. He is in very good spirits and is not worried about his foot at all. He takes it for granted that he won't be able to walk for quite a while and right now he is amusing himself making leather billfolds etc. The Red Cross gives him the leather etc. for the work.

It has warmed up again after the rain – really quite nice out.

I saw an English stage show last night. It was the corniest thing I ever saw no lie. It was supposed to be a tragedy but it was so silly everyone laughed in the wrong places. Oh well, I had to go to one before I left the country anyway.

I got a letter from Henry Lodge yesterday. It was nice to hear from him. He tells me he has a job in a wholesale house but that he's not too fussy on it. Oh well, he'll find a job one of these days that will keep him happy for the rest of his working days. From what he told me he had both a goiter and an obstruction in his throat.

Today one of the boys got a parcel that was forwarded from CIRU so perhaps my tobacco will come along one of these days

Have you received the first cheque from the govt yet, mom? If not let me know and I'll check up at this end. I know they will come along o.k. after the first one but the first one might give a little trouble.

I guess Pete will be going back to school pretty soon. He starts the 10th doesn't he?

Any word yet about when Junior is coming? I guess you won't actually know until he arrives on the other side, though.

Say hello to Ma for me and tell her that I hope she had a pleasant trip.

All for now sweetheart

Love & kisses

Grant

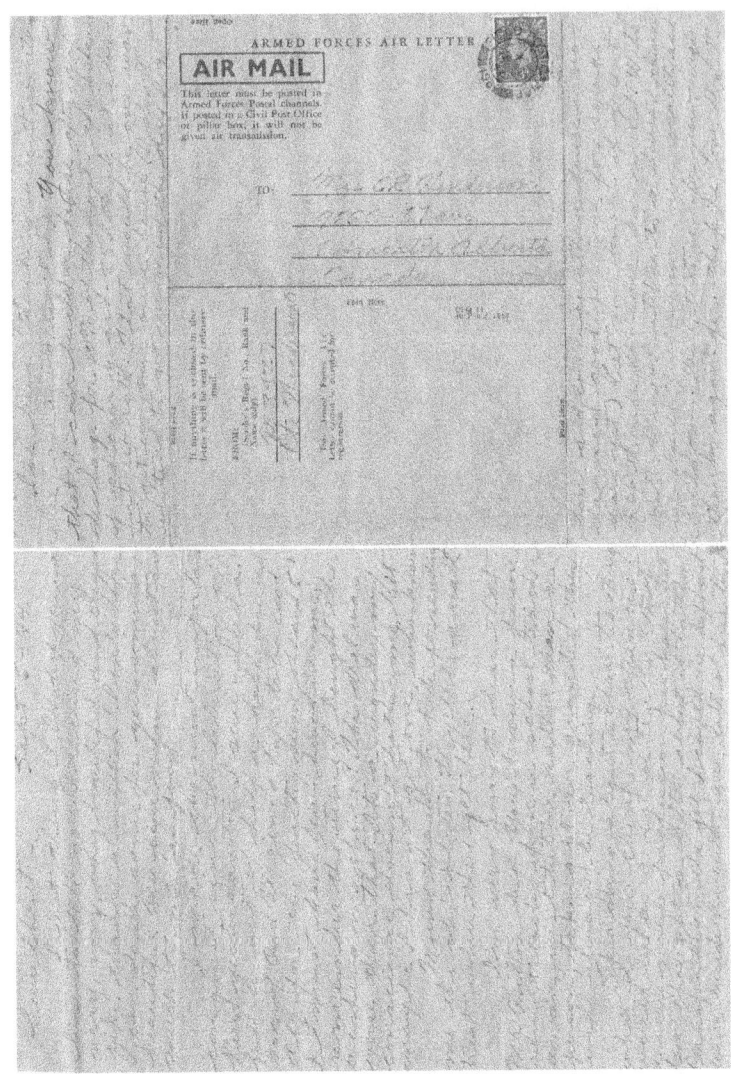

ARMED FORCES AIR LETTER

AIR MAIL

This letter must be posted in Armed Forces Postal channels. If posted in a Civil Post Office or pillar box, it will not be given air transmission.

TO:

Sept 6, 1944

Sweetheart:

I just thought I'd drop you a line to tell you I received my very, very, very beautiful and elegant pipe. Thanks a million! I only hope that I can do the same for you someday, beautiful. My pipe means almost as much to me as food.

I made the most important conquest since the liberation of Paris yesterday too. I swindled a fellow out of half a half pound box of Old Virginia Pipe tobacco. All for the paltry sum of 1 and 6! I must have Jew blood in me; remember the time I bought the washing machine? This deal was worse than that. It's a wonder my conscience doesn't bother me, but maybe I haven't got one, who knows.

Many thanks to Pete for sending me the chocolates. They'll be a real treat when they get here.

I am very sorry to hear that Mrs. Hilton died. You know a person almost looks upon a school teacher as an institution rather than a person, taking for granted they will always be teaching.

Speaking about school teaching what do you think my chances would be as a school teacher? Not a very noble profession perhaps but I thought a little about it lately. Perhaps that's the job I could be happiest doing besides I would have lots of free time to travel etc. if I wanted to.

I've been thinking about something else (amazing isn't it). You know that I can build a house after my discharge for 10% of the cost, the balance being spread over years 25 I think at a low interest rate. That would be one way to get *our own house (*I don't intend to get married the day I get home and consequently a house is no dammed good for me for several years yet) Let me know if you & pop think the idea has merit. With Doug & I entitled to a house, I think we should find us some nice locality and build one. Well that's all for now sugar.

Thanks again for the pipe.

Love Grant

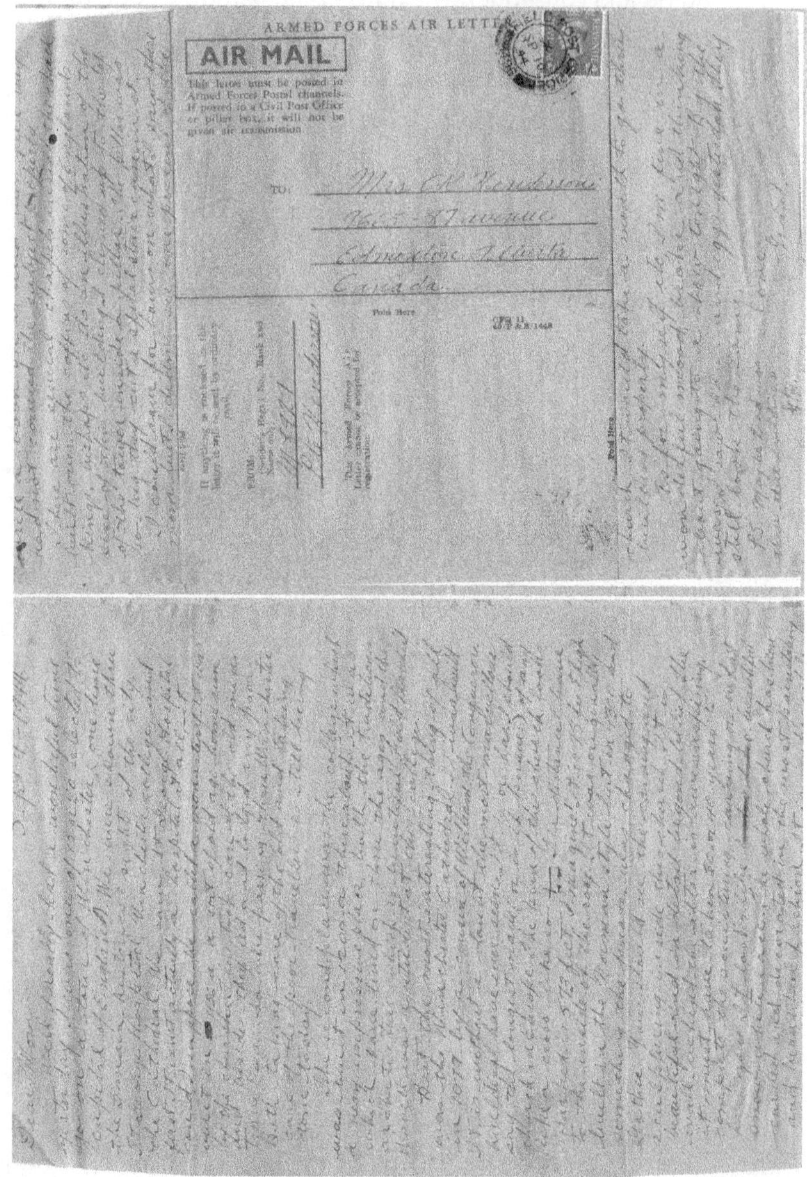

ARMED FORCES AIR LETTER

AIR MAIL

This letter must be posted in Armed Forces Postal channels. If posted in a Civil Post Office or pillar box, it will not be given air transmission.

TO:

Canada

Sept 9, 1944

Dear Mom:

Well I really had a wonderful time yesterday. I was one of 15 or 20 selected to go on a tour of Winchester, (one time capital of England). We were shown the 3 main historical sights of the city, St George Hospital, Winchester College, and the Cathedral. We saw St George Hospital first. It isn't actually a hospital at all, it could I suppose be a monastery. It was built in 1136 as a sort of old age home run by the church. They took care of the old men and besides they fed and lodged any poor travelers who were passing thru Winchester. Both taking care of the old and taking care of the poor travelers is still being done today.

The second place was the college which was built in 1200 or thereabouts. It was a very impressive place, both the traditions which have lived on thru the ages and the architecture which is beautiful. Field Marshall Worrall was a student at this college.

But the most interesting thing of all was the Winchester Cathedral. It was built in 1079 by a cousin of William the Conqueror. It is without a doubt the most marvelous building I have ever seen. It is or has, I should say the longest nave (or is Knave) of any church in Europe. The plan of this church looks like a cross like +- . The distance I have marked is 573 feet. Imagine! It is 78 feet high to the inside of the roof. It was originally built in the Norman style but in 1300 and something. The knave was changed to Gothic. You should see the carving and sculpturing inside this church. It is beautiful and in detail beyond belief. The wall behind the alter is awe inspiring, it must have taken 30 or 40 years to complete the sculpturing, carving or what have you. It looks like beautiful snow white lace. The whole church has been carved and decorated in the most painstaking and beautiful fashion. It is impossible for me to describe this place. One could write a book on it and then feel they had not covered the subject properly.

There are several chapels inside the church built over the coffins of some of England's kings, bishops, etc. As an illustration of the size of this building, I climbed up to the top of the tower inside a pillar. The pillar was so big they cut a spiral stair case in it.

I could rave for hours on what I saw there, mom, but I didn't see one percent of the church. It would take a month to go thru the buildings properly.

As for myself etc, I'm fine in a wonderful mood, broke and thinking about going to a show tonight. By the way, I saw ham and eggs yesterday. They still look the same.

Love Grant

P.S. Maybe Dad was thru these buildings

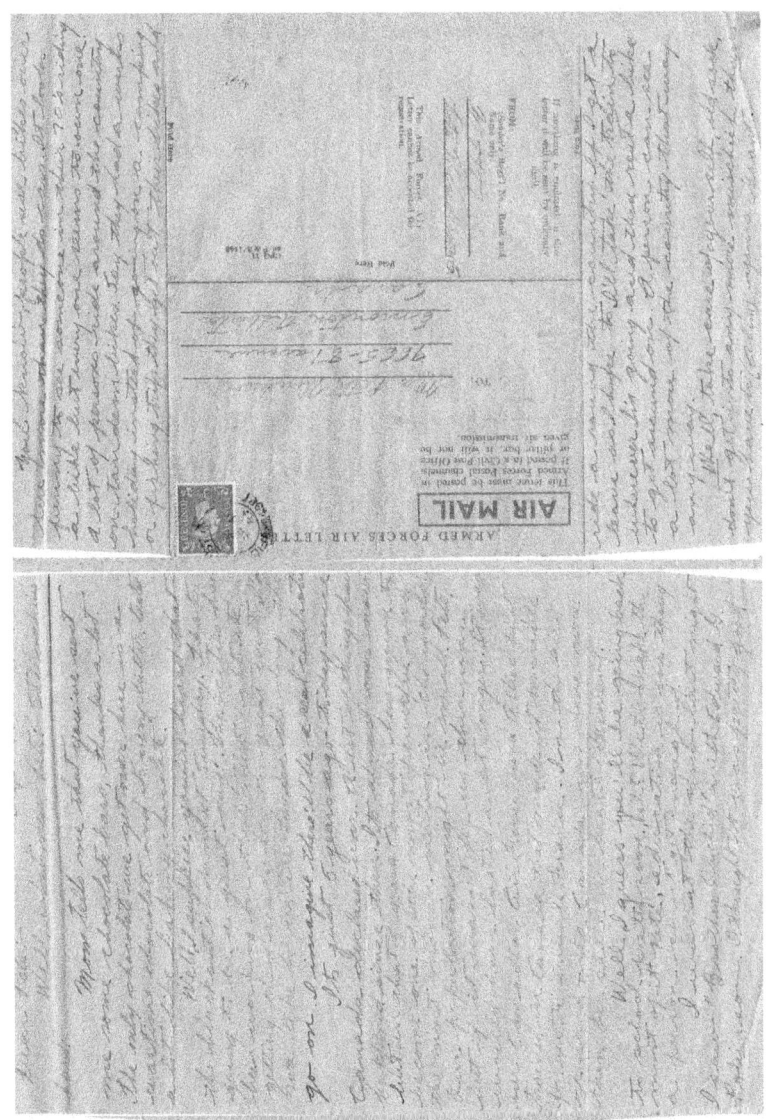

Sept 10, 1944

Dear Pete:

Well, what's new Pete? Still working hard?

Mom tells me that you've sent me some chocolate bars, thanks a lot. The only chocolate we get over here is wartime chocolate and it's very bitter, tastes a lot like baking chocolate.

Well, I suppose you've heard that the blackout ends next Sunday. That's going to be a great day! The cities have been working on their street lights etc. getting them ready for the great event. I'd sure like to be in London the day they go on. I imagine there'll be a real celebration.

It's just 5 years ago today since Canada declared war. A lot of things have happened since then. It's almost over now but in that 5 years Canada has grown to become one of the most powerful and the most modern nation in the world. Our population might be small, Pete, but if it wasn't for us this war would have lasted a lot longer. It was our Canadian Air Force and Allied pilots trained in Canada that made it possible for us to invade France. In the air, on land & sea, Canada has done more that her share in beating Germany.

Well, I guess you'll be going back to school pretty soon, eh? Well make the most of it Pete, education is one thing a person can't get enough of.

I was at the show last night. I saw "Brother Orchid" with Edward G Robinson. I thought it was pretty good although I suppose its 2 or 3 years old.

You know, people use bikes over here more that they do cars. It looks funny to see someone in their 70's riding a bike but everyone seems to own one. A lot of persons ride around the country on tandem bikes. Say they had a week's holiday instead of going on a camping or fishing trip they get out their bikes and ride around the country. If I get leave as I hope to, I'll take the train to wherever I'm going and then rent a bike to get around on. A person can see a lot more of the county that way anyways.

Well, take care of yourself, old sock, don't get into anymore mischief then you have to (ahem).

Yours

Grant

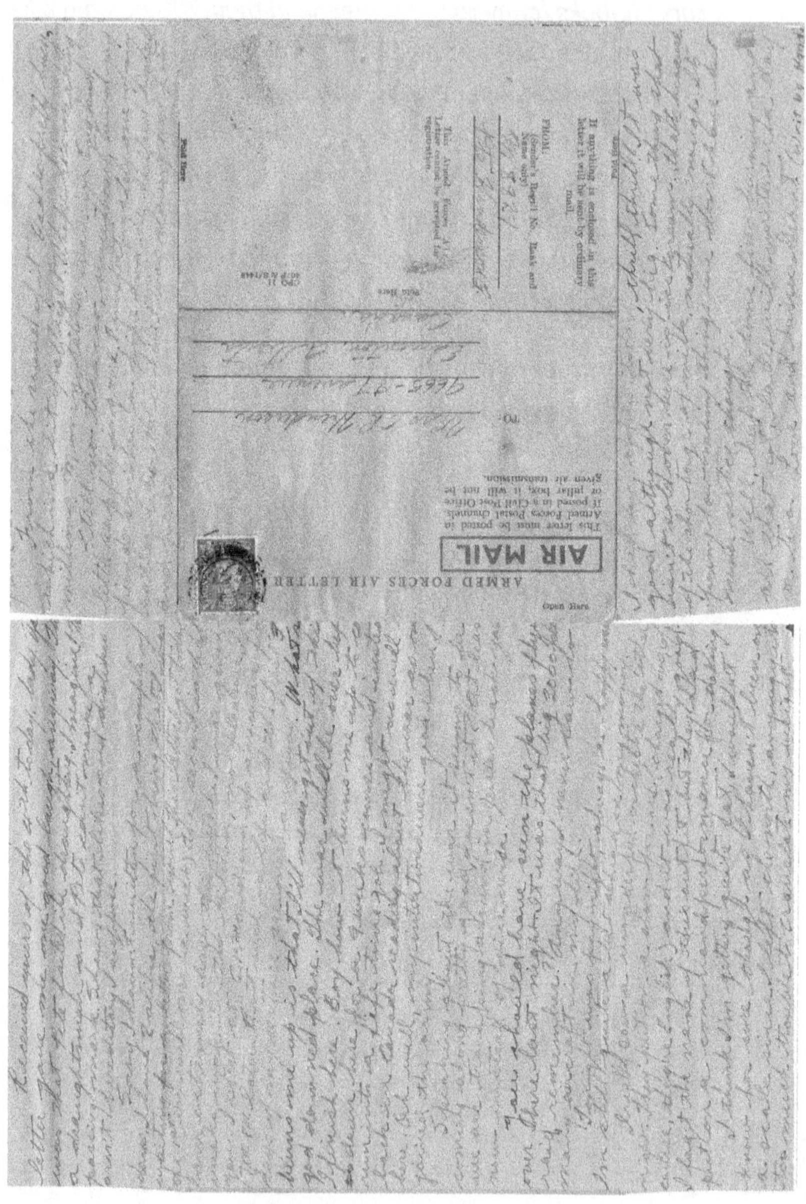

Sept 13, 1944

Dear Mom:

Received yours of the 4th today, lady. Your letter gave me a good laugh anyway. That was that Pete failed in draughting. Imagine! Me a draughtsman and Pete can't make a passing mark. Shows that likes and dislikes aren't hereditary I suppose.

Sorry I haven't written for a couple of days. I have 2 alibis, the first being that I was waiting for a letter from you. (This letter I got today is the 1st in well over a week) The second is that I am extremely busy this week. I was given a week's work in the kitchen, no pleasure. I assure you I start at 6:15 am and end anywhere from 7:00 pm later. But such is life and the first 3 days of my sentence are over anyway. What really burns me up is that I'll never get out of this God Damned place. The war will be over before I finish here. Boy how it burns me up to come down here for a 9 week course and instead run into a life time job. I might as well be back in Canada reading about the war as over here. Oh well, my intentions were good when I joined the army.

Speaking about the war it seems to be coming along pretty good, doesn't it? At least we are tramping around in Jerries back yard now instead of vice versa.

You should have seen the planes flying over here last night. It was that big 3000 plane raid, remember? Anyways I've never seen so many aircraft in my life.

Tonight was pay night, always a happy event. I'm still quite bit a head on my money.

I really saw a wonderful orchestra the other night. They put on a show for us (charged us of course, they're English) and it was really good. I forgot the name of this outfit but they had put on a command performance for the King.

I think I am getting quite fat. I wouldn't know for sure though as I haven't been on a scale since I left the north, anyway it's too much trouble to translate my weight from stones to lbs.

From the sound of it Dad is pretty busy which is a bit of all right. I hope he's making millions. Money talks, even in England.

Still no tobacco, sweetheart, and my little supply is gone. Unfortunately one of my friends smoke a pipe and he helped himself rather liberally while I was slaving over pots and pans.

I had an apple today, thrill thrill! It was good although not very big. Something that isn't sold over here is ice cream. That's because of the shortage of milk, naturally enough. It's funny how many thing we don't have but never notice though.

Well, keep the home fires burning and all that rot, lady, will write in a day or two.

Love and Kisses

Grant

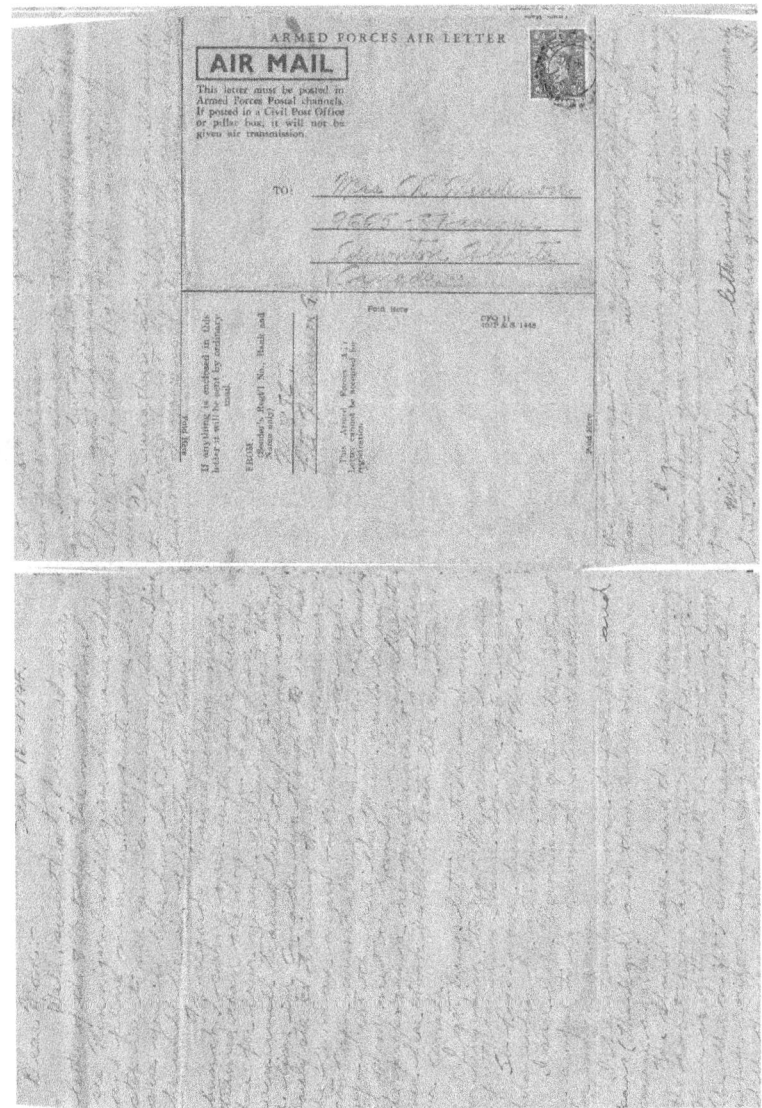

ARMED FORCES AIR LETTER

AIR MAIL

This letter must be posted in Armed Forces Postal channels. If posted in a Civil Post Office or pillar box, it will not be given air transmission.

TO:

Edmonton, Alberta

Canada

Fold Here

If anything is enclosed in this letter it will be sent by ordinary mail.

FROM:
(Sender's Regt'l No., Rank and Name only)

This Armed Forces Air Letter cannot be accepted for registration.

Fold Here

CFO 11
4017 A.S. 1945

Fold Here

September 16, 1944

Dear Mom:

Well, sweetheart, I received your letter of the 8th today. The next time I see Hennigar I shall give him our address and phone number. I'm quite sure he'll stop in to see you on his way home. I'm sure you'll like him but I don't expect he will be in Alberta till Nov.

As regards trained soldiers, mom, the bunch I came over with were better trained that the boys who had been over here for four years, believe it or not. We were well trained but they strung us such a line Canada we thought we had barely started training. As you can see now the German army met its end back at Caen and Falaise and it was the Canucks who beat the best the Hun could throw at them not the Yanks or Limeys. Despite the propaganda no great amount of soldiers over here took battle drill etc. like we took in Canada.

I got Doug's letter yesterday and am writing him tonight. He seems to be having a pretty fair time. I sure hope he gets a commission.

So Ross is over here. My, my he'll be a hero when he gets home how.

I sure hope Verne's leg gets better; it must be awful to have something like that. Give her my regards.

I have only one more day on pots and pans (Thank God) and then back on my course again.

You should have heard the shells banging the coast from France this a.m. I guess the Hun is getting rid of all he's got in hurry. The other night I saw a beautiful sight. The whole horizon was red glow from one of the German held towns on the coast of France. It must have been quite a fire to be seen that distance.

I'm rather surprised the war is still going on but glad of it. We'll pound the bloody guts right out of the Germans if she'll only keep fighting for another few weeks.

The weather is still quite nice. It's similar to the weather at home. A little cooler perhaps but not freezing cold like it is up north.

Well tomorrow we shall have lighting. Some thrill, not for me, but it will be for the Limeys.

I guess L.Jenkins didn't get in the army from what you say. Oh well, there's no sense in enlisting anymore at this stage in the game.

Well, I hope this letter isn't too dull mom, but I haven't done anything all week.

Love and a million kisses

Grant.

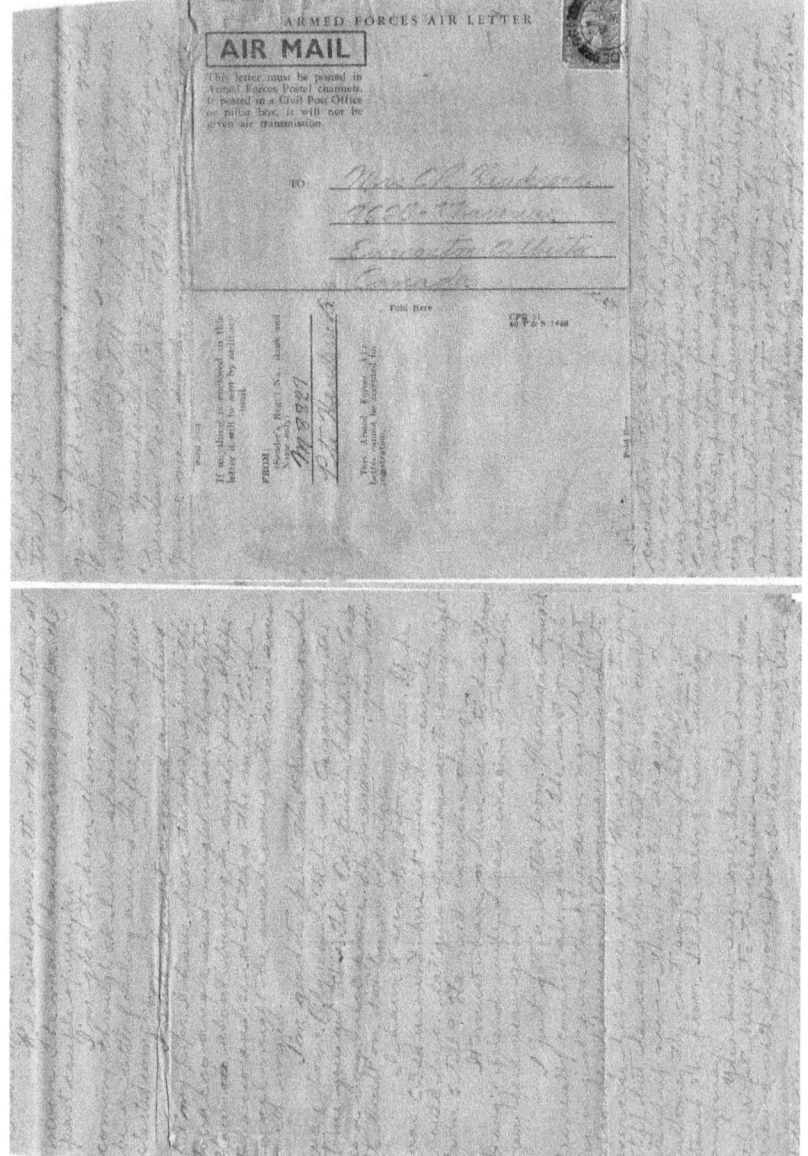

ARMED FORCES AIR LETTER

AIR MAIL

This letter must be posted in Armed Forces Postal channels. If posted in a Civil Post Office or pillar box, it will not be given air transmission.

TO:

Fold Here

If anything is enclosed in this letter it will be sent by ordinary mail.

FROM: (Sender's Regt'l No., Rank and Name only)

This Armed Forces Air letter cannot be accepted for registration.

Fold Here

Sept 19, 1944

Dear Mom:

Received your letter of the 11th today at noon. The mail has been very good for the past couple of weeks.

I glad to hear the money is coming through o.k. I was afraid there would be a little fooling around before the cheques started coming.

I still haven't received anything but my pipe. I have been thinking about the tobacco angle and might have the solution. How about buying a small plug of pipe tobacco and sending it thru the mail. Such a parcel might be small enough to come across with the mail.

I'm glad to hear that Junior is on his way home (I guess he will be in Calgary by the time you get this) The Col. Belcher hosp. in Calg is a very nice place. It's brand new, you know. It's built on Pat Burns' old estate.

I haven't seen Bud for weeks. If he was C.B ed around here it would mean he would be on fatigues of various sorts every night from 6 till 9. He needs exercise though.

It must have been nice to hear from Doug's friend's wife. I can imagine it made you feel very good.

I just got a letter from Hennigar tonight; he's really coming along swell. The cast on his leg is just from the knee down now (his foot is completely encased). Anyway he is able to exercise his knee joint. He says that it's very stiff but seems, very excited that he could stand up now – there's a steel do gigger on the bottom of the cast so that his foot doesn't touch the floor. I'll be seeing him Saturday anyway.

You know even over here the boys from the west keep to themselves – we never go around with anyone from Ontario east, we call each other down something awful too, but all in fun.

I guess when I finish this letter I'll go to the stage show that's on at 7 o clock. Every time I see one, I swear that I'll never see another but I still keep going to them.

You should have read an article in the "Sunday Pictorial" about Alberta and Sask. You've no idea how ignorant about our country these people are mom. The article was in connection with the hardships the Limey war brides would have out there such as – cooking on open fires, a dozen miles to the nearest neighbor, putting on snowshoes, hitching up dog teams and driving to the store where gas and electricity are unknown. These poor girls have been going to gov't schools for months now learning how to cook Canadian style. I've never heard of the dishes they mentioned.

Love

Grant

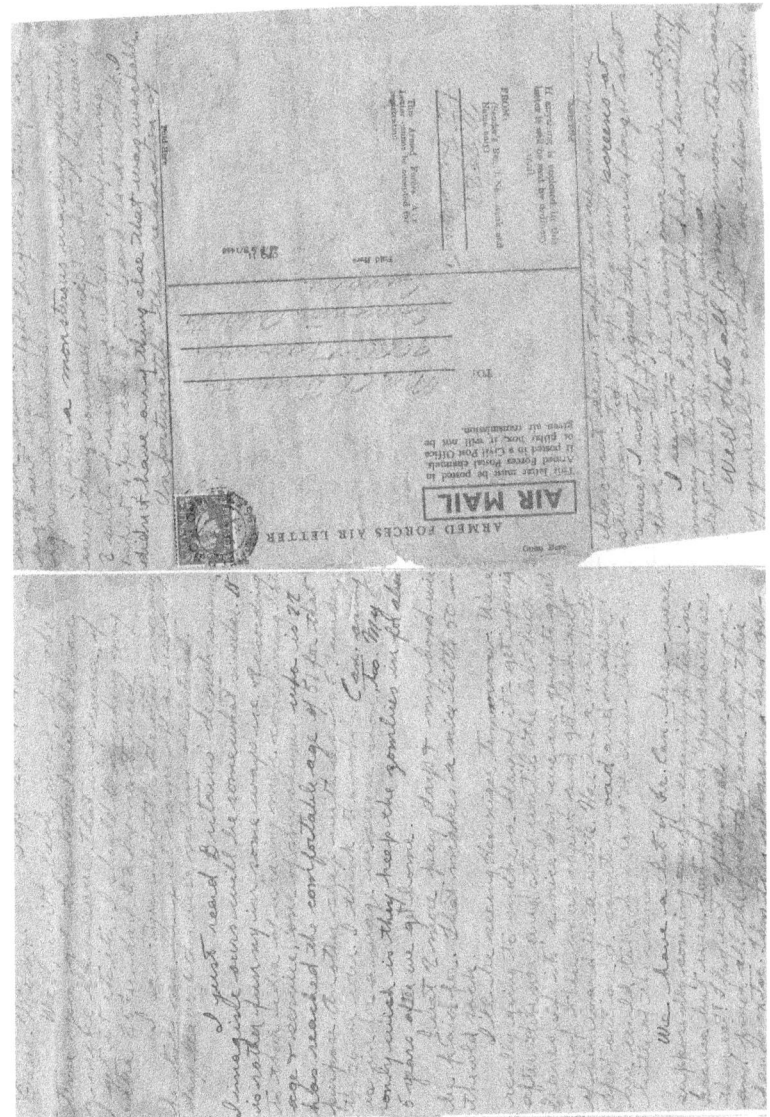

Sept 22, 1944

Dear Mom:

Well, with luck, mom, by the time you get this letter I should be on a nine day leave. That is of course, if I get it, etc.etc. I should be making my extra 25 cents a day too by next week.

I saw your brother the other morning; he told me he just came off a nine day leave. Otherwise, nothing of interest.

I just read Britain's demob. Scheme. I imagine ours will be somewhat similar. It is rather funny in some ways i.e. according to their idea of releasing men combining both age & service, one of my chums who is 22 has reached the comfortable age of 51 for that purpose. Another chap with us is 67 under the same idea. I think the whole Can. Army is in for a wage increase soon, too. My only wish is they keep the zombies in for about 5 years after we get home.

Just 2 more pay days & my bond will be paid for. That makes a nice little 50 in the old sock.

I'll be seeing Hannigar tomorrow. We're really going to make a day of it – get up right after dinner and stay until the last bus leaves. If it's a nice day we are going to grab one of those wheel chairs and get him out of his ward for a while. He's in a very pretty spot out on a country road and maybe we could take him out & show him a little of the scenery.

We have a lot of Fr. Can. here – were supposedly coming over for security police in France but were sort of fooled. You should see them eat! They eat 2 full meals for everyone and pinch all the food they can lay their hands on too. Then they sit around and gab away in French for a couple of hours after lights out every night. They're certainly an ignorant bunch.

I did a monstrous washing yesterday, everything I owned except what I was wearing. 2 suits of winter underwear, 1 of summer, I shirt, 4 pairs of socks, towel and handkerchief. I didn't have anything else that was washable.

Unfortunately this relaxation of blackout doesn't affect us much; we still have to put up blackout screens at sunset. I sort of figured they would forget about them now but I guess not.

I seem to be having more luck with my money lately. Last payday I had a few shillings left which is rather unusual.

Well that's all for now, Mom, take care of yourself & all that.

Love & Kisses

Grant

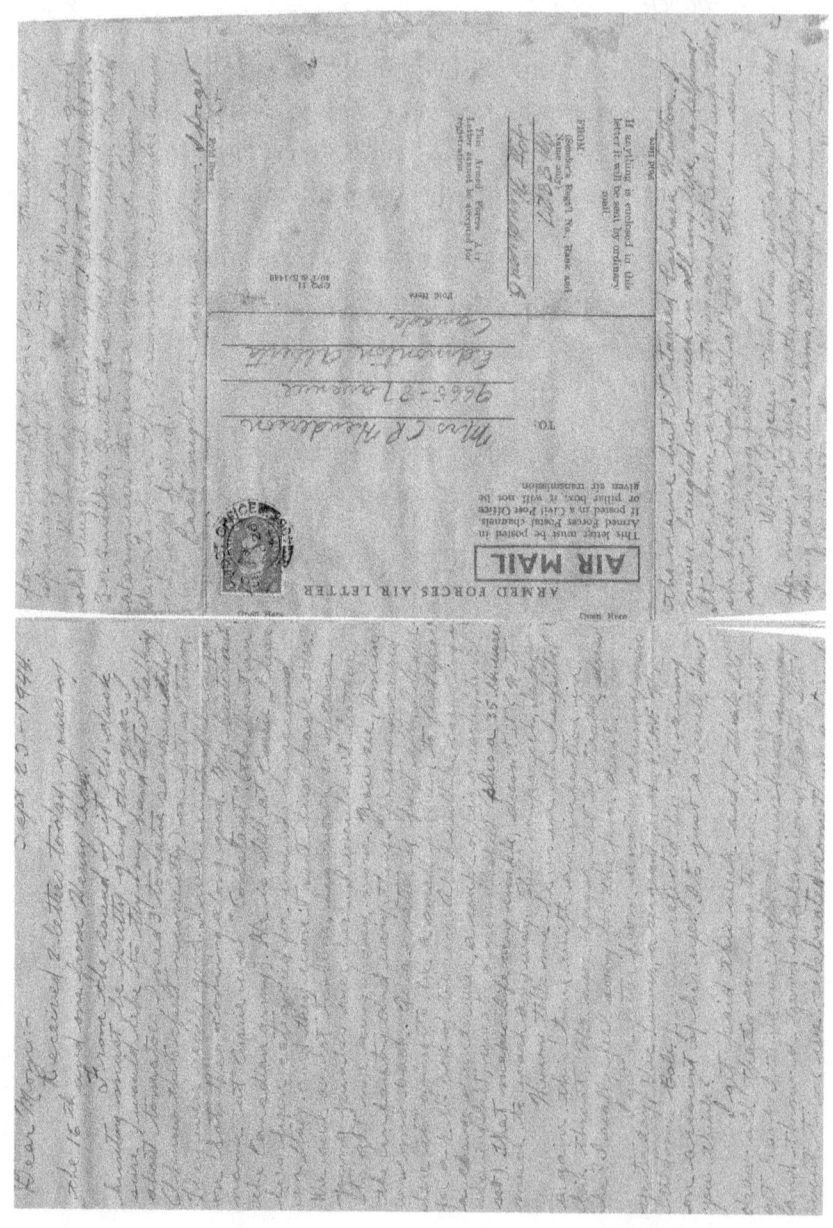

Dear Mom:- Sept 23-1944.

Received 2 letters today, yours of the 16th and one from Henry too.

ARMED FORCES AIR LETTER

AIR MAIL

This letter must be posted in Armed Forces Postal channels. If posted in a Civil Post Office or pillar box, it will not be given air transmission.

TO: Mrs C R Henderson
9665-87 avenue
Edmonton Alberta
Canada

If anything is enclosed in this letter it will be sent by ordinary mail.

FROM (Sender's Regt'l No., Rank and Name only)

This Armed Forces Air Letter cannot be accepted for registration.

September 25, 1944

Dear Mom:

I received 2 letters today, yours of the 16th and one from Henry Lodge.

From the sound of it the duck hunting must be pretty good this year. I sure would like to try my hand at it. Talking about tomatoes, I had 3 tomato sandwitches (I know that's spelt incorrectly) on Sat. afternoon. They were really good. I was with Hennigar on Sat. He's coming along good. My lieutenants' name at Currie was "Constant" (the best in the Canadian army) He is still at Currie, I hear he's been categorized for wounds he received in Italy and they won't send him back over. We owe a lot to him; he's worth 10 of these young punks over here.

I wouldn't bother to get me any honey, mom. You see, I'm in the infantry and everything I possess is carried on my back. As a matter of fact after I leave here it's going to be a small problem to find space for a ½ lb box of tobacco. All I will be carrying is a change of underwear, a couple of pair of socks, towel, shaving kit, sweater & ground sheet (plus 35 lb wireless set). That makes life very simple, doesn't it? Not too much to wash anyway. Still no parcel, lady.

Henry tells me he is in the hospital again, this time with an infection in his throat. He sure has a lot of trouble, doesn't he? I really feel sorry for the poor devil.

I got a letter from another chum of mine yesterday, Vic Turner, a sergeant in RCAF. He told me Bob J. was rejected by the army on account of his eyes. It's just as well don't you think?

I get paid this week and I think I'll draw all that's coming to me. If we don't get leave I think we'll get the weekend anyway and throw a good old fashioned party. It's about time we celebrate something, although for the world of me I can't think of any special event or anything.

What do you know! We had a good old buzz bomb last night! That's the first in 3 or 4 weeks. Quite a dif from when the old alarm used to ring a dozen or so times a day. To hear the siren now is like seeing an old friend.

Last night we saw a show. I forget the name but it starred Barbara Hutton. I never laughed so much in all my life, so help me! It was some crazy thing and it ended up that she had six kids, all at once. She can sure act a crazy part.

Well, I guess that I'm just about finished for now, old girl, by the way let me know how Doug does in his exams, although I know he will do all right.

By for now

Love Grant

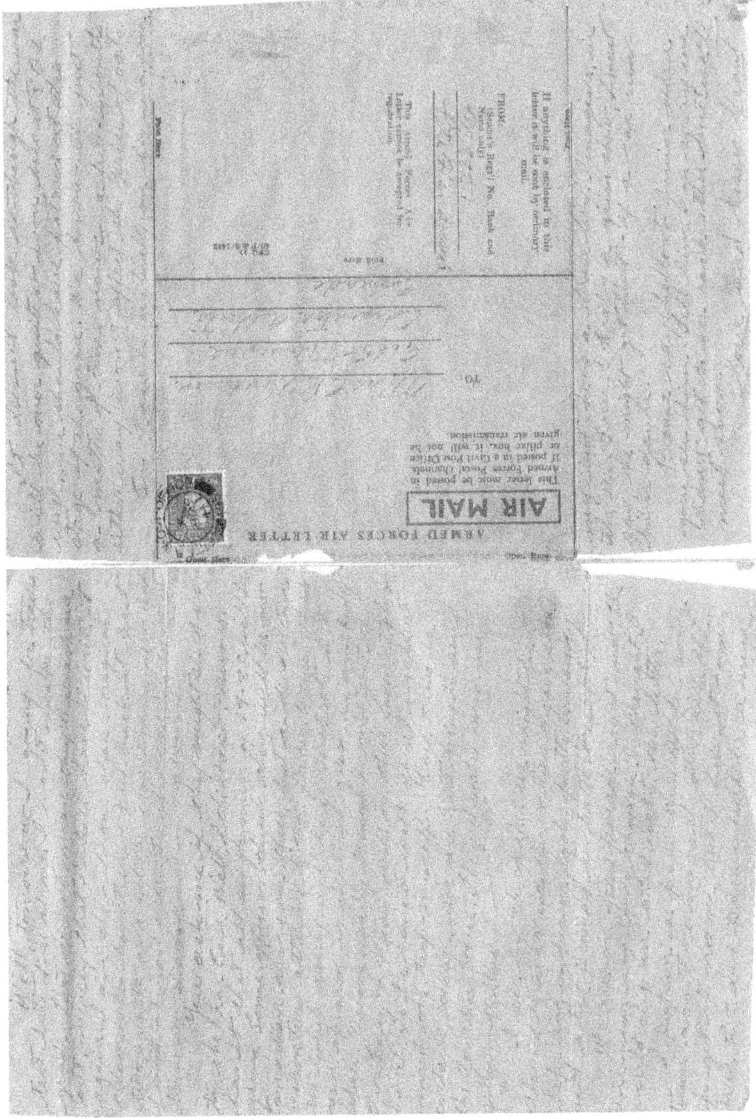

ARMED FORCES AIR LETTER

AIR MAIL

This letter must be posted in Armed Forces Postal Channels. If posted in a Civil Post Office or pillar box, it will not be given air transmission.

TO:

If anything is enclosed in this letter it will be sent by ordinary mail.

FROM: (Sender's Regtl. No. Rank and Name only)

This Armed Forces Air Letter cannot be accepted for registration.

Sept 28, 1944

Dear Mom:

Well tomorrow I go up for trades test but I'm afraid I won't make the grade. That doesn't mean they'll wash me out, merely that I shall have to write it again. I am the only one of our original class who hasn't been put back at least two weeks and the class I'm in now have failed at least once. So if I don't make it tomorrow, I shall not cry about it.

You asked me if they might send us to the Far East. Well, I think so, rumor has it that all single men of 19 -28 will be going. Some officers think there will be no Canadian army in there, but a div. of Can. Volunteers attached to the U.S. forces. Others think the whole army will be going etc, etc. but your opinion is just as good as anybody else's. No one really knows except that the Air Force & Navy will be there lock stock and barrel. To be honest with you I wouldn't mind the trip myself. One thing is certain, though we are not going to send Zombies there. They'll want men not yellow bellied.....

I see by the paper we might be allowed to wear collars & ties again soon. I hope so, a person looks pretty swanky with a tie (provide his battle dress fits).

We are on pay parade right now. The line was so long though I thought I would slip out and write this letter.

I put in a pass this am for some town about 20 miles the other side of L. I forgot its name but I hope it comes thru. A 2 day pass would be nice break about now.

It doesn't look as though the war will be over quite so soon does it? Oh well, we should have patience at this stage of the game. We know it's just a matter of time now – a few moths either way won't affect the price of oats.

So Ross is actually on his way over, my but he's a brave boy. Imagine in the air force! Really a grim show, I must say, he might get hurt if a car runs him down.

Please say hello to Junior when you see him. Tell him I'm sorry we didn't get to see each other but we'll meet soon.

Love and Kisses

Grant

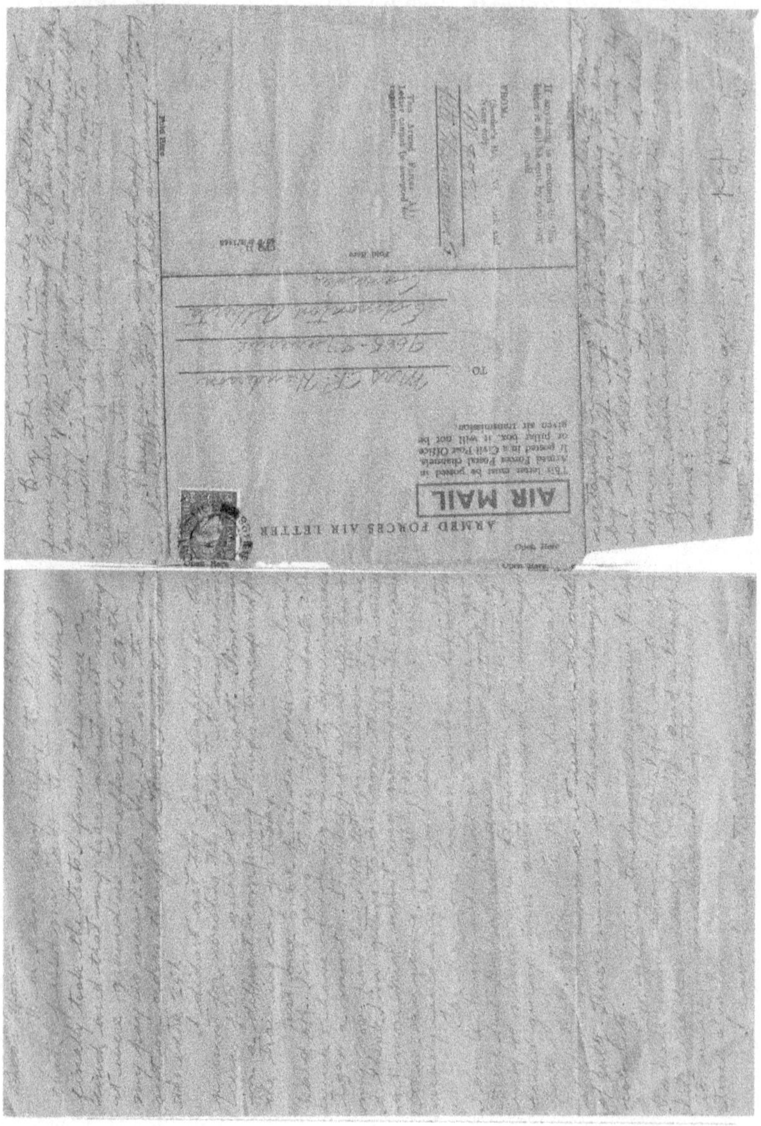

ARMED FORCES AIR LETTER

AIR MAIL

This letter must be posted in Armed Forces Postal channels. If posted in a Civil Post Office or public box, it will not be given air transmission.

TO

Oct 1st, 1944

Dear Mom:

Well, I am very happy to tell you that I passed my trades test o.k. When I finally took the test I found they were a cinch and that my fears about not making it were groundless. So effective the 29th my pay is now $1.75 a day. It has to come out on orders though before I start to draw the extra 25 cents.

I didn't get the leave I applied for. As a present for writing the trades test my section was put on guard that night. I'm now in a different company. I was transferred from the training coy yesterday.

Just one more pay day and my bond is paid off. I'm going to see the paymaster this week to have my assignment to you increased to $30 a month. It will probably be effective on my Nov. pay but I'll let you know for sure. I think I'm getting to be something of a miser. I get more kick about my growing bank account than anything, probably because I've never really saved any money before.

The ban on London is being lifted tomorrow. I don't know when I'll get a chance to go there but perhaps I'll get up next Saturday. Its only 45 minutes away by train, you know. I could go up there quite nicely on a midnight pass.

Well it's the 1st of Oct. today but the weather is still about the same as it was in the middle of July. There is no sign of the leaves changing colour etc.

I'm getting the travel bug again. Perhaps I shall move soon. I hope I feel as though I'd lived here most of my life and although it's a very nice place, I'm getting fairly tired of it.

I saw Bud yesterday; he seems to be enjoying himself.

By the way, in the last letter I got from you, you mentioned Mr. Davis. How is he anyway? He didn't look so hot when I left, I wonder if he's picked up since. I sorta liked the old boy; I wouldn't want anything to happen to him.

I suppose that Ma is quite happy now that Tommy is home. It must be a help anyway. It certainly wasn't good for her to be all by herself. If Junior is going to in the Belcher for any length of time, why doesn't Ma take a room in a hotel down there until he's ready to come home? Then she could see him every day anyways.

Well, I guess the paper has run out so good bye for now

Love Grant

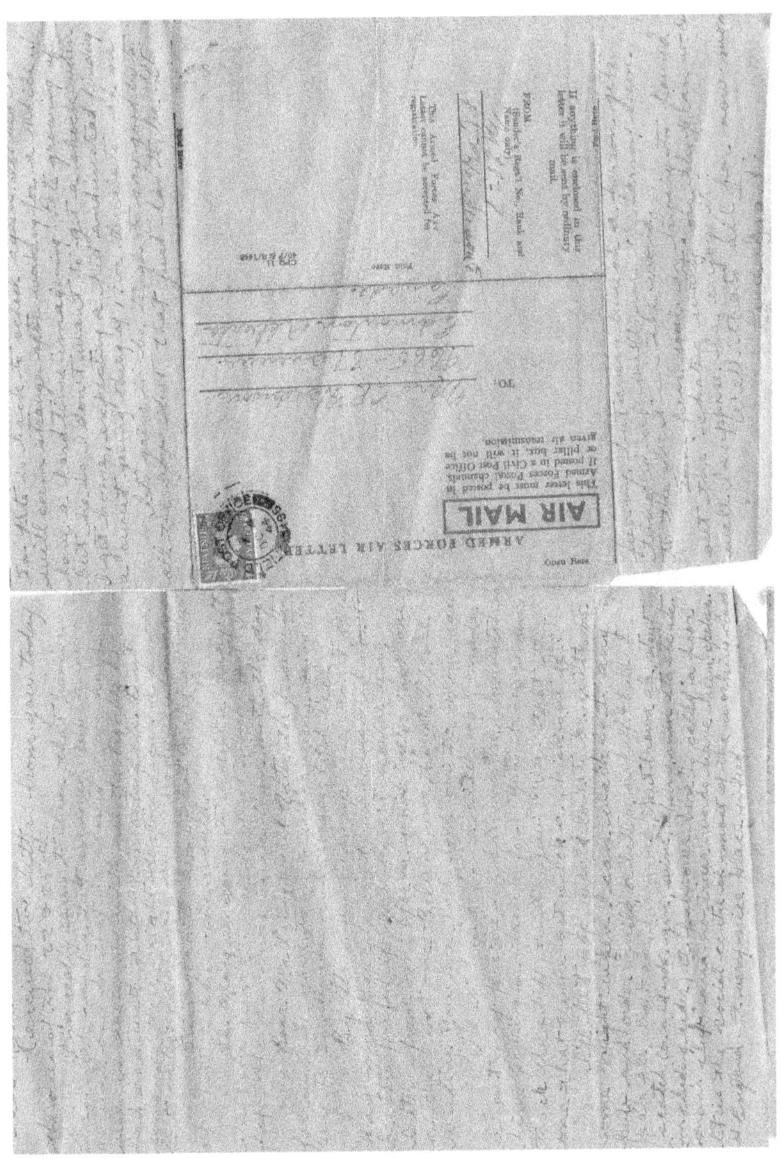

ARMED FORCES AIR LETTER

AIR MAIL

This letter must be posted in Armed Forces Postal channels. If posted in a Civil Post Office or pillar box, it will not be given air transmission.

TO:

If anything is enclosed in this letter it will be sent by ordinary mail.

FROM: (Sender's Regt'l No., Rank and Name only)

This Armed Forces Air Letter cannot be accepted for registration.

Oct 3, 1944

Dear Mom:

Received two letters from you today, the ones of the 22 & 25th.

I'm really sorry to hear that Junior is so sick and a bit annoyed. You know as well as I do that he should never have been in the army with all the troubles he had had with asthma, mastoids etc. But some of these bright doctors figure a person is 'A' category so long as his body is warm.

Sure glad to hear that Doug got thru o.k., but I knew he would.

So Marg is going to adopt a baby! It will be fun to see how it works out. I hope she has more luck than with the dog.

Poor Mr. Dingwall, after the pessimistic farewell he gave to me what is he going to say to Sandy when he leaves? Oh well.

By the way lady please don't send any more parcels to this address and don't be surprised if you don't receive any letters from me for a while after this one or the next one. Believe me though, I'll be writing. You see lady; I'm on the move again.

That was some crack dad made about my picture – what would I be watching him pouring a drink for? You know that I never touch the stuff, or do you? Was that the one that Verne got such a kick out of?

I'll bet pop would love to be with me some night when I can walk into any pub and order mild, or bitter, or half & half or scotch (or and soda), gin, wine, cherry, rum etc, etc,etc (including cider). A pub over here is called "a poor man's club" and no truer words have ever been spoken. It is the social centre of most of the working class of England. A very nice place indeed.

So Pete is back to school again. I'll bet it will seem strange after working for a while. I have a hard time imagining Pete growing up but he is. I don't want to get a shock when I get home, expecting a kid and instead finding a sweet young thing of 17 or there abouts, ah me.

It's going to be tough to say good bye to all the boys but that just has to be. It's funny, but every bunch a person gets tangled up with in the army seems to be the best in the world.

Some poor soul is trying to pound out the "skaters waltz" on the piano. Oh well, I suppose he enjoys it.

Well, that's all for now mom.

Love Grant.

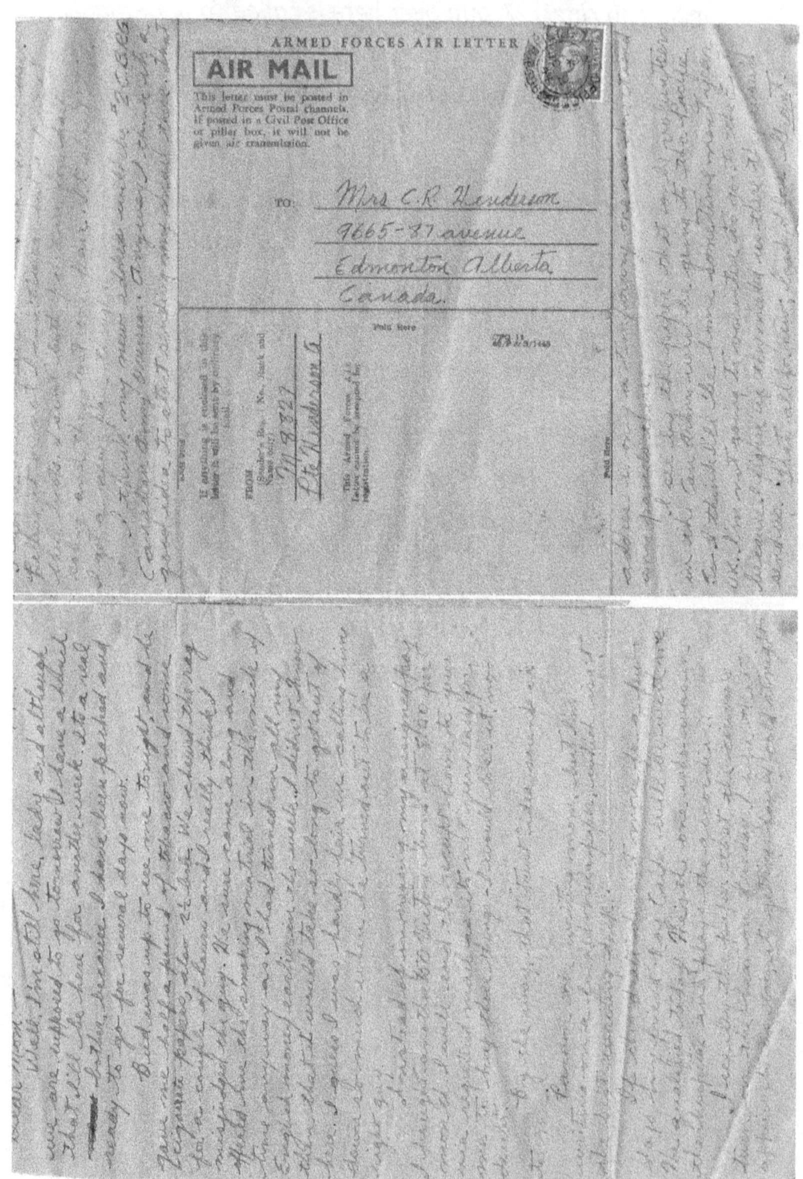

ARMED FORCES AIR LETTER

AIR MAIL

This letter must be posted in Armed Forces Postal channels. If posted in a Civil Post Office or pillar box, it will not be given air transmission.

TO: Mrs C.R. Henderson
9665-87 avenue
Edmonton Alberta
Canada.

FROM
M8327
Pte Henderson

Oct 6, 1944

Dear Mom:

Well, I'm still here, lady and although we are supposed to go tomorrow I have a hunch that I'll be here for another week. It's a real bother, because I have been packed and ready to go for several days now.

Bud was up to see me tonight, and he gave me a half a pound of tobacco and some cigarette papers, also 2 ½ bob. We chewed the rag for a couple of hours and I really think I misjudged the guy. He sure came along and offered me the smoking material in the nick of time anyways, as I had turned in all my English money earlier in the week. I didn't know then that it would take so long to get out of here. I guess I was hardly fair in calling him down so much when he turned out to be a right guy.

Instead of increasing my assigned pay I bought another $50 Victory bond at 8.40 per month. I will send the receipt home to you via registered mail as it's not very easy for me to keep those things & I would lose it, no doubt.

By the way, that "trust" idea sounds o.k. to me.

Pardon the writing mom, but I'm writing on a folded newspaper, which isn't the best writing desk.

If this draft doesn't move for a few days my friend Roy Calder will be with me. He qualified today. He's the one who was in the hospital and plays the accordion.

I see by the paper that civvy's turned on the heat on Sunday. I hope that applies to us too, it's getting fairly cold at night.

I got a new pair of boots the other day. Believe it or not I can't wear out a pair of these boots. I sent both pairs in for half soling and they lost one pair. It's about time I got a new pair though.

I think my new address will be #2CBRG Canadian Army Overseas. Anyway I think it's a good idea to start sending my mail there. That address is only a temporary one so don't send any parcels there.

I see by the paper that only volunteers in the Can. Army will be going to the Pacific. So I think I'll be home sometime next year o.k. I'm not going to volunteer because I figure if they needed us there, they would send us.

That's all for now.

Love Grant.

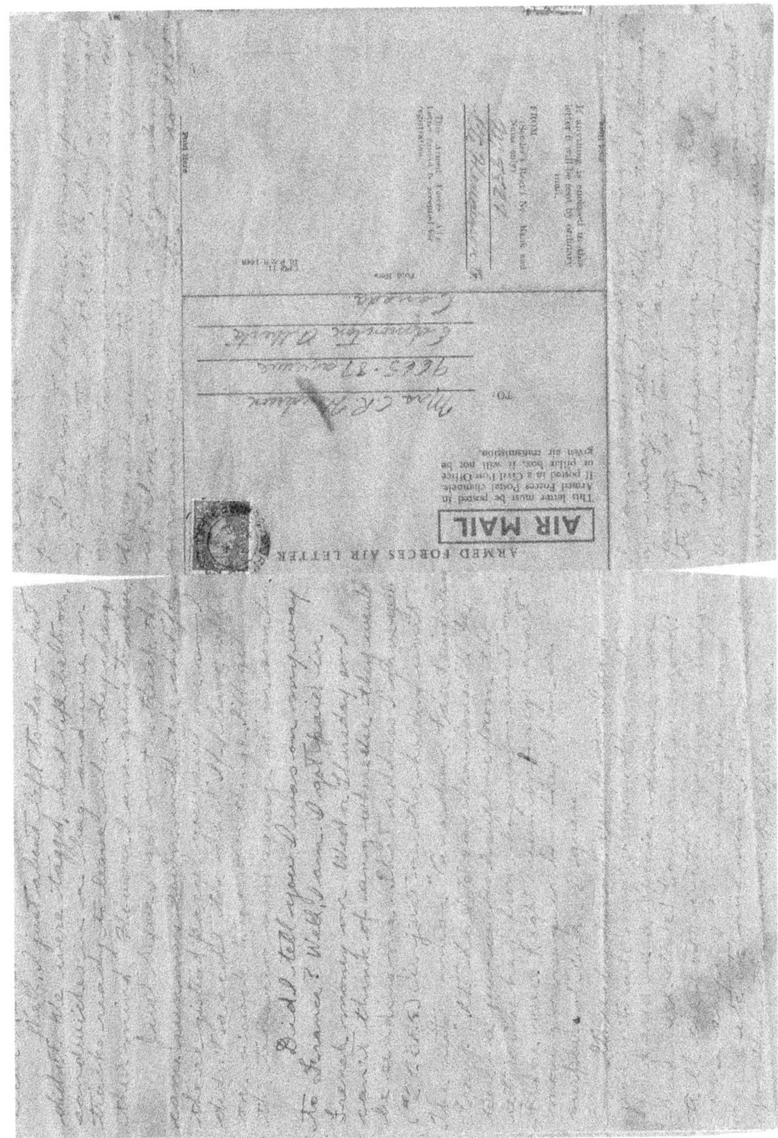

ARMED FORCES AIR LETTER

AIR MAIL

This letter must be posted in Armed Forces Postal channels. If posted in a Civil Post Office or pillar box, it will not be given air transmission.

TO:

Oct 8, 1944

Dear Mom:

Well, I just about left today – but didn't. We were tagged, had life belts on, sandwiches in a bag and were in trucks ready to leave when they changed their mind. However, I am going tomorrow.

Just before I got on the truck, they came running down with the chit for the registered parcel you sent me so I didn't accept the chit. If I leave after one o'clock tomorrow though, I'll get the tobacco and squeeze it in somewhere.

Did I tell you I was on my way to France? Well, I am. I got paid in French money on Wed or Thursday so I can't think of anywhere else they would be sending me. That address I gave you (#2CBRG) is just another holding unit. The letters mean "Canadian Base Reinforcement Group" It's hard to say how long I'll be there - a few weeks I suppose from the letters I've had from the boys who went over before me. Right now inf. sigs. aren't moving very quickly – they have a surplus of them, I guess.

It's really funny you know. I said good bye to all my friends, the cook prepared us special dinner – we had beef steak! Boy was it good! All the boys with cease fire badges were saying they wished they could come etc etc and now I guess that we'll go through the same performance again tomorrow but without the frills.

I haven't had any mail from you after the letter of the 25th, but I might get some tomorrow before I leave. All the mail seems to have been slowed up. I'm carrying a dozen stamped airmail forms with me so that I can keep the letters going to you o.k. anyways – the boys tell me that airmail forms and stamps are sometimes hard to get.

I just heard over the news that Wendell Wilkie died – I never knew he was sick.

Well that's all for now, mom, don't worry about me and I'll write often.

Love & Kisses

Grant

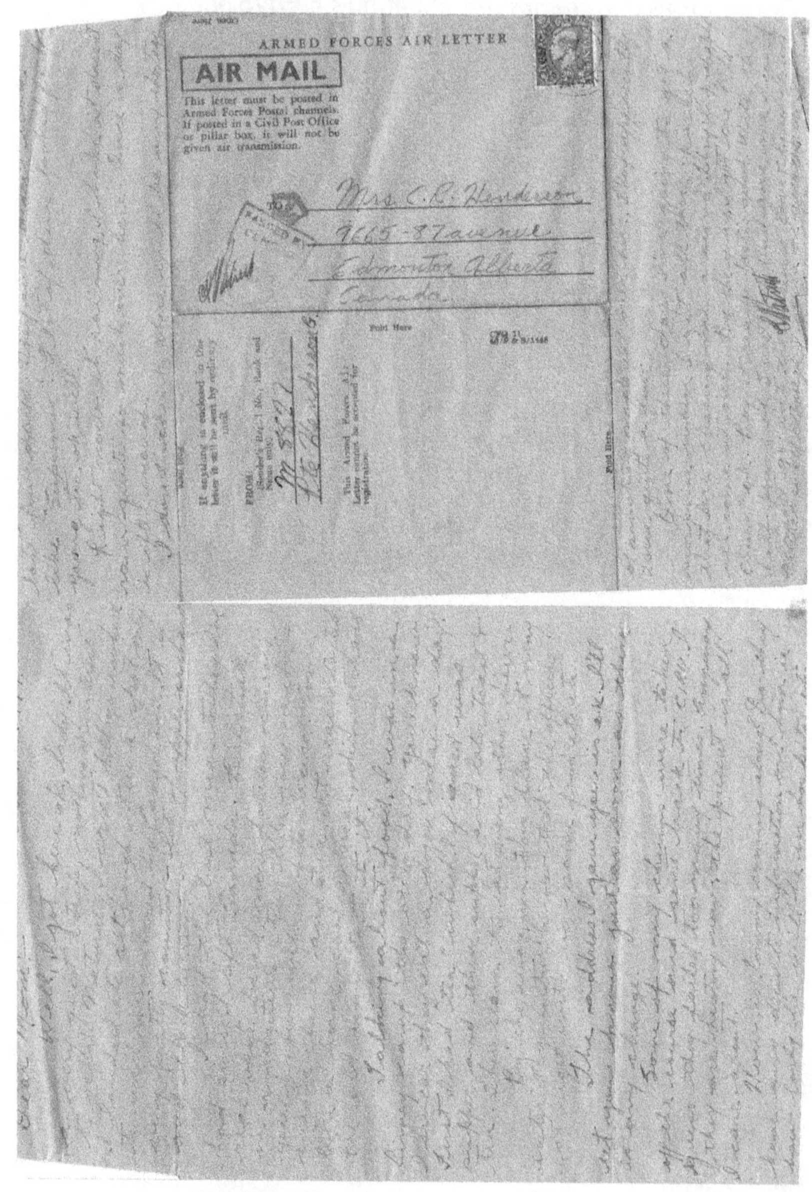

ARMED FORCES AIR LETTER

AIR MAIL

This letter must be posted in Armed Forces Postal channels. If posted in a Civil Post Office or pillar box, it will not be given air transmission.

TO Mrs C.R. Henderson
9665-87 avenue
Edmonton Alberta
Canada

PASSED BY CENSOR

Fold Here

If anything is enclosed in this letter it will be sent by ordinary mail.

FROM: Sender's Unit, No. Rank and Name only.
M 5521
Pte Henderson, S.

This Armed Forces Air Letter cannot be accepted for registration.

Fold Here

Oct 11, 1944

Dear Mom:

Well, I got here o.k. lady. It was a very quiet trip, nothing of interest to report. Naturally I can't tell you where I landed etc although it is a spot only too well remembered by Canadians. It is very pretty country – lots of apple orchards and blackberries.

I had the best meal today I've had since I left Canada. Beef steak, real white bread, new potatoes, carrots in a vegetable, stew like you make- you know with white sauce. Some cream cheese and tea. It really tasted like a home cooked meal, didn't have the old army taste to it.

Talking about food, I was in a Limey camp the other day. You know I swear they eat a dozen meals a day. First I had "tea" which I figured was supper and then supper and later toast & tea. They seem to eat every other hour.

By the way, in this place it may interest you to know that the officers eat right with us – same food etc etc.

The address I gave you is O.K. I'll let you know just as soon as there is any change.

Some of my chums were taken off the course and sent back to CIRU. I guess they failed too many times. Anyways they are history now; the present is all I care about.

How is Tommy coming along? Do they have any definite information on him i.e. how long he will be in hospital etc.

I've seen a lot of Jerry prisoners in the last few days. They sure didn't look like "Supermen". A lot of them look fairly young, too, oh well.

Right now it's raining; I hope it doesn't rain quite so much over here. Once a day is often enough.

I don't think there will be any shortage of smoking materials over here. They apparently issue quite a few.

One of these days I'm going to get a surprise when I get all those parcels that are chasing me around. They'll probably all come at once. By the way, I got the "Old Chum" o.k. Boy it really tastes good. With the half pound of sweet Bud gave me I could almost go into the business.

Love & Kisses

Grant

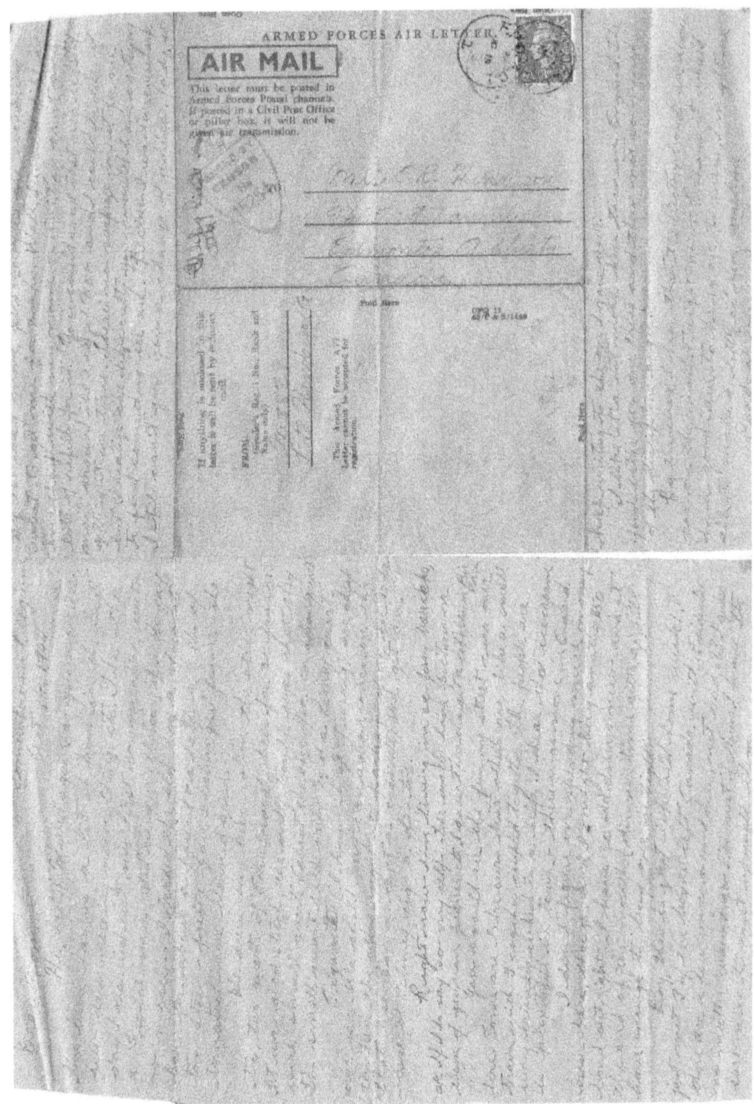

ARMED FORCES AIR LETTER

AIR MAIL

This letter must be posted in Armed Forces Postal channels. If posted in a Civil Post Office or pillar box, it will not be given air transmission.

Somewhere in Belgium

Oct 14, 1944

Dear Mom:

Hi, lady! Moved again as you can see. I've been having a lot of fun in the last few days – seeing new things etc. The other day I carried out my first conversation with a French man, did very well too, if I do say so myself. I trades the old boy a chocolate bar for about a pound & a half or 2 lbs of tomatoes – pretty fair exchange I figure – the tomatoes were darned good.
We drew pour beer ration the other night too, two quarts of Edinborough beer for 30 Francs. It was good stuff; the only trouble was that they were small quarts (about the size of a Canadian quart). The small quart only 2/3 of a Limey quart. Cigarettes (I know it's spelt wrong) are cheap over here. We could buy Canadian ones in the canteen the other night – 2 packages of 20 for 15 Fr. That's less than a cent a cigarette. We get an issue of 7 limey cigs a day too. Right now I'm living in ex-Jerry barracks. O.k. If I do say so myself. The walls have pictures on them of German planes etc. I guess they thought a lot of their Air Force.

You should see the funny street cars over here. Some are like ours but others are like a small train with 3 coaches coupled together. The people are very friendly which is a help. I hear that ice cream is plentiful in town – there was none in England.

I don't figure on spending much money over here, I might buy another bond our right. I have 30 odd dollars now and at the end of the month (dinner time gotta go) I'll have enough to buy one out right.

Boy this is just like old home week. I just met 3 of the boys I left Canada with. Evidently there are a few more around here, not bad eh? I guess no matter where I go I'll meet fellows I know. It's sure nice to meet up with them.

By the way mom, perhaps you were wondering what to get me for Xmas. Well, I would like an eversharp with my name or initials on it and lots of refills for it. You could send that via registered mail around the end of Nov. and I could be sure of getting it in time. There's no surprise in it for me but I realize the difficulty you would have in trying to find something for me. Besides I want an eversharp. I still can't give you a change of address lady, so keep writing to the one I gave you.

I like it a lot more here than in England. The food's better for one thing and there's not so much of the discipline angle. By the way, I hear that the Victory bonds are above par on the market right now. Perhaps it would be a good idea to hang on to mine, I might be able to make a little on them sometime.
Loads of love
Grant

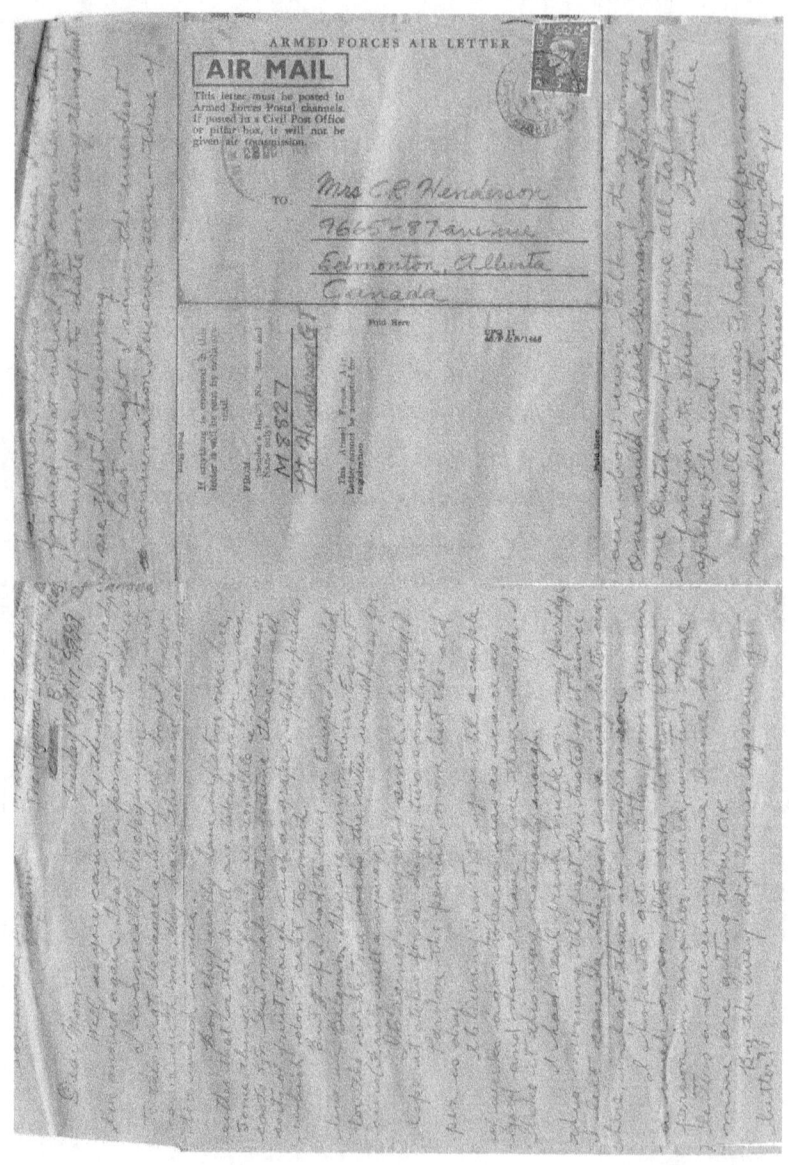

ARMED FORCES AIR LETTER

AIR MAIL

This letter must be posted in Armed Forces Postal channels. If posted in a Civil Post Office or pillar box, it will not be given air transmission.

TO: Mrs C.R. Henderson
7665-87 avenue
Edmonton, Alberta
Canada

Fold Here

FROM: M 8827 Pt. Henderson

Somewhere in Belgium

Tuesday Oct 17, 1944

Dear Mom:

Well, as you can see by the address, lady I've moved again. That is a permanent address.

I was really lucky when I was sent to this regt. Because a lot of the boys I knew came with me, they have the same job as me too which is nice.

Boy, they really have inflation over here; either that or the people are taking us for a run. Something's are fairly reasonable i.e. ice cream costs 5 Fr. But meals cost a fortune. There is all sorts of fruit, though, such as grapes, apples, peaches which don't cost too much.

But If I had to live in Europe I would live in Belgium. They are very modern. Except for the cobblestone roads, the cities would pass for our s(Fairly well anyway).

It's rained every day since I landed. I hope it stops for a day or two sometime.

Pardon the pencil, mom, but the old pen is dry.

It's funny isn't it ,up until a couple of weeks ago tobacco was as scarce as gold and now I have more than enough. I like it this way, naturally enough.

I had real fresh milk on my porridge this morning, the first I've tasted of it since I left Canada. The food is way better over here, in fact there's no comparison.

I hope to get a letter from you in a week or so. It's like talking to a person in another world, writing these letters and receiving none. I sure hope mine are getting thru o.k.

By the way did Verne's legs ever get better?

You know, it's funny how little news a person hears over here. I sorta figured that when I got over here that I would be up to date on everything but I see that I was wrong.

Last night I saw the weirdest conversation I've ever seen – three of our boys were talking to a farmer. One could speak German, one French and one Dutch and they were all talking in a fashion to this farmer. I think he spoke Flemish.

Well, I guess that's all for now mom, I'll write in a few days

Love & Kisses

Grant

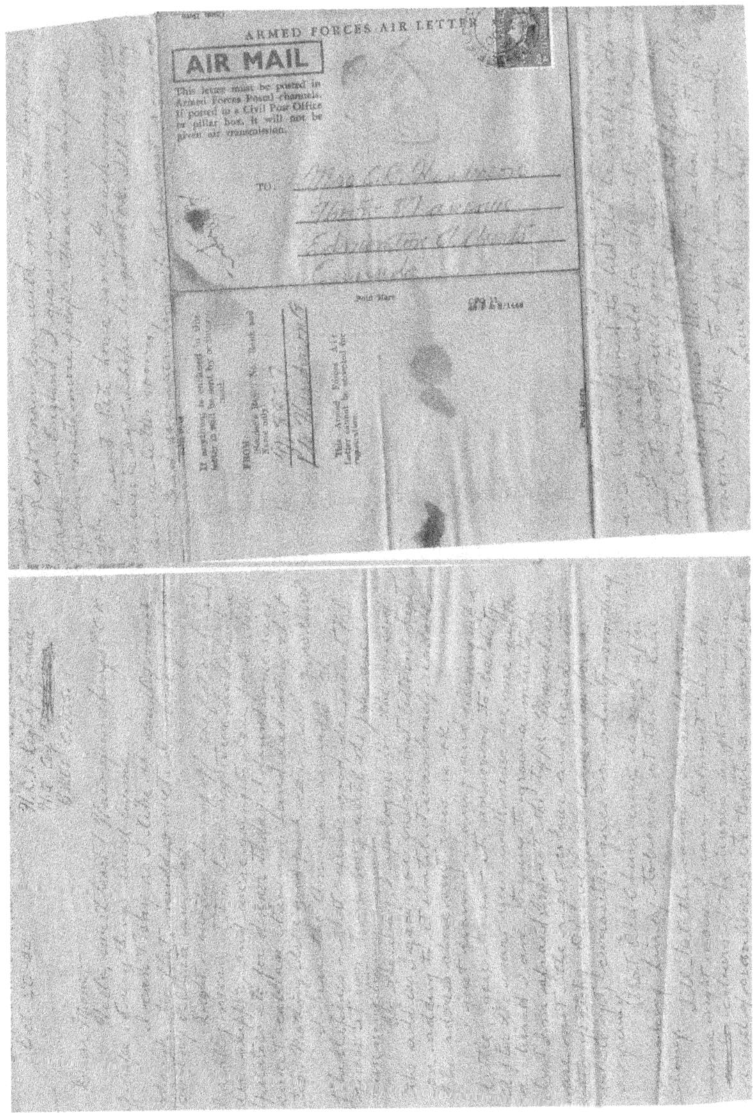

ARMED FORCES AIR LETTER

AIR MAIL

This letter must be posted in Armed Forces Postal channels. If posted in a Civil Post Office or pillar box, it will not be given air transmission.

TO:

Somewhere in Holland

Oct 20, 1944

Dear Mom:

Hello, sweetheart! How goes things? O.k. I hope. Everything's swell by me.

I can't say as I like the country much though, too flat, muddy & wet. Give me old sunny Alberta any day.

Right now I'm living off the fat of the land; I really mean it, too. Last night we had chicken for supper and we're going to have pork chops, potatoes etc for dinner today. I found some nice sweet cabbage this am and had lots of that too. Nothing like good fresh raw cabbage is there?

I hear the Americans invaded the Philippines – that sounds good doesn't it? I guess it won't be long before Japs are running too.

By the way, I apologize for the mess of the address I gave you on the last letter. I kept on adding to it until it was barely readable. The address above sent as is, is o.k.

I just finished shaving and cleaning up a little, you know it's annoying to be dirty. After the war you will never see me with a beard. I am trying to grow a moustache but I'm afraid I'm not the type. My whiskers are not the right colour and besides it too patchy. Oh well, I'll leave it go for a while yet, curiosity I guess or vanity – something anyway.

That "Old Chum" sure was good, after smoking Limey tobacco it tastes like honey.

I'll bet the country is really pretty at home right now. I can almost see the colours of the leaves, bright sunshine, smell of cranberries etc. Boy its wonderful place.

Right now I'm with one of the boys I met back in England. I guess in the army a person meets more people that in any other job.

I sent Pete home some French money about a week ago. I hope he got it o.k. I'll be writing him a letter soon.

Did you ever hear if Ross got across o.k.?

How is Junior? Is he up and around at all or is he confined to bed? Is he still in the army?

I've had a cold for the last couple of weeks but it's pretty well gone now. My old nose runs pretty fast but that's probably from the dampness. Well that's about it for now, mom, I hope to hear from you soon.

Love & Kisses

Grant

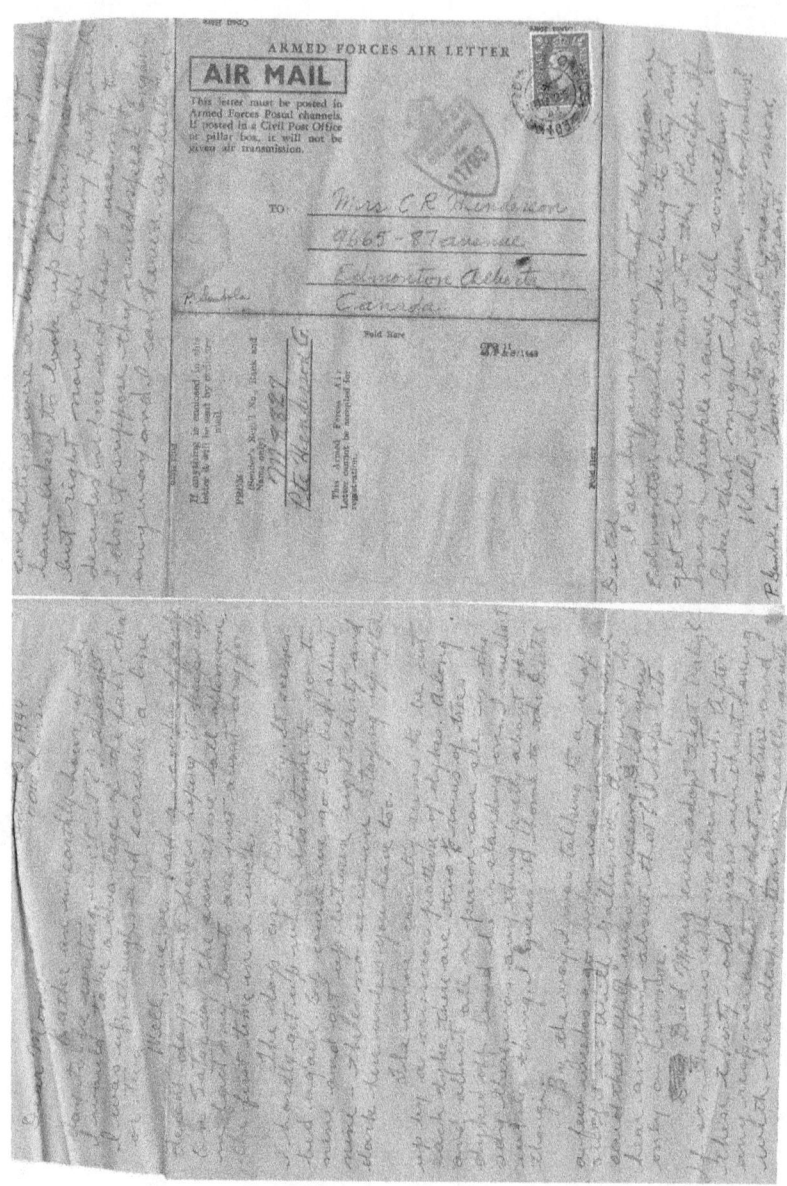

ARMED FORCES AIR LETTER

AIR MAIL

This letter must be posted in Armed Forces Postal channels. If posted in a Civil Post Office or pillar box, it will not be given air transmission.

TO: Mrs C R Henderson
9665 - 87 avenue
Edmonton Alberta
Canada

If anything is enclosed in this letter it will be sent by ordinary mail.

FROM: Pte Henderson G

This Armed Forces Air Letter cannot be accepted for registration.

Somewhere in Holland

Oct 23, 1944

0010 hours
Dear Mom:

Rather an unearthly hour of the day to be writing, isn't it? I thought I would take advantage of the fact that I was up, though and scribble a line or two.

Well, we've had a couple of fairly decent days now, here's hoping it keeps up. On Saturday the sun shone all afternoon, in fact my boots are just about dry for the first time in a week.

They days are flying by. It seems I hardly get up when it time to go to bed again. Of course we got to bed about nine and get up between eight thirty and nine – there's no sense in staying up after dark here unless you have to.

The whole country seems to be cut up by a crisscross pattern of dykes. A long each dyke there are two rows of trees and about all a person can see is the dyked off land he is standing on. I wouldn't say there was anything pretty about the whole thing. I guess its home to the Dutch though.

By the way, I was talking to a chap a few weeks ago who was in the same outfit as Wilf Gallimore. Anyway he said that Wilf was missing. Did you hear anything about that? I hope it's only a rumor.

Did Marg. Ever adopt that baby? If so, how is she making out? After these thirty odd years without having any responsibilities of that nature and with her disposition I'm really quite curious about the whole thing. If conditions were a bit different, I would have liked to look up Chris's relatives but right now the army pretty well decides where and how I use my time. I don't suppose they could speak English anyway and I can't even say "hello" in Dutch.

I see by our paper that the Legion in Edmonton has been kicking to try and get the zombies sent to the pacific. If enough people raise hell something like that might happen, who knows?

Well that's all for now, mom.

Love & Kisses

Grant

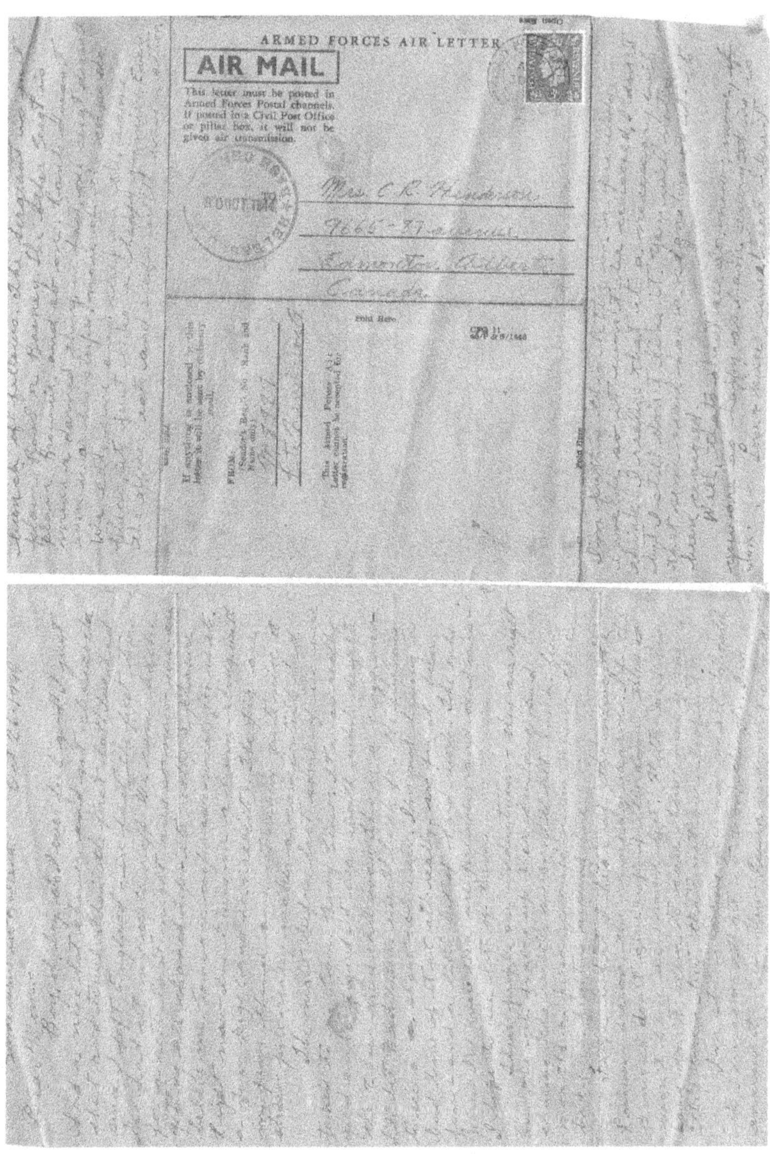

ARMED FORCES AIR LETTER

AIR MAIL

This letter must be posted in Armed Forces Postal channels. If posted in a Civil Post Office or pillar box, it will not be given air transmission.

Mrs. C.R. Henderson

Edmonton, Alberta

Canada.

Fold Here

Somewhere in Holland

Oct 26, 1944

Dear Mom:

Boy oh, boy, do I ever feel good! I just had a nice hot shower and got clean socks, shirt and towel. That's the first bath I've had since I left England – in fact the first time I've had all my clothes off. We came back for a rest last night and so now we are getting all cleaned up – it's really a pleasure, believe me. Someone cooks our meals for us etc. Right now I'm living in a barn along with a few pigs (and 4 or 5 rabbits). The pigs are in pens though and it's really quite nice. A straw pile really makes a comfortable bed.

The night before last some of us were taken to a Can. Army show. It was really quite good and I figured it was worth while despite the 2 hour drive each way. This is a crazy war – I'll bet dad never went back for the evening to see a show – oh well. I'm not having a bad time of it at all really so far it's been fun and a little bit of hard work. The only Jerries I've seen are prisoners and dead ones – I hope to see lots of them.

These people are industrious – they are right on the job fixing up their buildings and clearing the rubble away. I'll bet in a few months a person would never know there had been fighting around here.

From what I hear of the news, the Russians are on the rampage again. If the Germans don't give up pretty soon they won't have any men left. Hitler and his gang don't seem to care how many men they lose – but that's not our lookout.

I'm still waiting for my mail to catch up; I imagine I'll get it soon though. I am anxious to hear how Doug is coming along.

In case you're interested, I'm with a swell bunch of fellows. The Sergeant is just plain "Ross" or Barney. other Sergt. Is plain Brownie and so on. Ranks doesn't mean a darned thing in fact one sergt. Doesn't even wear his stripes, none of the corps do. We eat, live and sleep in the same places, it just like a happy family. Even the officer eats and sleeps with us in action.

I'm putting this letter in a privileged envelope so it won't be censored, I don't think. I realize that it's a necessary evil but I still don't like it. You will notice that some mail has a signature on it – it's been censored.

Well, that's about all for now, mom, if you are as happy as I am everything is o.k.

Love & kisses, sweetheart

Grant.

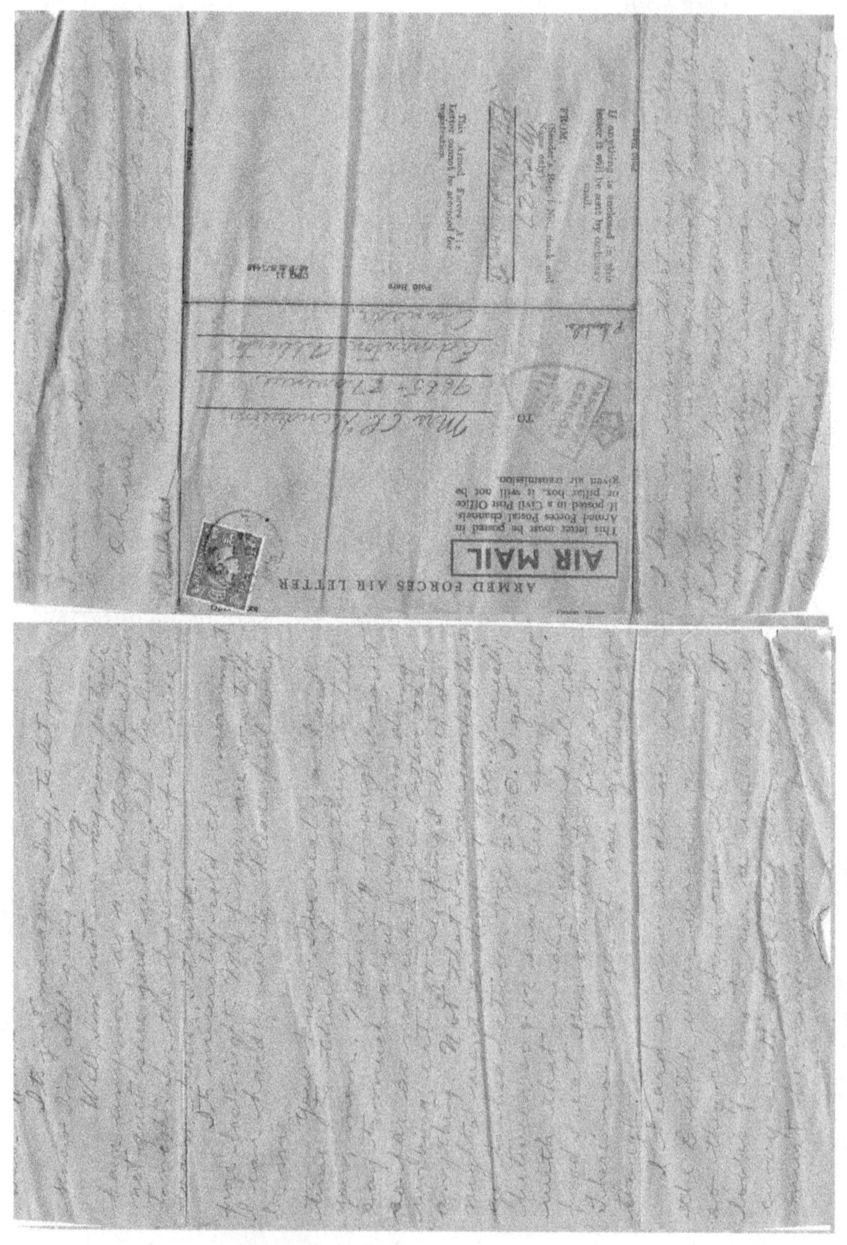

Oct 30, 1944

Dear Mom:

It's just me again, lady, to let you know I'm still going strong.

Well, I'm not in my comfortable barn anymore, as a matter of fact, I'm not quite sure just where I'll be living tonight. In the basement of a nice warm house, I think.

It's miserably cold this morning, it froze last night. My fingers are so stiff I can hardly write. Please feel sorry for me.

You know, I've really a hard time of anything to tell you, mom. Naturally enough, I can't say too much about what I'm doing so far as my work goes. Other than working, eating and sleeping, I don't do anything. Not that I'm over worked, last night I went to bed at 7:30. I usually go to be between 7:30 & 8:30. I get between 10 & 12 hours sleep every night. With that much sleep and all the food I eat I'm starting to fill out. There's no danger of me getting fat though.

I heard a new angle on why the Dutch wear wooden shoes. It's so they can skim over the mud. It looks funny to see a well dressed civvy with those bit shoes on. They must be awfully uncomfortable.

I hear a rumor that we get heavy underwear and great coats issued today, I hope so. I'm really colder in this dampness than I ever was at home.

I saw a show a couple of days ago "Captain Blood" with "Errol Flynn". A good old pirate picture – remember it?

I have to laugh every time that I think that you know more about the war than I do – even in the sector I am in. I have no interest at all in what's happening – strange isn't it. Oh well, that's the way things go.

Love & Kisses

Grant

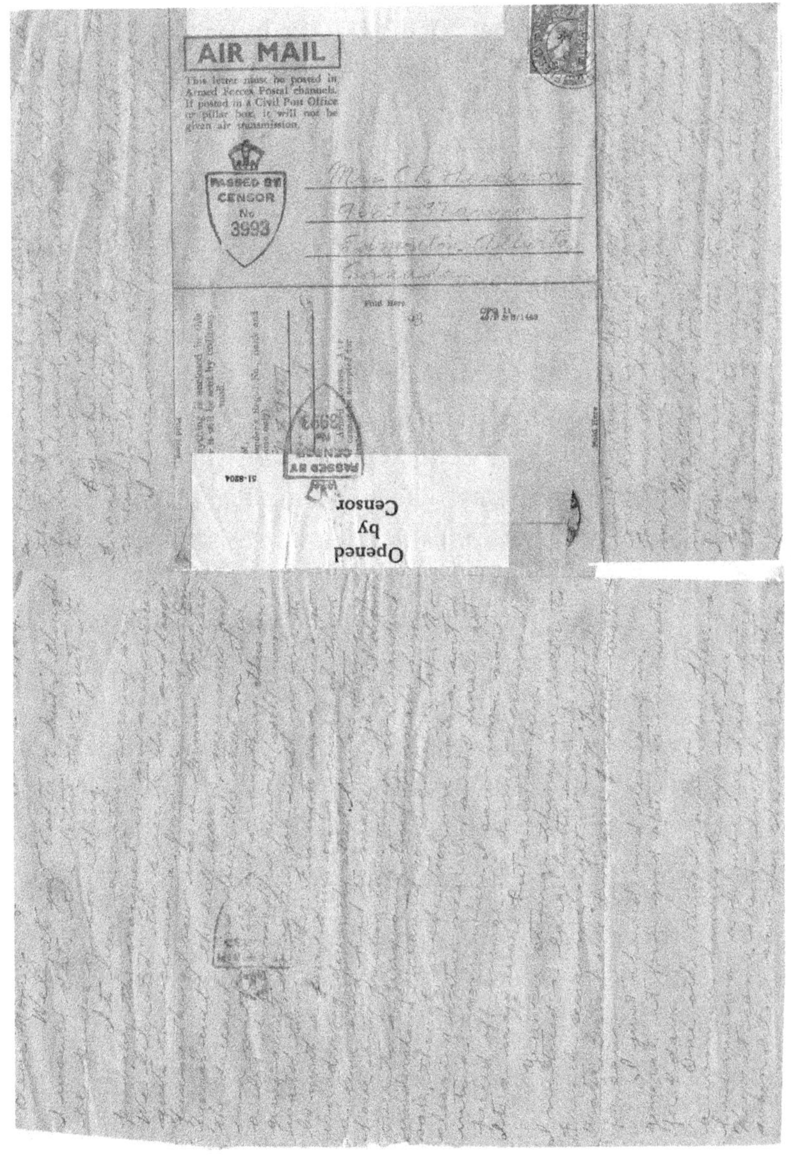

AIR MAIL

This letter must be posted in Armed Forces Postal channels. If posted in a Civil Post Office or pillar box, it will not be given air transmission.

PASSED BY CENSOR No 3993

Canada

Opened by Censor

Nov 2, 1944

Dear Mom:

Well, it's just 5 after 12 but I thought I would date the letter the 2 just to be precise or something.

It's been a rather screwy day, probably the craziest in my army career. We "liberated" this place today and bagged quite the occasional Jerry in doing so. One funny thing I saw was a German Military funeral with the pall bearers, mourners and the deceased going down the street on their own without a guard or anything. There were a lot of Jerry medical personel (spelt wrong) going about doing their job with no one to watch them either. Funny to see a truck go by with a Jerry driver or a couple of them wandering down the street. I was stringing a line and had to make a joint. I did not have any friction tape though so I wandered over to a Jerry and tried to make him understand I wanted some adhesive tape. No sale, though, so he took me into a sort of clearing station nearby and I finally got into a room where I saw some, so I peeled off enough to do me & scrammed. It's a crazy war. But a lot of fun.

You see strange things in bottles, too. I noticed a large bottle and if my French serves right it says "Filtered Water, Drinkable" Imagine bottled water for sale.

I just shaved and cleaned up in general, it feels good after not even washing for 4 days.

One other thing I saw today, there was a woman howling her eyes out. Her husband was a German we had captured. How it came about I don't know but when I last saw her she was in with her husband, had his pack on her back and was marching down the road with them. I wonder what will happen to her in the end, they must separate them some time or other I guess.

By the way, I shaved off my mustache. Frankly, it didn't look so hot but curiosity kept me from doing so before.

I have only a few airmail forms with stamps left, mom and the Lord only knows where I can get more stamps so I guess I'll have to start writing regular mail soon. I hope you don't mind.

My mail hasn't caught up with me yet but it should anytime now. I figure mail written to this address will probably get to me before the stuff posted to England etc.

That's all for now, lady.

Love and Kisses

Grant

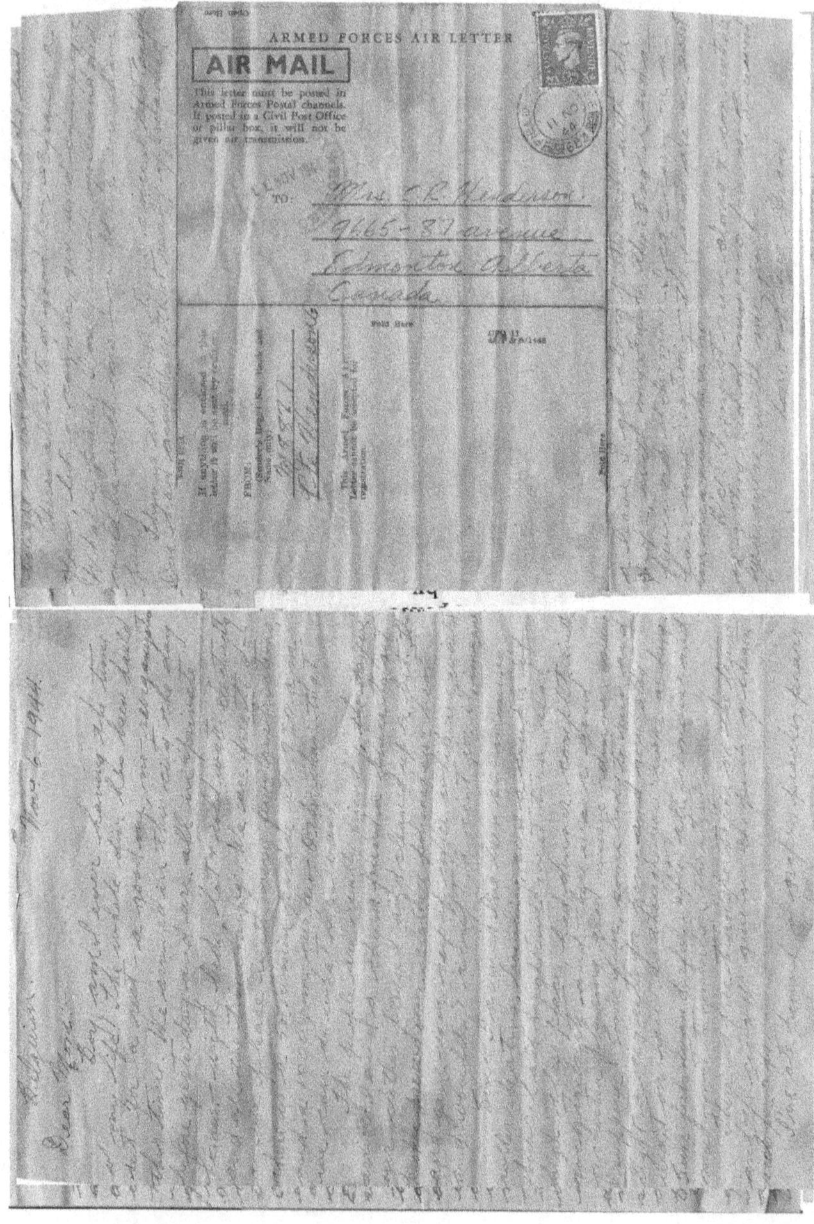

ARMED FORCES AIR LETTER

AIR MAIL

This letter must be posted in Armed Forces Postal channels. If posted in a Civil Post Office or pillar box, it will not be given air transmission.

TO: Mrs. C.R. Henderson
9665-87 avenue
Edmonton Alberta
Canada

Nov 6, 1944

Belgium

Dear Mom:

Boy, am I ever having the time of my life! The whole div. has been hauled out for a rest – a good one, no reorganization this time. We arrived in this city the day before yesterday and are all in private homes with beds, hot & cold water electricity and all the trimmings. We are free to do as we please with very few restrictions. There is a 5 or 10 min. parade at 9:30 am and a 10:00 pm curfew. Other than that we can do what we want.

The people are really friendly, the day we arrived I and a chap found a place to get our clothes pressed and cleaned up a bit. The people presses our clothes, polished our boots and gave us a cup of coffee while we waited and wouldn't accept a cent for it, imagine.

Since I arrived I've been swimming, roller skating, bowling, seen a couple of shows. Last night we went to a real high class place, had dinner complete with cocktails etc. and there was a good orchestra playing good music – dinner music, I suppose. Some fun, somebody to run and light a cigarette for you and generally wait on you as though you were a king. Sure feels wonderful after all the noise and mud – not to mention the stink.

There was free transportation on the trams and the civvies give us the pick of theatre seats for 5 Fr.

I've ate pounds of grapes, peaches, pears and apples, gallons of ice cream, and bought a lot of candy.

There's all sorts of good beer – 3 franks a glass, lots of cognac, gin and champagne. What a place! I only wish you and dad could be with me – could we ever have fun!

This is the first time since I left Canada I've had anything that really approached a leave. I get along pretty well with the people, with my French, their English and a few words of German. I can carry on a fair conversation – the hands are an asset in speaking here to.

Well I must run along & concentrate on getting rid of my 1000 francs. Sure wish you were with me folks.

Love and Kisses

Grant

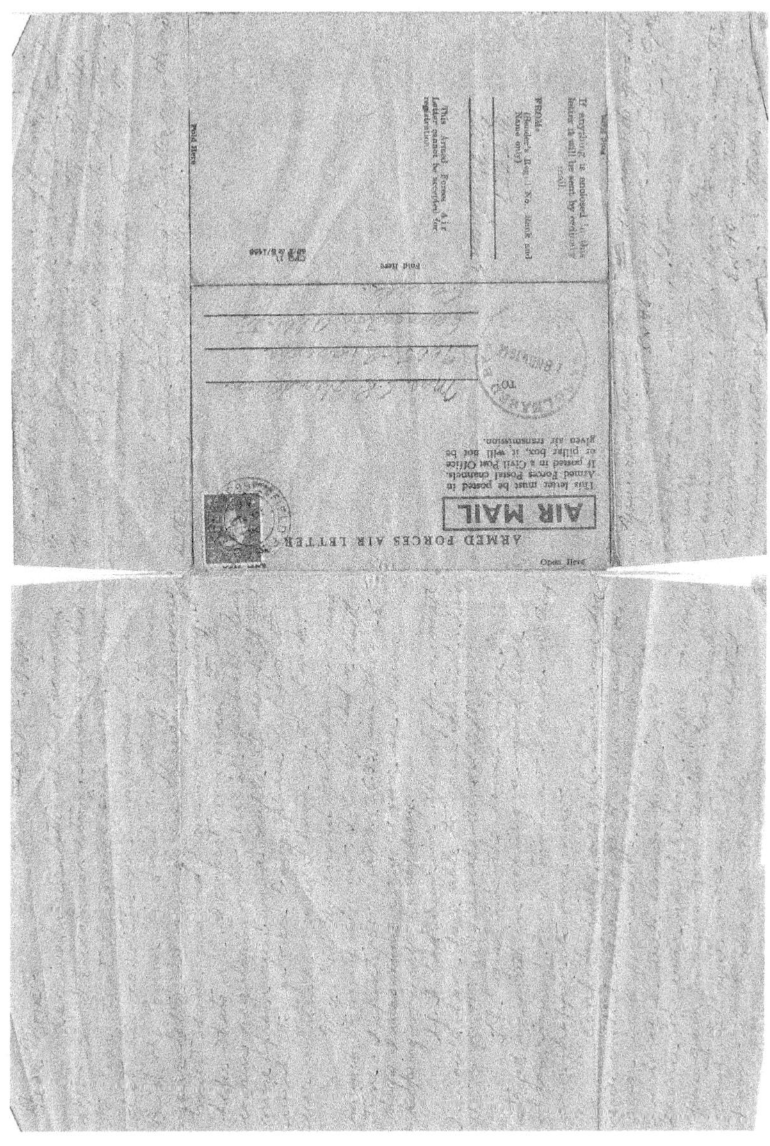

ARMED FORCES AIR LETTER

AIR MAIL

This letter must be posted in Armed Forces Postal channels. If posted in a Civil Post Office or pillar box, it will not be given air transmission.

Open Here

Fold Here

If anything is enclosed in this letter it will be sent by ordinary mail

FROM:
(Sender's Regt'l No. Rank and Name only)

This Armed Forces Air Letter cannot be accepted for registration.

Fold Here

Nov 10, 1944

Dear Mom:

Received your letter of Oct.30 today, also the Glen Cannon Story. I was shocked to hear that Doug was sick and I hope that his condition has improved by now.

Did the Legion find out anything? From your letter it sounds as though his nerves must of cracked from over studying. I hope that's all. I expect my mail to be coming regularly now. I shall probably hear more from you in a couple of days. If you wish to go and see Doug please feel free to use whatever money I have in the bank.

My holiday ended yesterday morning much to my sorrow. I really had a swell time. I spent 1000 francs (25.33) in the 4 or 5 days I was there so you can see I was keeping myself fairly busy.

If I had been in the city for a month, I would have been able to speak Flemish. I was doing pretty good by the time I left.

The girl in the house where I stayed insisted in sewing a good luck charm inside my tunic so I guess nothing can happen to me now.

Confidentially, old girl, I have an idea you will be hearing good news regards the war in a few weeks. There is in the words of a well known person "a 50 – 50 chance the war will be over before the New Year given 5 weeks good weather". Naturally I can't tell you more but from what I know it looks reasonable.

You mentioned that HQ sounds good, it is. I'm not at BNHQ anymore but in a Coy HQ which is a real set up. It means that I have a roof over my head, in a house or barn. All I have to do is maintain communication with BNHQ by telephone on wireless. Although I go in on attacks etc, I don't use my weapons except for defense.

I just heard that we (me & my friends) are going to the rear for a week – some fun. So you can see I'm leading a pretty soft life.

I heard from Hennigar today, too. He has been moved to a different hospital and is coming along fine.

Well I hope to hear that Doug is better by the next letter, mom.

Love & Kisses

Grant

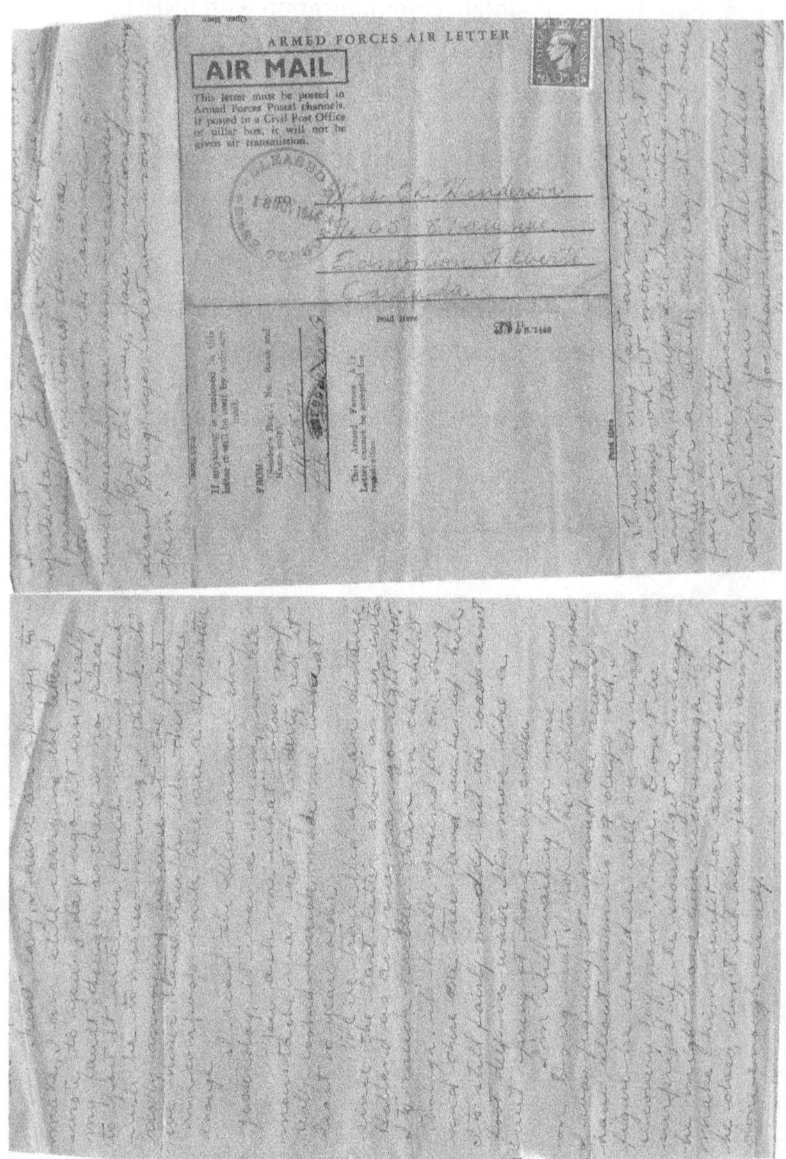

ARMED FORCES AIR LETTER

AIR MAIL

This letter must be posted in Armed Forces Postal channels. If posted in a Civil Post Office or pillar box, it will not be given air transmission.

Mrs. C.R. Henderson

Edmonton Alberta

Canada

Nov 13, 1944

Dear Mom:

First, lady, I have an apology to make, I am still carrying the letter I wrote to you 3 days ago. It isn't really my fault though, as there is no place to post it until we finish moving which will be tomorrow morning. I think it is really annoying because at the front we never have trouble like this. These nincompoops back here are a dif matter though.

I read the Glen Cannon story yesterday, it was seriously no lie.

You asked me what colour my moustache was, sort of a dirty red. It really looked horrible, made me look at least 10 years older.

We've travelled a fair distance since the last letter as far into Holland as anyone can go right now. It's much prettier than in the Scheldt though, its higher ground for one thing and there are trees and bushes up here. It's still fairly muddy but the roads aren't foot deep in water. It's more like a wet spring at home only colder.

I'm still waiting for more news on Doug but I hope he's better by now. I was figuring it up and the news I have about him is 19 days old. I figure he should be well on the road to recovery by now. I hope. Don't be surprised if he should get a discharge, he might have been sick enough to make him unfit for aircrew duty. If he does, don't let him join the army, he's done enough already.

I met 2 of my chums from CSRU yesterday, Callinane & MacKenzie, I have probably mentioned them some time or other they are in the same div so I will probably see them occasionally.

By the way you mentioned something about Doug's eyes, what was wrong with them.

This is my last airmail form with a stamp on it mom, if I can't get any more stamps I'll be writing regular mail for a while, they say it goes over fast anyway.

Let me know if any of my letters don't reach you – they should.

Well, I'll go thaw my fingers now, lady.

Love & Kisses etc.

Grant.

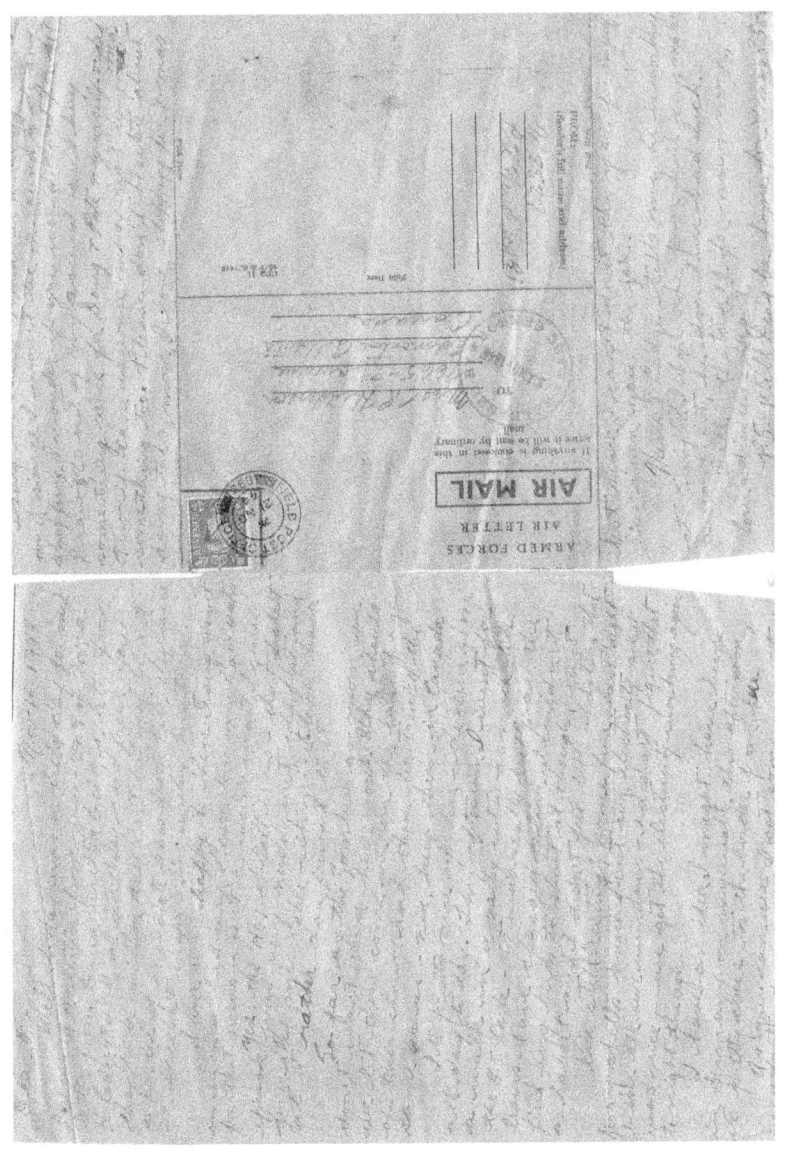

ARMED FORCES
AIR LETTER

AIR MAIL

If anything is enclosed in this letter it will be sent by ordinary mail

TO:

FROM:
(Sender's full name and address)

Nov 16, 1944

Dear Mom:

Well today was a field day for me. I received 2 letters from you – 2 & 4 of Nov, a letter from Doug written on Oct 2 and H.Lodge 19 of Oct., a birthday card from you, thanks a million and last but not least a parcel of chocolate bars from Pete. They were in excellent shape. I am writing him today.

I am very happy to hear Doug isn't in such a bad way. I sure tore my hair waiting for that news – just a worry wart I guess.

Yes, the ALI of Galt is us – that Scheldt episode was very muddy, wet, cold, flat and generally miserable – it's nice to look back at it rather that forward to it.

So far as the Zombies go mom, we don't want them here now. Why should we let them come in on the last page of this show and then be treated the same as us - keep them in Canada.

It's pretty nice up here – the sun shone all day today. This afternoon I went for a walk in a valley – it was much like the S.S. Park – it was really pretty, all the leaves have changed colour. I couldn't find any birds to shoot at though; just a rabbit and I didn't feel like shooting that.

I'm still "resting" some fun. Last night Jerry shells knocked out our electricity and broke all our windows – I didn't figure that was nice – we got the electricity working again tonight though.

I have an idea I might have been in German y on my walk this afternoon, it's pretty close to the border from here.

As you can see, I got some more stamps enough to do me for a couple of months.

Seeing as how Xmas is drawing near and since I won't be around to do any shopping, I wonder if you would do it for me.

Draw $20 out of my account and buy something nice for Doug & Pete &yourself & dad. Also if there is some money left buy Ma something too. Please don't hesitate about doing this, mom, I love shopping for Xmas but since I can't do it this year for myself, I've given you the job.

Henry Lodge tells me he is working at Swifts. I hope the poor devil can make a go of it, he does have bad luck.

Well that's all for now, Mom,

Love and Kisses

Grant

P.S. Will Doug be home for Xmas?

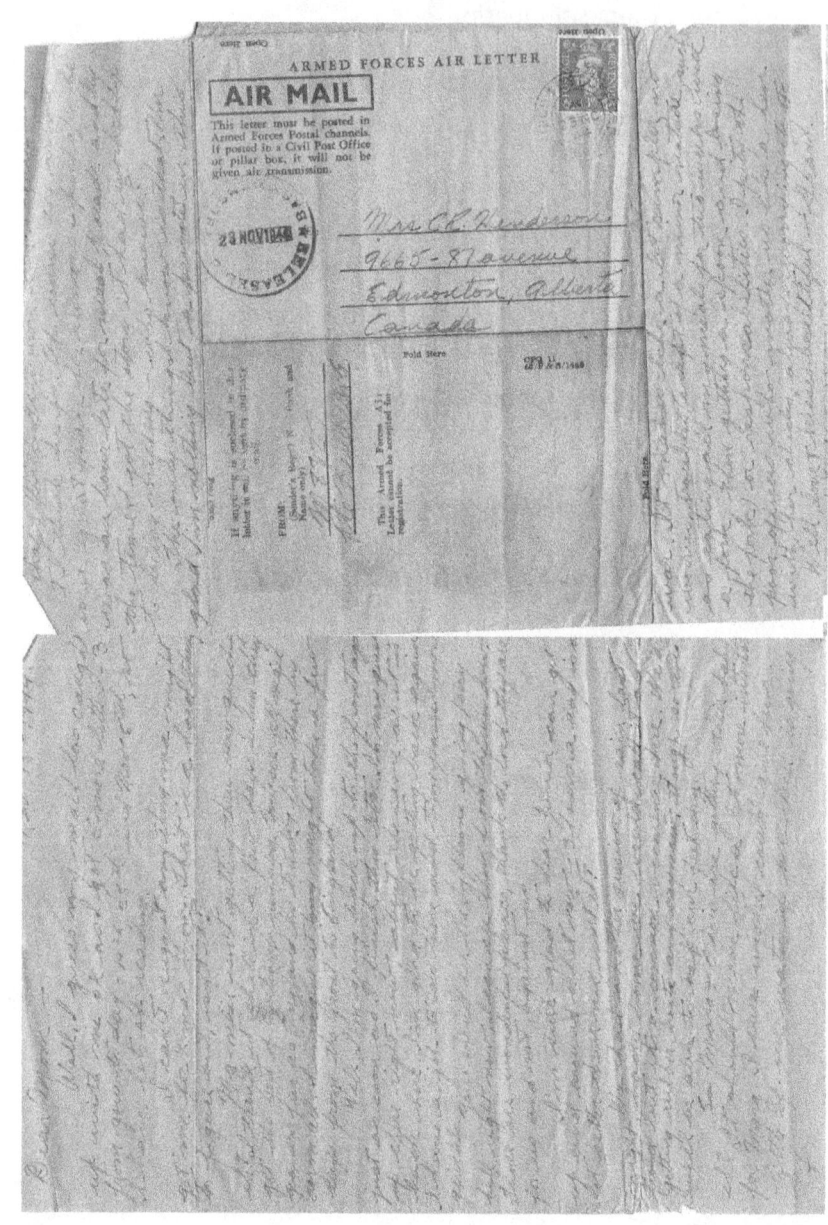

ARMED FORCES AIR LETTER

AIR MAIL

This letter must be posted in Armed Forces Postal channels. If posted in a Civil Post Office or pillar box, it will not be given air transmission.

Mrs C.L. Henderson
9665-87 avenue
Edmonton, Alberta
Canada

Nov 18, 1944

Dear Mom:

Well I guess my mail has caught up with me ok as I got 5 more letters - 3 from you today – 14th, 28th and Nov 6th, so I have lots of reading.

I can't suggest anything Ma might get me for Xmas, Mom. That is a hard thing to figure out, isn't it?

My mail isn't getting there very quickly eh? I think it shall in a few days when they get the port authority running. You see all mail goes as far as England by truck. I imagine that it might take a few days from the front to England.

Well I'm going back to the front again just as soon as I finish this letter. It's very quiet up there right now, about the same as it is back here. I'm glad to be getting back again. I have a job to do there and the time passes more quickly.

You should see the Typhoon giving Jerry hell right now; I can see them from the window. Those wonderful planes, thank the Lord they are for us and not against us.

I am sure glad to hear that Junior can get up and around a bit now – 3 hours a day is a lot better than nil, isn't it?

We had another session of rain last night, back home we would call it a flood but it's a common occurrence here. We are getting rubber boots any day now though so we will be able to keep our feet dry.

So Marg & Chris are getting their baby eh? It should make life a lot more interesting for Marg. I sure wish I could give her a little of our water if her well Is going dry.

Perhaps Wilf Gallimore isn't missing but I think he is. Of course the army is a great place for rumors perhaps he was an hour late for meal parade and by the time I got the story it had worked up to being missing – who knows?

The only thing I know is that I'm glad I'm nothing but a private in this war. It makes life a lot simpler no worries, troubles (except of a minor nature, such as eating all my meals for two weeks with a fork, then getting a spoon and losing the fork) or responsibilities. I pity the poor officers who mother us like a hen with her chicks, always worrying etc.

Well, Love & Kisses beautiful

Grant

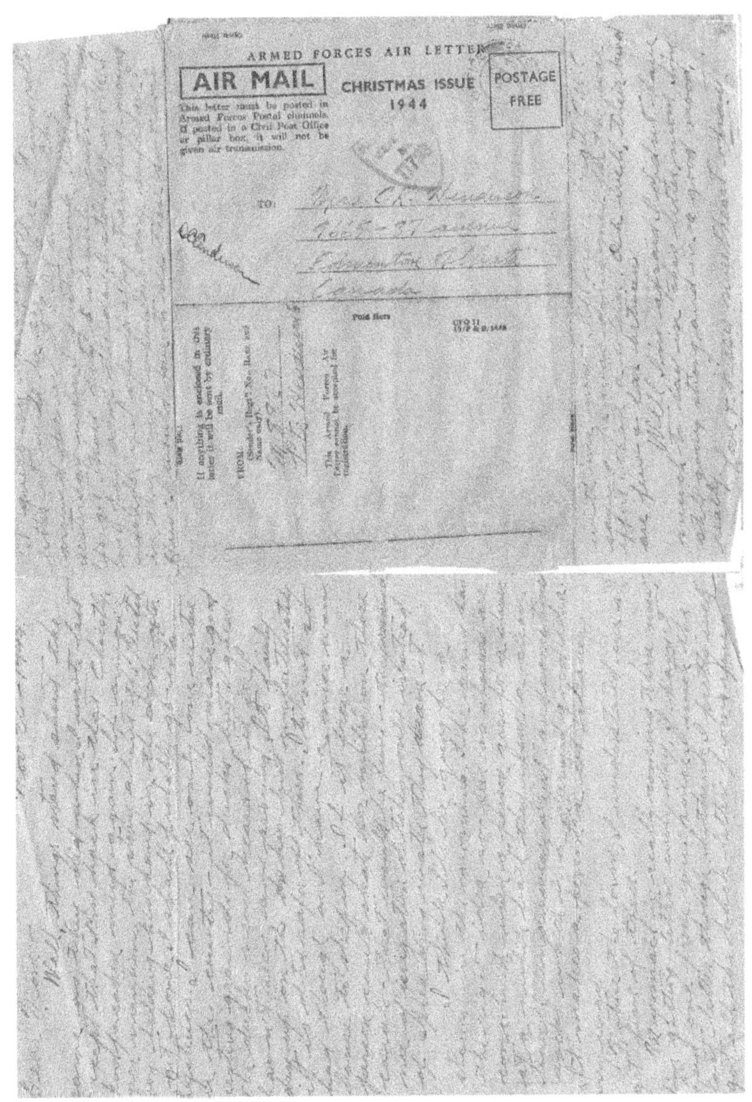

ARMED FORCES AIR LETTER

AIR MAIL

CHRISTMAS ISSUE 1944

POSTAGE FREE

This letter must be posted in Armed Forces Postal channels. If posted in a Civil Post Office or pillar box, it will not be given air transmission.

TO:

Canada

Fold Here

If anything is enclosed in this letter it will be sent by ordinary mail.

FROM:

Nov 20, 1944

Dear Mom:

Well, things have stayed the about the same as they did when I wrote last except that I'm back in that Christly, Godforsaken mud again. If anyone ever mentions the story about the Dutch boy holding his hand in the dyke after I get home I shall probably go into hysterics. I can see only one virtue in this country – it would make good nesting ground for ducks but I guess ducks never heard of it for I haven't seen any around. It's fairly dry up on the dykes but unfortunately it is often safer off them. It's not so bad though as I have a nice warm house to sleep in. if it froze a person could skate for miles on those canals – that would be fun –they remind me of irrigation ditches only instead of spreading water they drain it.

I think I'll be going for a shower in the morning. The army had the right idea so far as showers are concerned, when a person goes for shower at a mobile bath they issue a clean towel, underwear, shirt and sometimes socks which is a darned good idea. It makes a person a lot cleaner anyway.

Notice the form; I understand we all get five of these.

My mail is really coming thru now. I am getting letters every day. I haven't got one from you since I wrote the last letter though. I think I pretty well got all the back letters from you.

I guess by the time you get this letter it will be the 1st Dec. Time rolls around doesn't it. It seems like yesterday when I quit work. I'll never forget those dirty skunks cutting off my pay as of the day I stopped work. I wonder if I should stop tramping around in the mud when I've done my share. How I would love to see those So & So's with me now. I'll never forget CWC saying he was doing more for the war effort than a soldier. Oh well their kind are few and far between.

Well I'm afraid I didn't have much to say in this letter, mom. I'm still going strong and in a good mood, really.

Love and Kisses sweetheart

Grant

Dear Mom:-

Received your letter of the 9th yesterday. So Doug is up for discharge, well I wasn't exactly surprised at that and I don't suppose you were. I know that whatever was wrong with him will be cleared up with a month or so of change. It is probable that he got kind of jumpy from working too hard like I did at the Ironworks. I was a changed person after being in the army a few weeks and away from worries and troubles etc. Anyway I know that you will take good care of him. It should take some of the emptiness out of the house to have him back again and I know you and Dad will like that. I hardly think the army will call him up and between you & me I would keep him away from recruiting offices. He has done his share. [illegible]

[illegible]

ARMED FORCES AIR LETTER

AIR MAIL

1 CANADIAN A.B.P.O. 28 NOV 4[illegible]

TO: Mrs C.R. Henderson
9665-87 avenue
Edmonton Alberta
Canada.

Nov 24, 1944

Dear Mom:

Received your letter of the 9th yesterday. So Doug is up for discharge, well I wasn't exactly surprised at that and I don't suppose you were. I know that whatever was wrong with him will be cleared up with a month or so of change. It is probable that he got kind of jumpy from working too hard like I did at the Ironworks. I was a changed person after being in the army a few weeks and away from the worries and troubles etc. Anyway I know that you will take good care of him. It should take some of the emptiness out of the house to have him back again and I know you and Dad will like that. I hardly think the army will call him up between you & me. I would keep him away from the recruiting offices. He has done his share. Let a zombie or a near zombie like Ross Mc take his place. So much for that.

Well I am "resting" again, in fact about all I've done lately is that. This a.m. our div. general came down and spoke to us for a while. He seemed to be a nice chap. Incidentally that place where we spent our 5 day leave was Ghent. We went up there from the Breskins pocket show. I can name any town I have been in more than two weeks ago so if you are curious about any place I might have been or anything like that let me know and I will tell you I'm in the 3rd div, 9th brigade (the only highland brigade in the Can. Army) so probably you can read more about where we are in the paper than I can tell you.

As usual it is dull and wet; one weather forecast could do this country for a year.

By the way, our div com. said this am that it could be over in a few weeks (I hope).

I had a letter from Bob Jenkins the other day. He is going to the Calgary tech.

By gosh, I almost forgot! I received that parcel with the soap & tobacco & tomato juice, grapefruit juice & cherries. It was really swell. I'll be able to wash Holland off now and smell good at the same time.

Love & Kisses

Grant

ARMED FORCES AIR LETTER

AIR MAIL

1 CANADIAN
CHRISTMAS ISSUE
1944
3 DEC 44

POSTAGE FREE

This letter must be posted in Armed Forces Postal channels. If posted in a Civil Post Office or pillar box, it will not be given air transmission.

TO: Mrs. C.R. Henderson
9665-87 avenue
Edmonton Alberta
Canada

Fold Here

Nov 27, 1944

Dear Mom:

Well, yesterday I received a letter written from you on Oct 23, a half pound of tobacco sent to CBRG and 300 cigarettes from Ma. A pretty good day, I'd say. The smoking situation is very good now and doesn't break my heart. Pardon the writing, lady, my fingers seem to be stiff. I am writing Ma today to thank her for the smokes.

You were asking me if your letters are censored, no they aren't. You should get quite a few from me that aren't censored. We get special envelopes sometimes and I always put your letters in them. Well I got another jab in the arm on Sat –typhus, I think they don't spare the needles in this racket. We got our beer issue yesterday – Guinness stout. I got 2 issue, one from Bre HQ & one from C coy HQ (I'm attached to them) I drank one bottle and 3 of us got together with our beer & rum and drew cards for the whole works of it. So the Coy runner (who now had six oz's of rum and 3 quarts of stout). The last time I saw *he was quite drunk. The rum we get I is like syrup and is powerful dope.*

Oh, but we got an awful scare the other day! When our div commander was talking to us he said the 3rd div had done everything but drop from an airplane. The way he said it, it sounded as though we were going to be paratroops and we all visioned ourselves flying thru the air. The old boy saw the glum looks on our faces and put us straight. What a relief!

I went to church yesterday, the first time in 8 weeks. It was a nice sunny day and we became parade square soldiers again for a while. We formed in a field and the pipe band led us to church. That was the first time I was on parade in several weeks.

I'm beginning to have an idea the weather's not so bad here. If it doesn't get any colder it will be O K for winter. There isn't any snow yet anyway.

By the way, I met one of the boys who was with me in Grande Prairie. He is an Edmonton, south side boy by the name of Roland. He stopped to ask me the way the other night and recognized my voice. We chewed the rag for a couple of hours. It was really swell to see him. I guess I know fellows in darned near every regiment in the Can. Army.

Love Grant

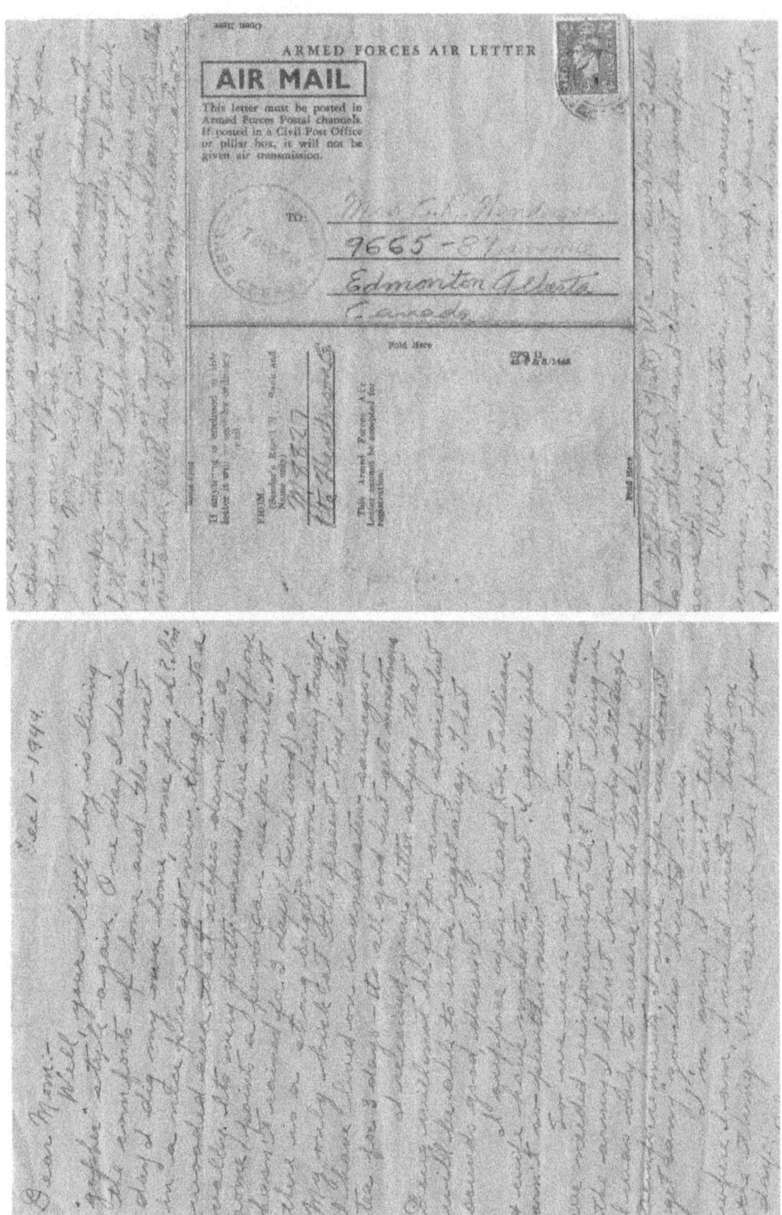

ARMED FORCES AIR LETTER

AIR MAIL

This letter must be posted in Armed Forces Postal channels. If posted in a Civil Post Office or pillar box, it will not be given air transmission.

TO: Mrs. C.R. Henderson
9665-87 avenue
Edmonton Alberta
Canada

Dec 1-1944.

Dear Mom:-
Well, your little boy is living

Dec 1, 1944

Dear Mom:

Well, your little boy is living "gopher" s style again. One day I have the comforts of home and the next day I dig my own home, some fun eh? I'm in a nice place right now, though it's a wooded area that slopes down into a valley. It's very pretty around here and from some points a person can see for miles. It hasn't rained for 3 days (touch wood) and there is a strong bright moon shinning tonight. My only kick at the present time is that I have lived on canned stew, sausages and tea for 3 days it's all good but monotonous.

I received your letter saying that Doug will not be fit for army service but will be able to work right away. That sounds good doesn't it?

I suppose you heard Ken Sullivan & wife have moved to the coast. I guess jobs aren't so plentiful now.

So we were out of action because we needed reinforcements eh? Just being in the army I didn't know why although I was only to aware of the lace of reinforcements. I sure hope we don't get any "zombies" busted on us.

I am sorry I can't tell you where I am, I could write a book on the things I've seen in the past few days.

Oh, yes I got a new pair of socks today, the first time they have been changed in about a month I guess. Even then there was only a hole in the toe of one of the ones I took off.

My cold is just about better. A couple of more days nice weather & I think I'll have it licked. I can't figure out how I ever got a cold. I've swallowed countless vitamin pills and drank my rum ration faithfully (oh Yeah?). We do swallow 2 pills a day though and they must be good for something.

Well Christmas is just around the corner, it sure sneaks up, doesn't it? I guess I won't have Xmas dinner in Berlin this year though.

Well that's all for now, Mom. Love and Kisses

Grant.

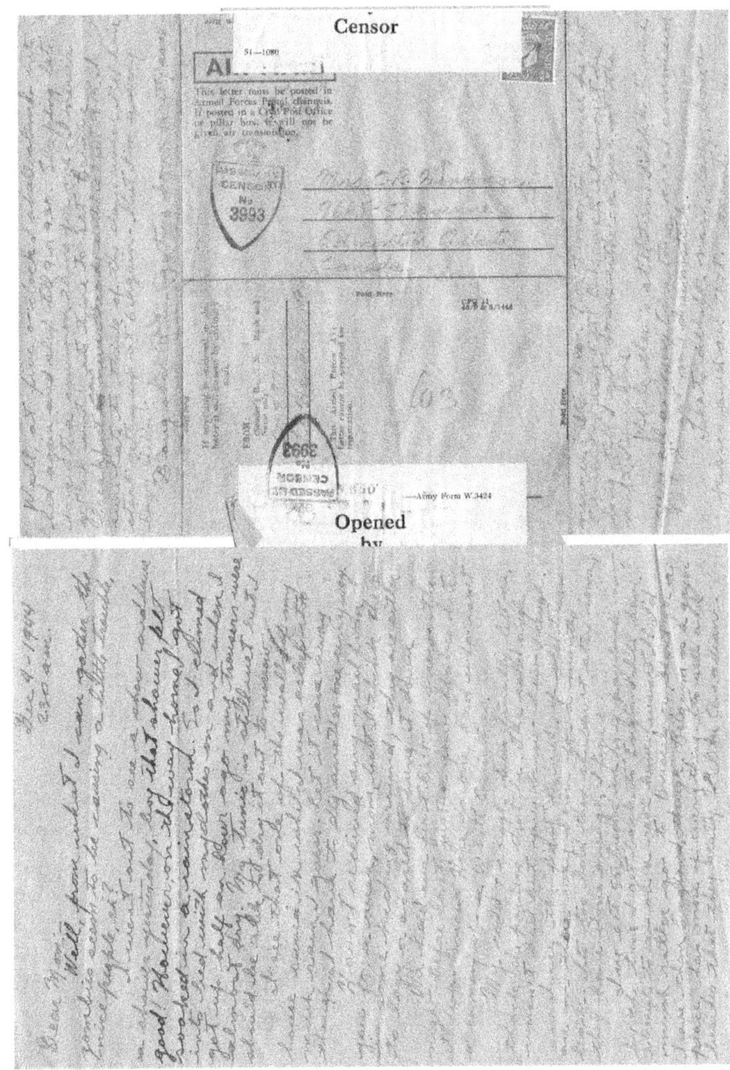

Censor

This letter must be posted in Armed Forces Postal channels. If posted in a Civil Post Office or pillar box, it will not be given air transmission.

PASSED BY CENSOR No 3993

Army Form W.3424

Opened by

Dec 4, 1944

2:30 a.m.

Dear Mom:

Well from what I can gather the zombies see to be causing a little trouble, nice people, eh?

I went out to see a show and have a shower yesterday, boy that shower felt good! However, on the way home I got soaked in a rainstorm. So I climbed into bed with my clothes on and when I got up half an hour ago my trousers were almost dry. My tunic is still wet but I should be able to dry it out tomorrow.

I see that one of the walls of my house caved in while I was a sleep. It's too much rain I guess. Let it cave away though, I have to dig another one anyway.

Haven't received any mail from you for a week, mom but I think there is some kicking around; they are either to lazy or scared to bring it down.

We had our first bit of snow the night before last, just a few flakes, but it was snow. Here is one lad who isn't dreaming of a white Christmas.

My cold and cough has finally left me thank the powers that be. The cold wasn't bad but you know how I cough.

I see that the first bunch of old timers are on their way home for a month leave. It's too bad they couldn't stay home, they have done enough, I figure.

I've got 55 bucks in my pay book now, by the time I get back to England I'll have enough to go on a real leave won't I? I'd much rather go to Brussels or Ghent for leave than England though. Belgium is a gayer place, has more of everything to see and besides they really like Canadians.

Well at five o'clock I shall climb into bed again and sleep till 9 or 9:30. Sleeping late is quite a common thing for me. I never get up until it's time to eat because breakfast never is ready until about 9:15. I sure hate to think of the days when I'll have start getting up at 6 again but I'm a very lazy fellow.

Doug should b e getting home pretty soon now eh? It's been 7 or 8 months since he left Edmonton isn't it? Oh well it won't be long till I get home either – a year at the most I imagine.

While there is still time I'd like to wish you all a Merry Christmas and I commission Pete to eat my drumstick.

That all for now, lady,

Love and Kisses and all that.

Grant

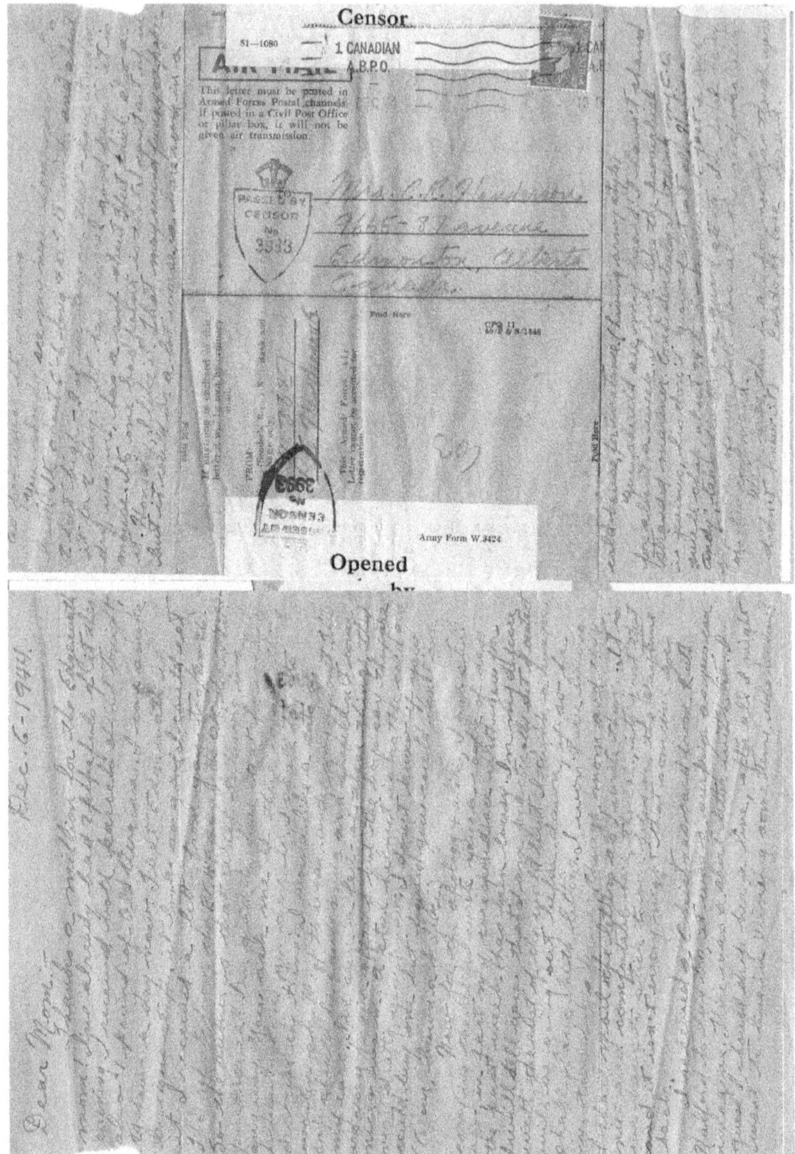

Censor

51—1080

1 CANADIAN
A.B.P.O.

AIR MAIL

This letter must be posted in Armed Forces Postal channels. If posted in a Civil Post Office or pillar box, it will not be given air transmission.

PASSED BY CENSOR No. 3933

Mrs. ... Edmonton, Alberta, Canada.

Army Form W.3424

Opened by

Dec. 6-1944.

Dear Mom:-

Dec 6, 1944

Dear Mom:

Thanks a million for the Edgeworth mom! I've already had 2 pipefuls of it this evening. I received both parcels of it tonight, also 1 pound of Old Virginia. I can smoke 24 hours a day now. That Edgeworth is luscious stuff. It looks so good I could eat it. I received a letter from you too (Nov 26). The reports from the RCAF sounds O.K., doesn't it? So the rumor is that Wilf Gallimore is a prisoner eh? I'm glad to hear that he is alive anyway. You asked me if there is anything I would like, yes there is, I shall try to describe the thing. I would like a sort of woolen skull cap to wear under my helmet. This cap should be fairly snug and shouldn't cover my ears. I've seen a few of these things, they are very plain affairs but the boys say they are nice & warm. A steel helmet is rather cold and very drafty, you know. I don't know if you could buy one but figured that you could knit one (colour, brown or khaki).

Now for the apology & alike, I am still carrying the letter I wrote you a couple of days ago, in fact my correspondence with you for the past week has been lousy. In my defense I will tell you that I am practically out of contact with the rest of the world but I think a runner will be going out before dawn, If so he shall have both letters. I won't be living in this hole forever though mom and then I shall mail the letters as I write them. It is nice and comfortable here though, it's just that we have to stick to our holes in the daytime and it isn't every night that someone goes back.

I received a Christmas card from Ruth Halford today too, it was a surprise as you can imagine. There was a short letter with it. I guess I should drop her a line, after all I might want to live in Winnipeg sometime, who knows?

As per usual it's raining.

You should see my new home mom, it's a beaut! It's about 6'—6 long 4 or 5 ft wide and about 2 feet high – 3 of us live in that – have lived in it for 2 days. It has several good points, it is dry, warm, has a roof about 3 feet thick also a mouse. It's one bad point is that I can't sit up in it. Honestly, I like it. That may sound funny on paper but it could be a lot worse, a bare room in a cold house for instance. (Living army style).

You should see my beard! I haven't shaved for about a week. I look like the proverbial stranded mariner. Confidentially I think my C.O. is jealous, his don't grow fast at all. He is a swell chap, about 24 or 25 – answers to just plain "Andy", takes his turn on guard etc, etc. In brief he just one of us but has all the responsibilities of his command.

Well lady, this is all for now. (As though you didn't know it)

Loads of love

Grant

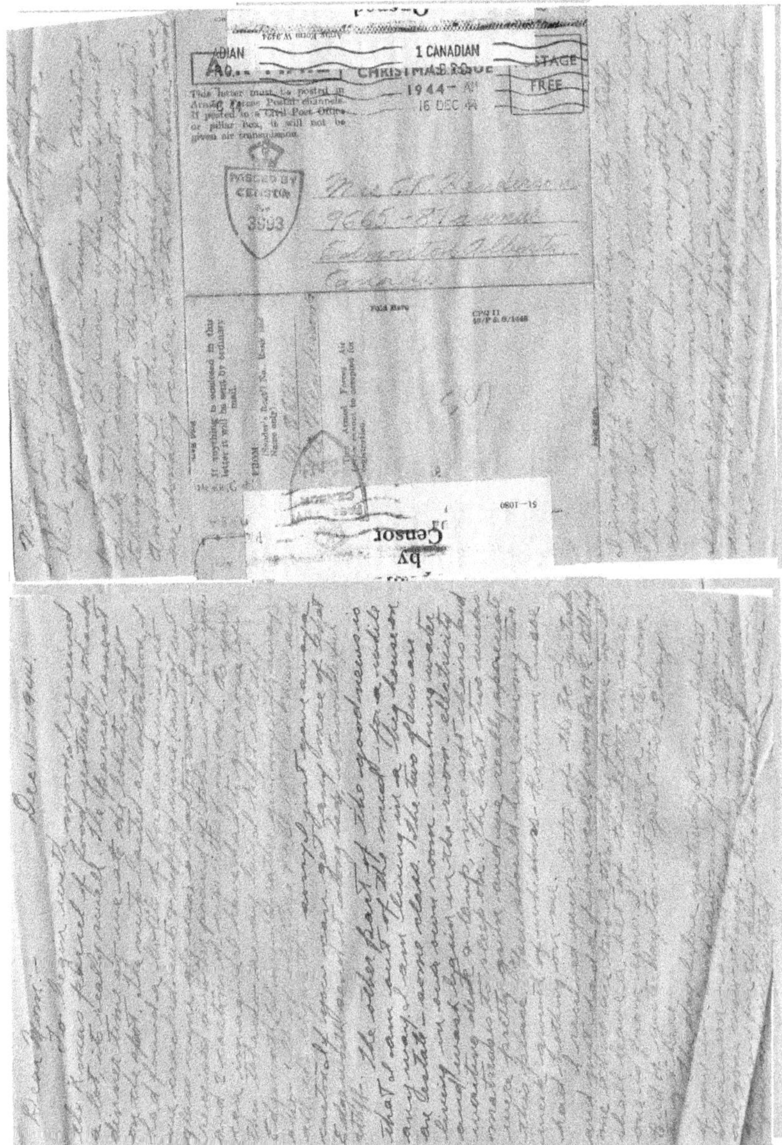

1 CANADIAN
CHRISTMAS ISSUE
1944
16 DEC 44
POSTAGE FREE

This letter must be posted in Armed Forces Postal channels. If posted to a Civil Post Office or pillar box, it will not be given air transmission.

PASSED BY CENSOR No. 3993

Fold Here

Censor

Dec 11, 1944

Dear Mom:

To begin with mom, I received the Xmas parcel of food yesterday, thanks a lot, it's really swell. The parcel came at dinner time so we ate the lobster right on the spot. The nuts lasted all afternoon; I had found a bottle of Bordeaux wine so we cracked nuts & sipped wine (out of cut glass wine glasses) all afternoon. I also received another pound of tobacco from you and 2 cartons of cigarettes from Ma. As you can imagine I have had to give some of this tobacco away but I kept all the Edgeworth (I would rather give my rifle away) also 1lb of old Virg. & ½ lb of Old Chum and all the cigarettes, sorry I just gave away a carton. If you can get any more of that Edgeworth send it along lady, it's wonderful stuff.

The other part of the good news is that I am out of the mud – for a while anyways. I am living in a big house on an estate – some classes. The two of us are living in our own room – running water and wash basin in the room - electricity writing desk & lamp, nice soft chairs and mattresses to sleep on. The last two weeks were pretty grim and we really appreciate this place. You should have seen my two week growth of my whiskers – Robinson Crusoe had nothing on me.

I received your letter of the 30th yesterday and just had a phone call from Batt Q telling me there are two letters there for me. So I shall leave a bit of this letter in case one is from your. I received a letter from Bud H. yesterday too – it just took 3 days to get here.

The day before yesterday, I crawled out of my hole and saw my first real snow of the season – about 4 inches of it. It has all gone now though. By the way I was in Germany for the past two in case you are interested.

Nope, no letter from you lady but I got one from Pete -- really got a kick out of it too.

We shall be having our Christmas party soon (I know when but I don't think the censor would appreciate me telling you when the outfit is going out). Anyway I think it will be fun, we are donating cake, etc to the cause and I imagine the unit will do itself proper too. Although I would much rather be with you folks for Xmas my next choice is the H.L.I boys, my other family.

Well as soon as I finish this, I think I will go & play pool for a while. This is the way I like to fight. Well I'll write in a couple of day's mom.

Love & Kisses

Grant

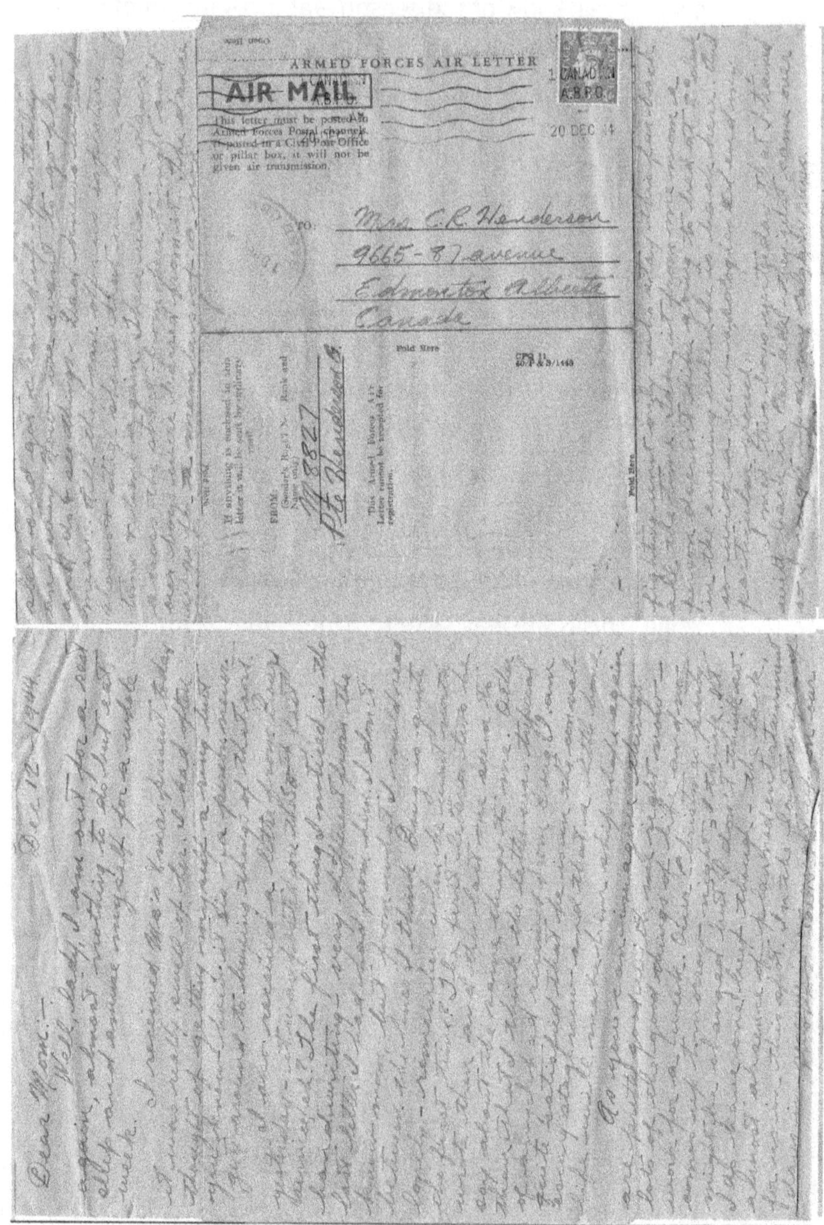

ARMED FORCES AIR LETTER

AIR MAIL

This letter must be posted in Armed Forces Postal channels. If posted in a Civil Post Office or pillar box, it will not be given air transmission.

CANADIAN A.B.P.O.

20 DEC 44

TO: Mrs. C. R. Henderson
9665 - 87 avenue
Edmonton Alberta
Canada

FROM: (Sender's Regt'l No., Rank and Name only)
M 8827
Pte Henderson

If anything is enclosed in this letter it will be sent by ordinary mail.

This Armed Forces Air Letter cannot be accepted for registration.

Fold Here

Dec 12, 1944

Dear Mom:

Well lady, I am out for a rest again, almost nothing to do but eat, sleep and amuse myself for a whole week.

I received Ma's Xmas present today; it was really swell of her. I had often thought of getting myself a ring but you know how it is – a person never gets around to buying things of the sort.

I also received a letter from Doug yesterday – it was posted on the 5th, fast service eh! The first thing I noticed is the handwriting – very different from the last letter I had from him. I don't know mom, but from what I could read between the lines I think Doug is quite lonely – remember when he went north the first time? The first letter or two he wrote the same things to me. Other than that I think the letter was typical of any I had received from Doug. I am quite satisfied that he is in the convalescing stage now and that a little home life will make him ship shape again.

As you can imagine things are pretty good with me right now -- lots of the good things of life and no work for a week. Our Christmas party comes up tomorrow night. It might be changed but I don't think so. I do have one beef though - the lack, absence of planned entertainment for us in this spot. In the last couple of days in reserve we caught up on our sleep and got cleaned up partially anyway. Now we want to go places and do & see things – Dad knows what I mean. All they can offer us is picture shows & stage shows that we have seen time & time again. There was a dance across the street from here tonight and our boys were barred from it. The dance was for members of a non-fighting unit only, who stay this far back all the time. Take it from me mom a person doesn't like going to bed at 8 o'clock in the evening when he is back here. And so with a few apologies end my particular grouch.

I met two boys yesterday that I trained with back in Canada – they just came over so I caught up on Calgary news.

Love and Kisses

Grant

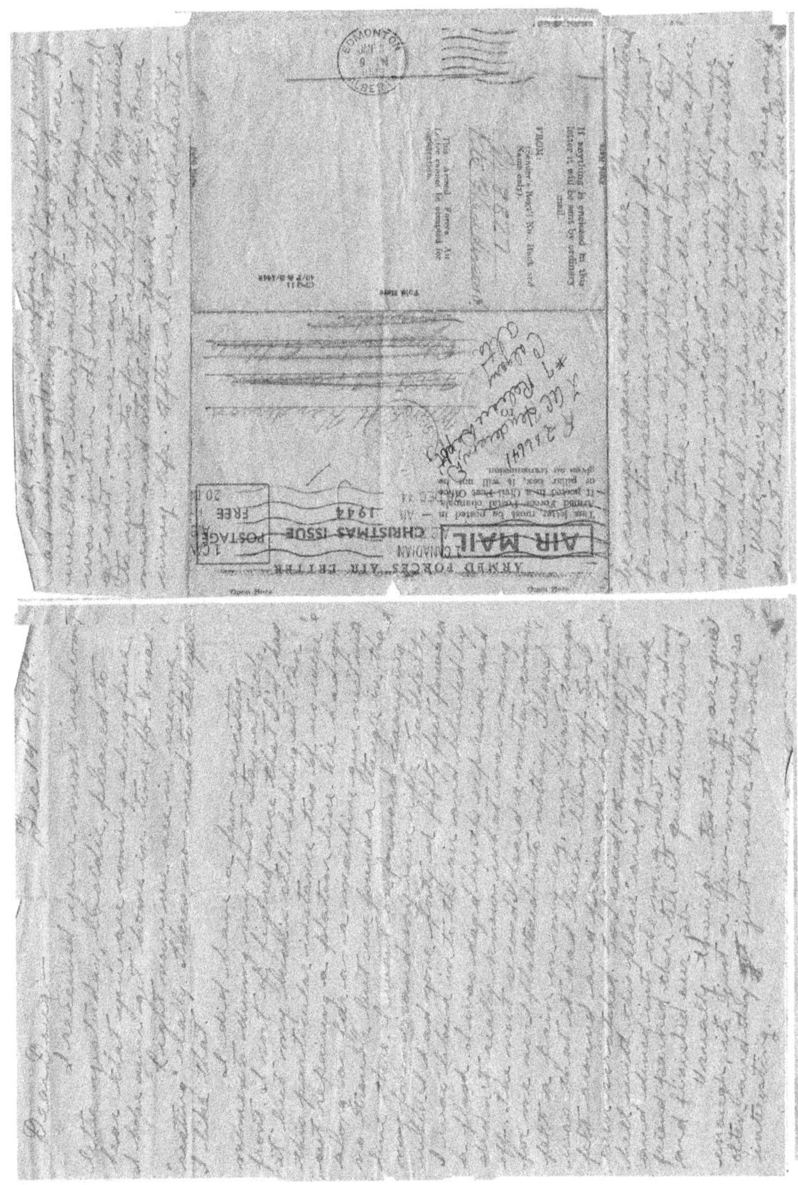

Dec 14, 1944

Dear Doug:

I received your most welcome letter yesterday, laddie, pleased to hear that you are coming along fine. I hope you get home in time for Xmas.

Right now we are in reserve "resting" really. There's no need to tell you I like that.

I did have a few exciting moments during my last stay at the front. I sort of figured once that I'd had it but my luck's still holding out. On this particular instance two of us were out repairing a platoon line. We had gone along as far as a machine gun nest with no trouble but we found a tangle in the line there. I sent forward carrying my friend's and my rifle. Suddenly when I had gone forty or fifty feet forward I was blown into the air and blinded by the flash. I was dazed by the explosion and didn't really know what was coming off. The next second I heard a mortar coming for me so I flattened into nothing. Then I felt a pain in my leg, my first thought was that it had been blown off. So I felt around and praise the Lord it wasn't even scratched. So I said (to myself) to hell with this place and galloped back and dived into the m.g. nest. So I and my friend parked there till it quieted down and finished our job.

Usually though things are quiet enough, it's just a few moments every so often and they just make life more interesting.

Well, Doug, I supposed you feel kind a bad about getting out of the Air force. I wouldn't worry about it though, it was just in the books that you would get out, no one can help it. My advice to you is to forget about the air force now and start to think about your civvy life. After all we all want to be civvys again and will be. You volunteered for active service and served for almost a year, you should be proud of that. But our future is before us, the army & air force is just an incident in our life, one we should forget about as quickly as possible. We are all civilians at heart.

Well here's to a Merry Xmas Doug and the best of luck in the New Year.

Love

Grant.

ARMED FORCES AIR LETTER

AIR MAIL

This letter must be posted in Armed Forces Postal channels. If posted in a Civil Post Office or pillar box, it will not be given air transmission.

TO: Mrs C.R. Henderson
9665-87 avenue
Edmonton Alberta
Canada

If anything is enclosed in this letter it will be sent by ordinary mail

FROM: (Sender's Regt'l No., Rank and Name only)
M 8827
Pte Henderson

This Armed Forces Air Letter cannot be accepted for registration.

NOTE.—Correspondence on this form is subject to censorship. The contents are liable to examination.

The following certificate must be signed by the writer:

I certify on my honour that the contents of this Armed Forces Air Letter refer to nothing but private and family matters.

SIGNATURE (Name only) A.L. Henderson

Dear Mom:— Dec 16 - 1944

Well, we have electricity tonight so I thought I would drop you a line before the wires burn up. The original wiring system went haywire so I turned electrician and put a line into our room. However I used my signal wire for the job and seeing as how it is kinda flimsy I expect to see the wire sizzling at any moment.

I had another bath & change of underwear yesterday - the second within a week. No amount of changing can keep my underwear clean, though, my trousers are so dirty. But it was a swell shower and I soaked for half an hour.

I'm bored with this place already, doing nothing much [illegible] dragging now. Oh well, [illegible]

It's still raining and dull. I guess this must be winter weather around here. I've been waiting patiently for the sun — that would come and stay but no soap. It only freezes at night but the dampness makes it seem much colder.

I really saw a good show yesterday, "The Adventures of Mark Twain". I had never seen it before and I figured it was pretty good.

Did I tell you I had an electric teapot? I found it at the last place we were at so I took it along with me. It's quite an affair, boils water in 2 or 3 minutes. I guess I'll have to leave it here unless I go through as I couldn't be bothered to lug a teapot around with me.

I'm afraid this is going to be dull [illegible] think of a darned [illegible]

[illegible] I can't think of anything to say. I can tell you [illegible] like, though. There's sort of a monthly parcel I've been thinking about. To begin with a couple of bars of face soap, a package of razor blades, shaving cream & tooth paste. There are other things that go good around here like chocolate, cheese, soup packages, cream cheese, chewing gum, [illegible] spreads and stuff like that. Everything good for [illegible] with little preparation [illegible]

I just received your letters [illegible] So pa is raising teeth again, some fun eh! You mention me writing Bud. I have written to & received a letter in answer from him. I'm glad to hear Dennis dropped by, he's a good lad. You should hear our pipers outside. I feel sorry for them, bare legs in this weather. Love [illegible]

Dec 16, 1944

Dear Mom:

Well we have electricity tonight so I thought I would drop you a line before the wires burn up.
The original wiring system went hay wire so I turned electrician and put a line into our room. However I used my signal wire for the job and seeing as how it is kind a flimsy I expect to see the wire sizzling at any moment.

I had another bath & change of underwear yesterday – the second within a week. No amount of changing can keep my underwear clean, though my trousers are so dirty. But it was a swell shower and I soaked for half an hour.

I'm bored with this place already, doing nothing is o.k. up to a limit but time is dragging now, Oh well, I've put in half my time here now.

It's still raining and dull; I guess this must be winter weather around here. I've been waiting patiently for the snow that would come and stay but no sale. It only freezes at night but the dampness makes it seem much colder.

I really saw a good show yesterday. "The Adventures of Mark Twain" I had never seen it before and I figured it was pretty good.

Did I tell you I had an electric tea pot? I found it in the last place we were at & so I took it along with me. It's quite an affair, boils water in 2 or 3 minutes. I guess I'll have to leave it here when I go though as I couldn't be bothered to lug a teapot around with me.

I'm afraid this is going to be dull reading mom. I can't think of a darned thing that's happened for days now – such is life. Since I can't think of anything to say, I can tell you something I would like, though This is a sort of monthly parcel I've been thinking about. To begin with a couple of bars of face soap, a package of razor blades, shaving cream & tooth paste. Here are other things that go good around here. Hot chocolate, those noodles soup packages, cream cheese, chewing gum, all sorts of sandwich spreads and stuff like that. Anything good for snacks with little preparation is what we like.

I just received you letters of the 4th 7 6th. So pa is losing teeth again, some fun eh? You mentioned me writing Bud, I have written to & received a letter in answer from him. I'm glad to hear Henry dropped by, he's a good lad. You should hear our pipers outside; I feel sorry for them, bare legs in this weather.

Love and Kisses sweetheart

Grant

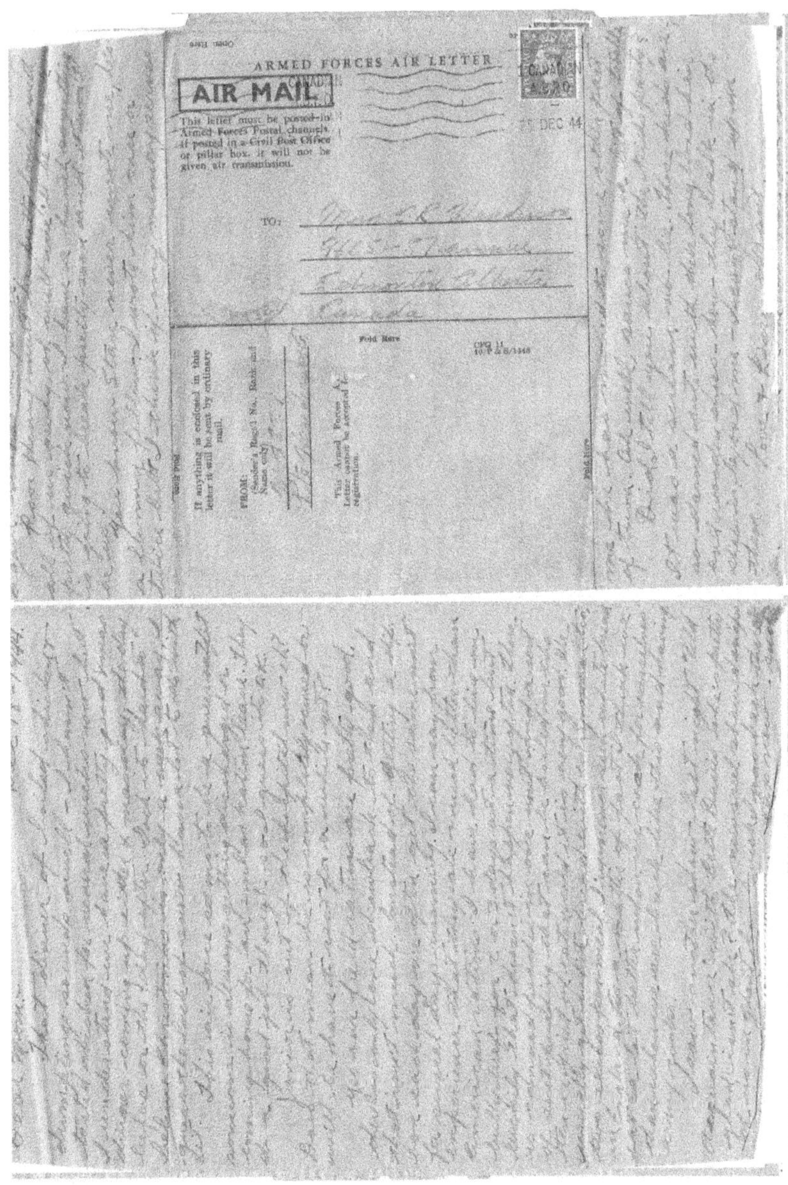

ARMED FORCES AIR LETTER

AIR MAIL

This letter must be posted in Armed Forces Postal channels; if posted in a Civil Post Office or pillar box, it will not be given air transmission.

TO:

If anything is enclosed in this letter it will be sent by ordinary mail.

FROM:

Dec 18, 1944

Dear Mom:

That dinner of boiled chicken & dumplings sounds swell – I haven't tasted chicken for several weeks now but I understand we have a pretty good Xmas dinner coming up either Xmas day, the day before or the day after. Gosh it's hard to believe Christmas is only a week away, I guess the lack of snow has a lot to do with it.

This air force seems to be a queer outfit someone is always getting discharged or coming home for an embarkation leave. They do a good job though so I guess its O.K.

Junior is out of the hospital now eh? Does that mean he is completely cured or will he have to rest for a while yet?

Yes our field rations are pretty good, there is only one drawback to them and that isn't much. Instead of getting a dif. Box each day we often get the American rations. I have had to live on bully beef for 2 or 3 days at a time but luckily that doesn't happen very often. There is canned peaches in one unit and a sort of suet pudding that can be boiled in the tin or fried or eaten cold it is very good. We usually get white bread with every meal too, two slices per meal. I've never seen white bread in England. As a matter of fact I think we eat a lot better when we cook for ourselves then when we are back like this and having army cooks.

I saw another show last night "Old Acquaintance" with Bette Davis she's pretty good isn't she? The newsreel showed snaps of us in Ghent. I wish that I was back there again – what a place.

Poor Henry must be pretty lonely with all of us away, oh well we'll be back pretty quick now. I have a hunch something is going to break pretty soon and it won't be us.

You know Stan never wrote me, he's a funny fellow. I wrote him once or twice but I think if my memory serves me he has moved to some other part of town. Ah well saves me a bit of trouble.

Did I tell you about the kid's party? It was a scream, no lie. Those kids are so darned cute with their long blond hair and wooden shoes – how they walk in the shoes is beyond me – I can't stand up in them.

Love and Kisses

Grant.

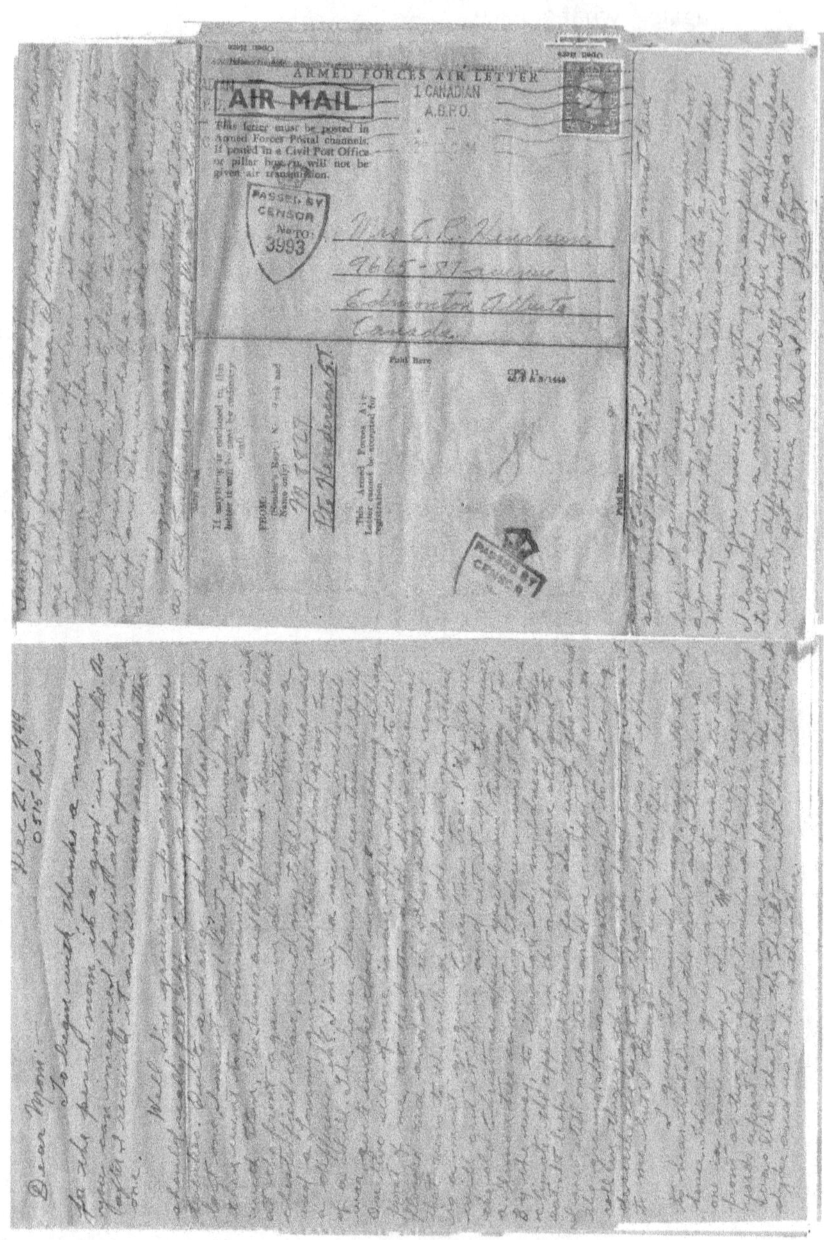

ARMED FORCES AIR LETTER

AIR MAIL

This letter must be posted in Armed Forces Postal channels. If posted in a Civil Post Office or pillar box it will not be given air transmission.

1 CANADIAN A.B.P.O.

PASSED BY CENSOR No. 3993

Mrs. C.R. Henderson
9615-81 avenue
Edmonton Alberta
Canada

Dec 21-1944

Dear Mom:

Dec 21, 1944

0515 hrs

Dear Mom:

To begin with thanks a million for the pencil, mom, it's good one, no lie. As you can imagine I had it all a part five minutes after I received it and I've never seen a better one.

Well I'm growing up aren't I? You should feel old, having a boy in the twenties. Quite a change, this birthday from the last one, I must say! Last year I worked and then went to a community affair at Scona rink with Stan, Vic Turner and Bob Jenkins. Now I'm back at the front again – Germany – sitting in a chesterfield chair with my telephones wireless set and a Tommy gun on the table in front of me. Sure a difference, eh? I'm in a nice house on the rise of a hill. The house hasn't been touched by the war quite unlike those in the neighboring village. On two sides of me is an apple orchard to the front of me at the bottom of the hill is the usual flooded area and at the other side is the road that runs to the village. In the back yard there is the most gorgeous Christmas tree. I think we will cut it down and set it up in the house, the old Christmas spirit, you know. Anyways it is a German tree so cutting it down won't bother me. By the way to illustrate the mildness of this climate, the apples in the orchard are still good to eat. It looks much like a fall day with the coloured leaves still on the trees and a carpet of leaves on the ground. It was a pretty sight to see the fog roll in through the orchard last evening. I can't describe the sight of that orchard as it appeared to me but I thought it was beautiful.

I guess it sounds funny, especially to Dad, to hear that I'm at the front and living in a house. This is a queer war, quite unlike the last one in some ways, I think. Many people see the front as two parallel trenches a couple of hundred yards apart with us in one and Jerry in the other. It was like that in the Scheldt with him behind one dyke and us behind the other. There we just chased him from one dyke to the next until he reached the sea. Of course sometimes there are no houses or if there is no houses or if there is it might be unwise to live in them – then we take to the ground. We have electricity of sorts here too. I found a line with juice in it half a mile away and brought it up and then we wired the house to suit our selves.

I guess jobs aren't so plentiful at the coast as Ken Sullivan imagined. What is the situation around Edmonton? I suppose things have slackened off a bit since I left.

I guess Doug will be home by now, here's hoping anyway. I wrote him a letter a few days ago and put the house address on it (as you very well know).

You know I'm getting an awfully fat face, I looked in the mirror the other day and even I can tell the difference. I guess I'll have to go on a diet when I get home.

Loads of Love

Grant.

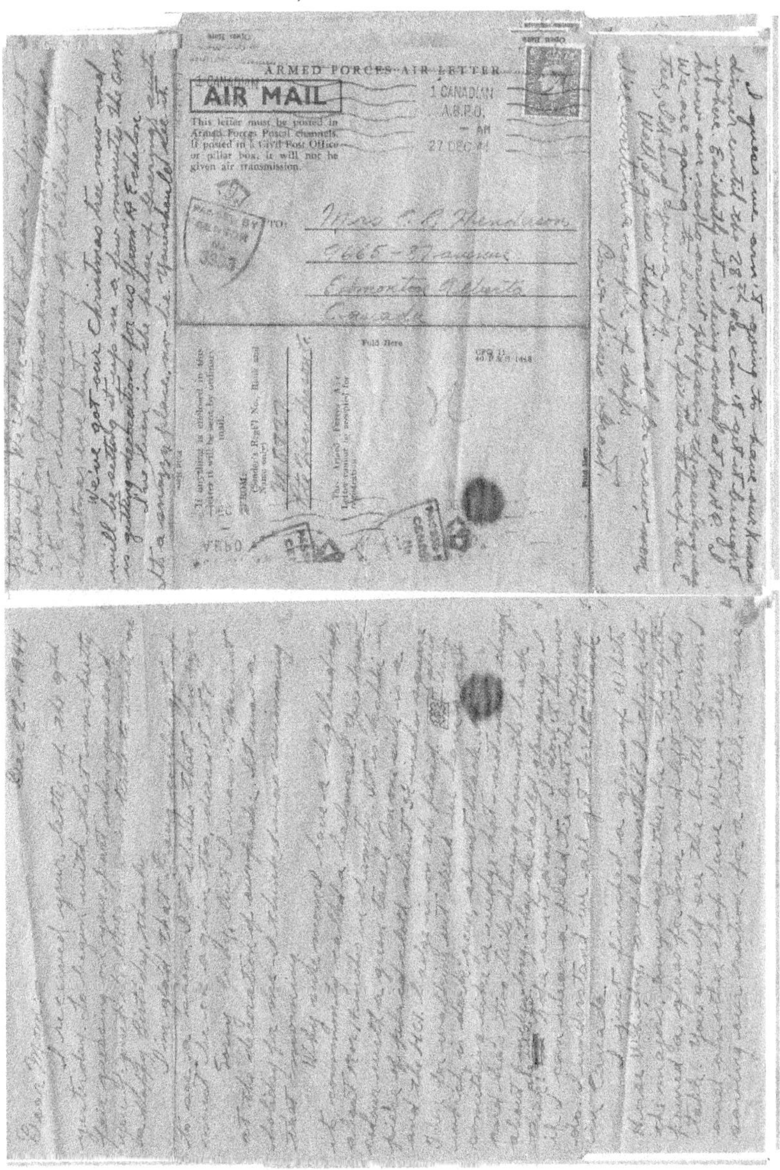

ARMED FORCES AIR LETTER

AIR MAIL

This letter must be posted in Armed Forces Postal channels. If posted in a Civil Post Office or pillar box, it will not be given air transmission.

1 CANADIAN A.B.P.O. - AM 27 DEC 44

TO: Mrs C. B. Henderson
- 97 avenue
Edmonton Alberta
Canada

Dec 22, 1944

Dear Mom:

I received you letter of the 9th yesterday. To begin with that was pretty fair guessing on your part when you figured the letter was in time to wish me a Happy Birthday, thanks.

I'm glad that Doug could get up to see a show. It shows that his eyes must be o.k. again too, doesn't it?

Sorry lady, but I wasn't present at the decoration of our padre. It was a holiday for me – I think I was swimming that morning.

Why sure mom I have a highland cap, it's commonly called a balmoral. You know about 12 or 14 inches in diameter. It is khaki in colour with a green tassel. On one side is a plaid cloth about 3 ½ inches square and the H.L.I badge on the plaid.

Then for walking our dress we have a cap which is dark green, almost black. It is something like a wedge hat – not much though, and has two tails hanging down the back about 6 inches long. They are called glengarrys I think, the whole hat. Nope, can't draw it I don't know if I can wear a plaid tie but the officers do. I understand we all get kilts back in Canada.

I just finished a glass of White Horse Whisky, awful aren't I? I think it is the major's anyway either he or the captain poured a glass for me and left it on the table. You should see the bottle of rum I and another chap have. We've been saving our ration for a while – it sure piles up. We'll be able to have a few hot drinks on Christmas Eve anyway. Perhaps it's not the churches way of celebrating Christmas Eve but-

We've got our Christmas tree now and will be setting it up in a few minutes. The Q.M.S is getting decorations for us from A Echelon.

I've been in the house of Goering's aunts. It's a snazzy place, no lie. You should see it.

I guess we aren't going to have our Xmas dinner until the 28th. We can't get it brought up here. Evidently it is being cooked at Bn HQ. I know our cooks aren't preparing the meal anyway. We are going to have a picture taken of our tree; I'll send you a copy.

Well, I guess that is all for now, mom. I'll write you in a couple of days.

Love and Kisses

Grant

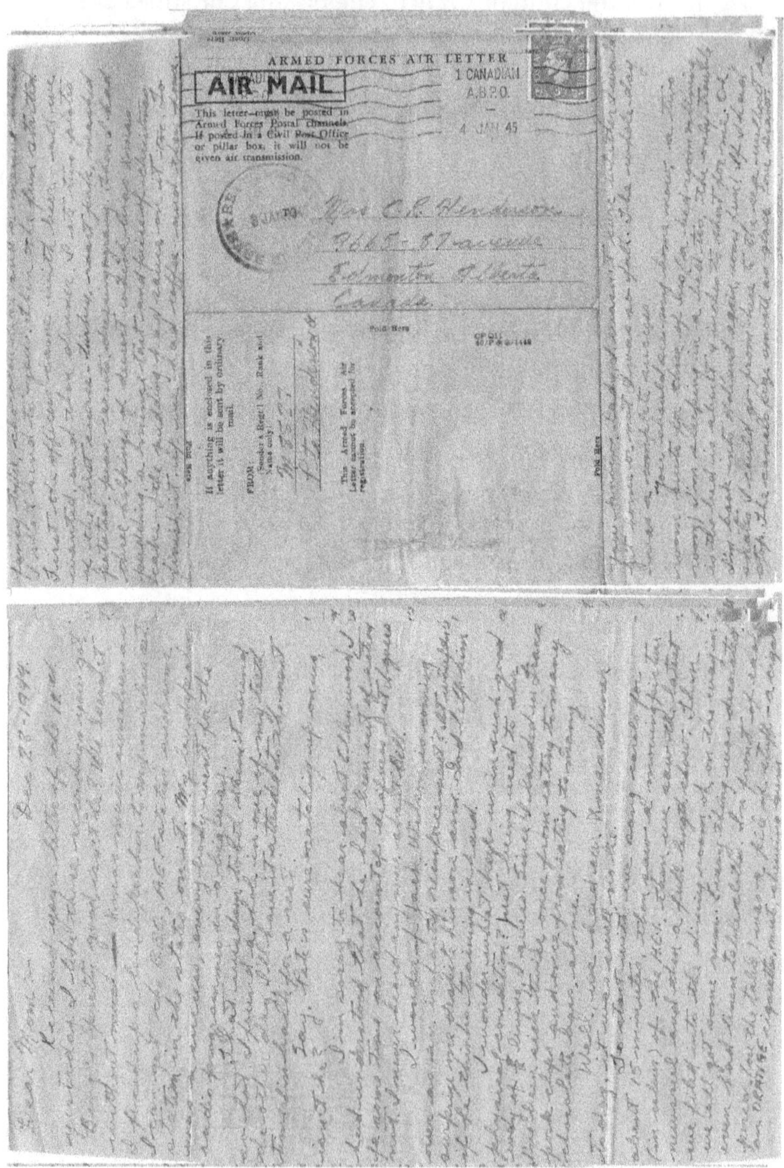

ARMED FORCES AIR LETTER

AIR MAIL

This letter must be posted in Armed Forces Postal channels. If posted in a Civil Post Office or pillar box, it will not be given air transmission.

1 CANADIAN A.P.O. 4 JAN 45

Mrs C.R. Henderson

Edmonton Alberta

Canada

Dec 28, 1944

Dear Mom:

Received your letter of the 12th yesterday. I liked those recordings you got. Bing is pretty good, isn't he? We weren't without Xmas music ourselves as I fixed up a loud speaker to my wireless set. I can get the B.B.C., A.E.F station and some station in the states on it. My loudspeaker was a success; everybody went for the radio programs in a big way.

That wisdom tooth doesn't sound so hot. I found a hole in one of my teeth the other day; I'll have it attended to the next time I'm back for a rest.

Say, Pete's sure catching up on us isn't he?

I'm sorry to hear about Ellen Wood. I had understood that he had been out of action for some time on account of deafness but I guess not. I never heard any more about Bill.

I wonder if Jack Wilson is coming over as infantry reinforcement? It wouldn't surprise me despite his sore arm. God help him if he thinks training is hard.

I wonder what keeps us in such good physical condition? Just being used to our way of living, I guess. Since I landed in France, I've been sick twice, once from eating too many pork chops and once from eating too many chocolate bars, ah me.

Well we had our Xmas dinner today; it was swell, no lie.

To start with we sang carols for about 15 minutes, then saw a moving picture (in colour) of H.L.I., then we saw the latest newsreel and then a full length show. Then we filed into the dining room, ok, on the way in we all got some rum. Everything was decorated even had linen table clothes. In front of each person(on the table) was a pile of stuff – a cigar, an orange, cigarettes, nuts, chewing gum, fancy toffee, chocolate bar and a menu which I shall send to you. Then the fun started. First the officers came with beer – all we wanted and then dinner. I ate two plates of first course – turkey, roast pork, mashed potatoes, peas, carrots, dressing and gravy. Then I had three helpings of desert which was Xmas pudding, a minced tart and piece of Christmas cake – the pudding had sauce on it too. To finish it up we had coffee and then home.

You know lady, I wasn't sure whether I would get home or not I was so full. The whole day was a complete success.

You should see my home now, a two room suite for three of us (a bedroom & living room). I'm sleeping on a bed too; the only trouble is the bed is about 4 inches to short for Me. O.K. I'm back into Holland again, some fun! If I had skates I could go from here to the sea without a stop. The canals freeze smooth as glass.

Love Grant

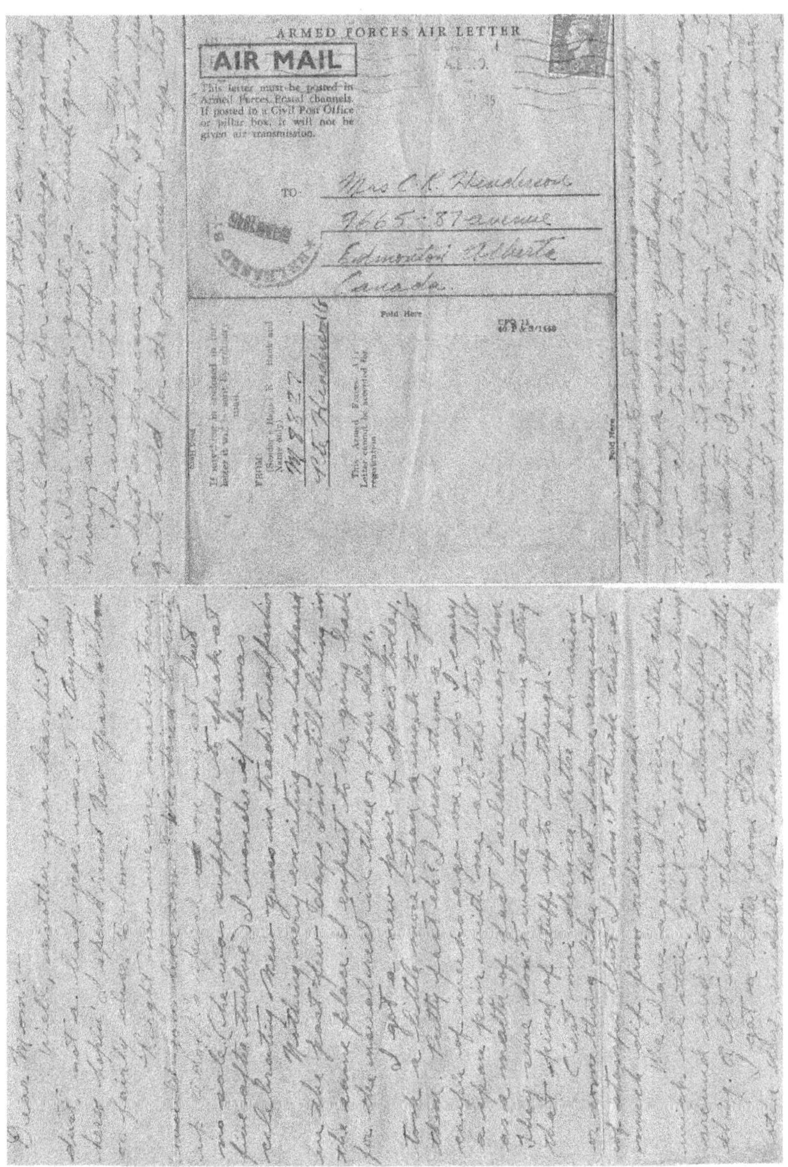

ARMED FORCES AIR LETTER

AIR MAIL

This letter must be posted in Armed Forces Postal channels. If posted to a Civil Post Office or pillar box, it will not be given air transmission.

TO: Mrs C.K. Henderson
9665 - 87 avenue
Edmonton Alberta
Canada

Fold Here

0045 hrs

Jan 1, 1945

Dear Mom:

Well, another year has bit the dust, not a bad year was it? Anyway here's hopin' I spend next New Year at home or fairly close to home.

Right how we are making a toast, would you like some? We tried to pick up Adolf's speech on my set but no sale. (He was supposed to speak at five after twelve) I wonder if he was celebrating New Years in traditional fashion.

Nothing very exciting has happened in the past few days. I'm still living in the same place. I expect to be going back for the usual rest in three or four days.

I got a new pair of specs today. Took a little bit more than a week to get them. Pretty fast eh? I broke them a couple of weeks ago on a do. I carry a spare pair with me all the time but as a matter of fact I seldom wear them. They sure don't waste any time in getting that kind of stuff up to us though.

C'est moi dernier letter par avion or something like that. I have run out of stamps but I don't think there is much dif from ordinary mail.

We have acquired a nice little three wick oil stove, just right for packing around and it's sure a wonderful thing. A lot better than my electric kettle.

I got a letter from Stan Mitchell the other day, evidently he has repented.

I went to church this a.m. It was a real church for a change, organ and all. I've become quite a church goer, you know, ain't it awful?

The weather has changed for the worst or best as the case may be. It had been quite cold for the past several days but at least it's not raining and muddy.

I had a shower yesterday. I should throw this tattered and torn uniform away. I've worn it ever since I left England, it's sure dirty. Going to get a haircut one of these days too. I've only had a neck trim in about four months. B.Hairy Joe, I was known as in my day.

Love & Kisses

Grant.

ARMED FORCES AIR LETTER

AIR MAIL

This letter must be posted in Armed Forces Postal channels. If posted in a Civil Post Office or pillar box, it will not be given air transmission.

TO: Mrs C.R. Henderson
9665 - 87 avenue
Edmonton Alberta
Canada.

Fold Here

CPO 11

If anything is enclosed in this letter it will be sent by ordinary mail.

FROM: (Sender's Regt. No. Rank and Name only) M 8827 Pte. Henderson

This Armed Forces Air Letter cannot be accepted for registration.

Fold Here

Jan 19, 1945

Dear Mom:

Still forgetting the year as you can see. Hope you don't mind the pencil; my pen gives me the willies, it's always running out of ink.

Well the highlight of the news, I suppose, is that I'm going on a 48 hour rest tomorrow morning. I was ordered to so I guess I'd better submit peacefully, I've been in action with Coy HQ longer than anyone without a break. They say they have quite a program for us so I guess I might have fun.

I received two old letters from you the other day, Sept 29 and Oct 4. In the one of the 29th you told me about Maurice Mather joining the army. It was rather ironical that I should read that now, I read his name on the Killed list a week or so ago. Naturally I was sorry, especially for Jessie and the kids but that which has happened is best forgotten.

Well this is the anniversary of my leaving home, remember? The old year has sure buzzed around, hasn't it? It 's been a good year for me, I've seen five new countries, travelled thousands of miles for free and have saved all sorts of money, $300 in gratuities, $50 in victory bonds, 80 odd dollars in my pay book and about the same at home. Not bad eh?

Well, I'll write as soon as I come off this rest.

Love & Kisses

Grant

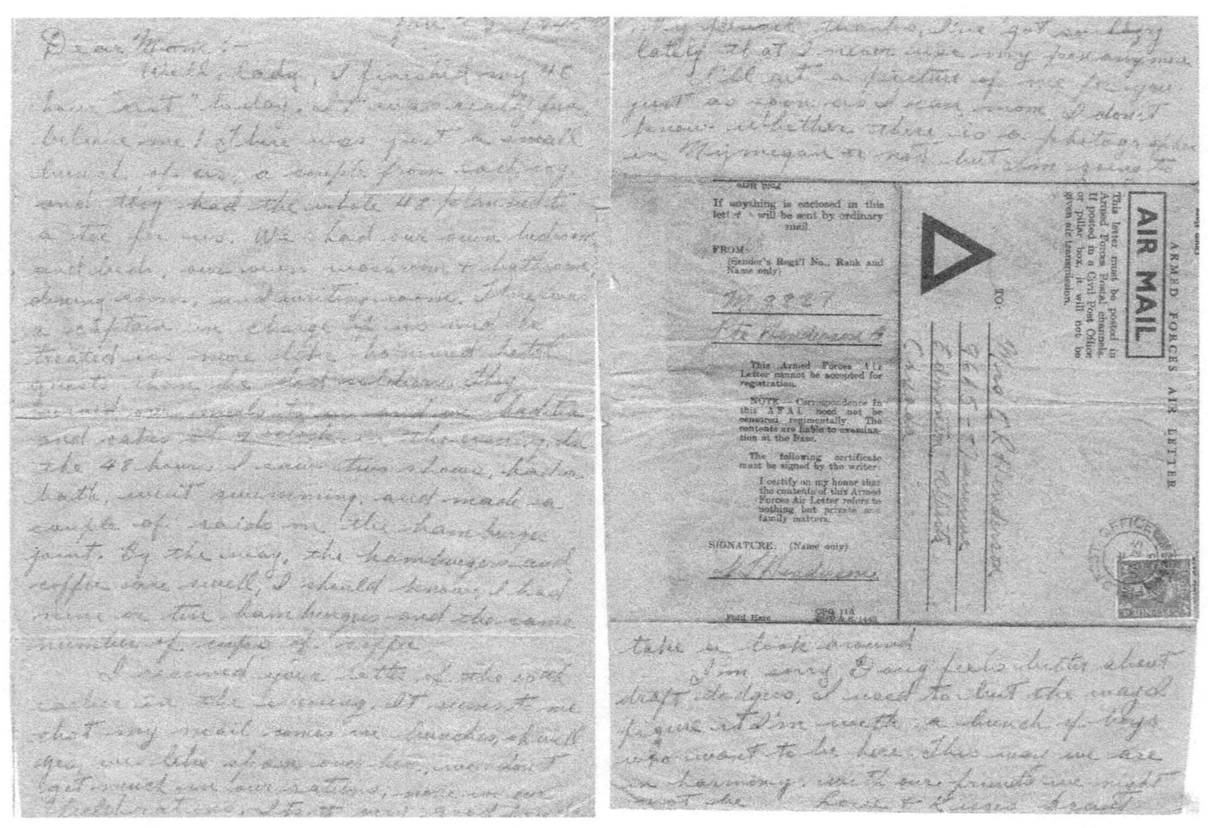

[illegible]

Dear Mom:-

Well, Lady, I finished my 48 hour "rest" today. It was really fun, believe me! There was just a small bunch of us, a couple from each coy., and they had the whole 48 planned to a tee for us. We had our own bedroom with beds, our own washroom & bathroom, dining room, and writing room. They had a captain in charge of us and he treated us more like "honored" guests than as [illegible] soldiers. They [illegible] and cakes at 4 o'clock in the evening. In the 48 hours I saw two shows, had a bath, went swimming, and made a couple of raids on the hamburger joint. By the way, the hamburgers and coffee were swell, I should know, I had [illegible] hamburgers and the same number of cups of coffee.

I received your letter of the [illegible] earlier in the evening. It seems to me that my mail comes in bunches, [illegible] you, we like [illegible] over here, we don't get much in our rations, [illegible] [illegible]

[illegible] thanks, I've got so [illegible] lately that I never use my [illegible] anymore.

I'll get a picture of me for you just as soon as I can. I don't know whether there is a photographer in Nijmegen or not but [illegible] going to take a look around.

I'm sorry [illegible] feels bitter about draft dodgers, I used to but [illegible] figure it [illegible] a bunch of boys who want to be here. This way we are in harmony, with our friends we might not [illegible]

Love & Kisses [illegible]

ARMED FORCES AIR LETTER

AIR MAIL

This letter must be posted in Armed Forces Postal channels. If posted in a Civil Post Office or pillar box, it will not be given air transmission.

TO: Mrs C R Henderson
9615 - [illegible]
Edmonton, Alberta
Canada

Fold Here

If anything is enclosed in this letter it will be sent by ordinary mail.

FROM:
(Sender's Regt'l No., Rank and Name only)

M 9927
Pte Henderson [illegible]

This Armed Forces Air Letter cannot be accepted for registration.

NOTE.—Correspondence in this A.F.A.L. need not be censored regimentally. The contents are liable to examination at the Base.

The following certificate must be signed by the writer:

I certify on my honour that the contents of this Armed Forces Air Letter refers to nothing but private and family matters.

SIGNATURE: (Name only) [illegible] Henderson

Fold Here

CFQ 11A

Jan 23, 1945

Dear Mom:

Well, lady, I finished my 48 hour "rest" today. It was really fun, believe me! There was just a small bunch of us, a couple from each coy and they had the whole 48 planned to a tea for us. We had our own bedroom and beds, our own washroom & bathroom, dining room and writing room. There was a captain in charge of us and he treated us more like honoured hotel guests than he did soldiers. They served our meals to us and we had tea and cakes at 9 o'clock in the evening. In the 48 hours I saw two shows, had a bath, went swimming and made a couple of raids on the hamburger joint. By the way the hamburgers and coffee are swell, I should know. I had nine or ten hamburgers and the same number of cups of coffee.

I received you letter of the 10th earlier in the evening. It seems to me that my mail comes in bunches, oh well.

Yes, we like spam over here, we don't get much in our rations, none in our field rations. It's very good fried.

Yes, you sent me lots of leads for my pencil thanks, I've got so lazy lately that I never use my pen any more.

I'll get a picture of me for you just as soon as I can, mom. I don't know whether there is a photographer in Nijmegen or not but I'm going to take a look around.

I 'm sorry Doug feels bitter about draft dodgers, I used to but the way I figure it I'm with of bunch of boys who want to be here. This way we are in harmony, with our friends we might not be.

Love and kisses

Grant

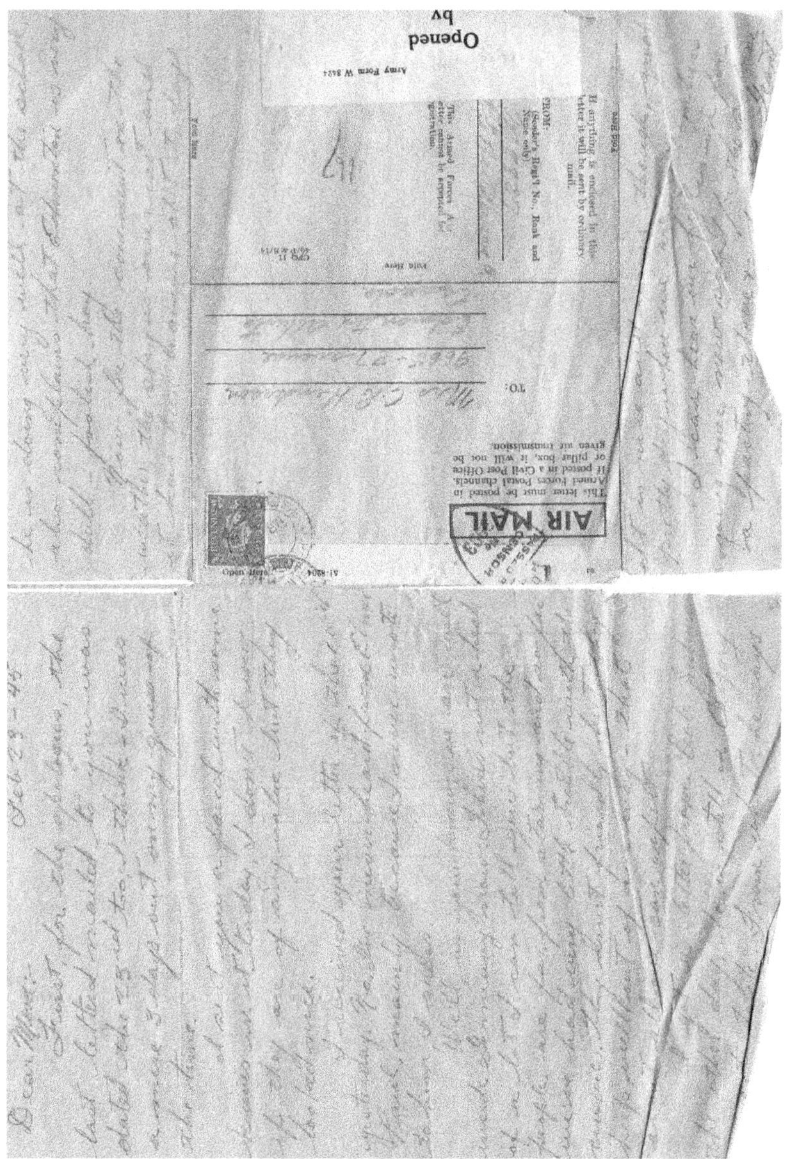

Feb 23, 1945

Dear Mom:

First, for the apologies, the last letter I mailed to you was dated the 23rd too, I think – I was a mere 3 days out on my guess of the time.

I sent you a parcel with some knives in it today. I don't know if they are of any value but they looked nice.

I received your letter of the 10th yesterday. No, I've never heard from Elmer Paul, mainly because I never wrote him, I guess.

Well, as you know we are well inside Germany now. There's not a heck of a lot I can tell you but the people are far from starving and so far we've had little trouble with the civvies. They aren't friendly but they keep well out of our way – that's all one can expect.

I got a letter from Bob Jenkins the other day; he is still in Calgary going to Tech. From what he says he is doing very well at the school also complains that Edmonton is very dull – foolish boy.

Now for the comment on the weather, the sky is overcast and it has been raining a bit today. It is nice and warm though, and pretty dry where we are.

I can hear our heavy bombers going over now so Jerry is in for a pasting – thank God for the Air force.

Love & Kisses Grant

ARMED FORCES AIR LETTER

AIR MAIL

This letter must be posted in Armed Forces Postal channels. If posted in a Civil Post Office or pillar box it will not be given air transmission.

Feb 25, 1945

Dear Mom:

Hi, Lady, I received two parcels from you today, the cookies and the soap etc. Thanks a million, the cookies have gone already; they brought back memories of the days when we used to raid the old cookie jar.

I also received your letter of the 15th, a straight 10 days.

I wonder if they actually did snag Art Middrie, I hope not, unless they have dieticians in the army now. I'd sure like to see C.W.C sporting a rifle though, it'd wear off his little paunch toute suite.

It's raining (as per usual) I think I'll be a farm boy after the war. I get more fun feeding the chickens and rooting them off their roosts (nests if you like) to get the egg. We go to check the egg situation about every hour and every time a hen crows. Some fun. There are a couple of monstrous pigs here too, no wonder they are fat, I don't think they walk ten feet a day. I've really had a lot of fun on this farm.

Well, Pete will be sixteen in a couple of days now, a young man, no less. The old family sure grew up in a hurry didn't it?

Well that's all for now, Mom. I'll write as soon as possible.

Love & Kisses

Grant

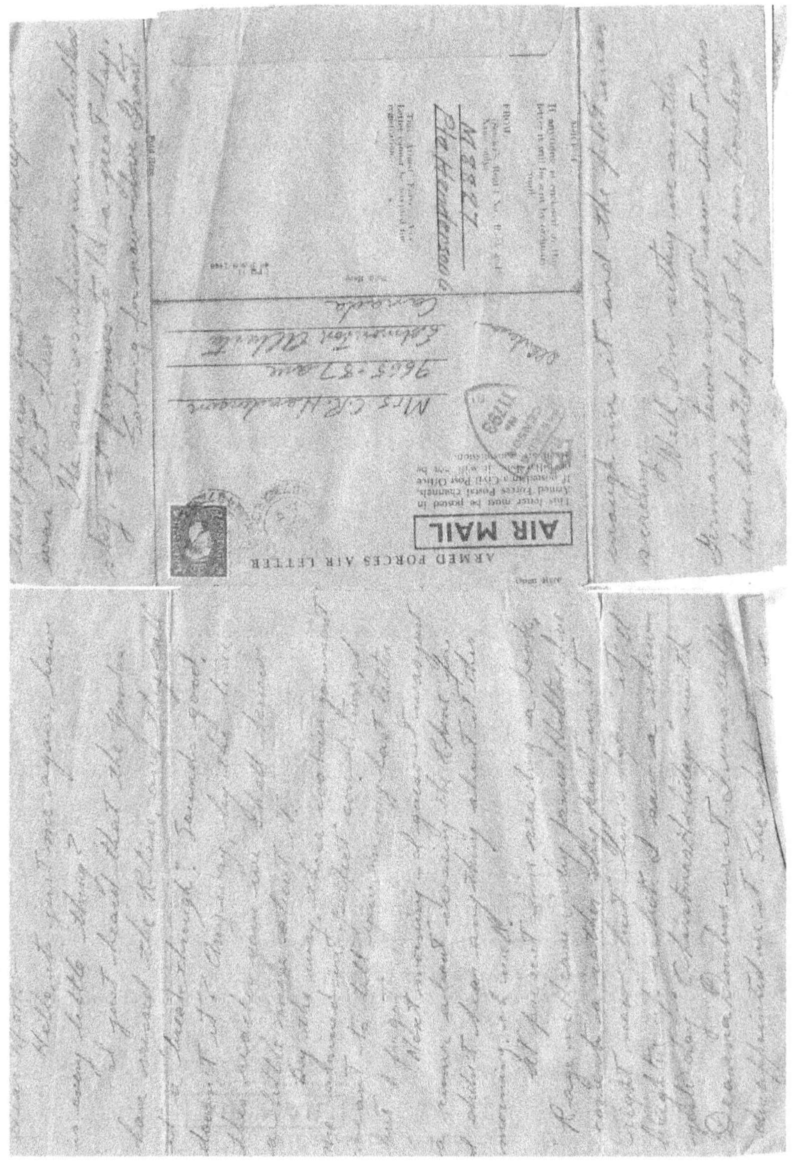

ARMED FORCES AIR LETTER

AIR MAIL

Feb 27, 1945

Dear Mom:

Hello, it's just me again, how is every little thing?

I just heard that the Yanks have crossed the Rhine, and they call it a break through. Sounds good, doesn't it? Anyway, by the time this letter reaches you we shall know a little more about it.

By the way, those cookies you sent me arrived in perfect condition. I meant to tell you in my last letter but forget.

Next morning – I guess it was just a rumor about crossing the Rhine for I didn't hear anything about it this morning, oh well.

At present I'm reading a book "Rage in Heaven" by James Hilton. I've come to a rather dry part in it right now but here's hopin it'll brighten up a bit. I saw a show yesterday "Christmas Holidays" with Deanna Durbin in it. I was really disappointed in it, she did not sing enough in it and the plot was screwy.

Well, I'm sitting in another German town right now that has been blasted apart by our bombers and arty. I often wonder what those places looked like before the war hit them.

The sun is shining in a cloudless sky. It promises to be a great day.

So long for now

Love Grant.

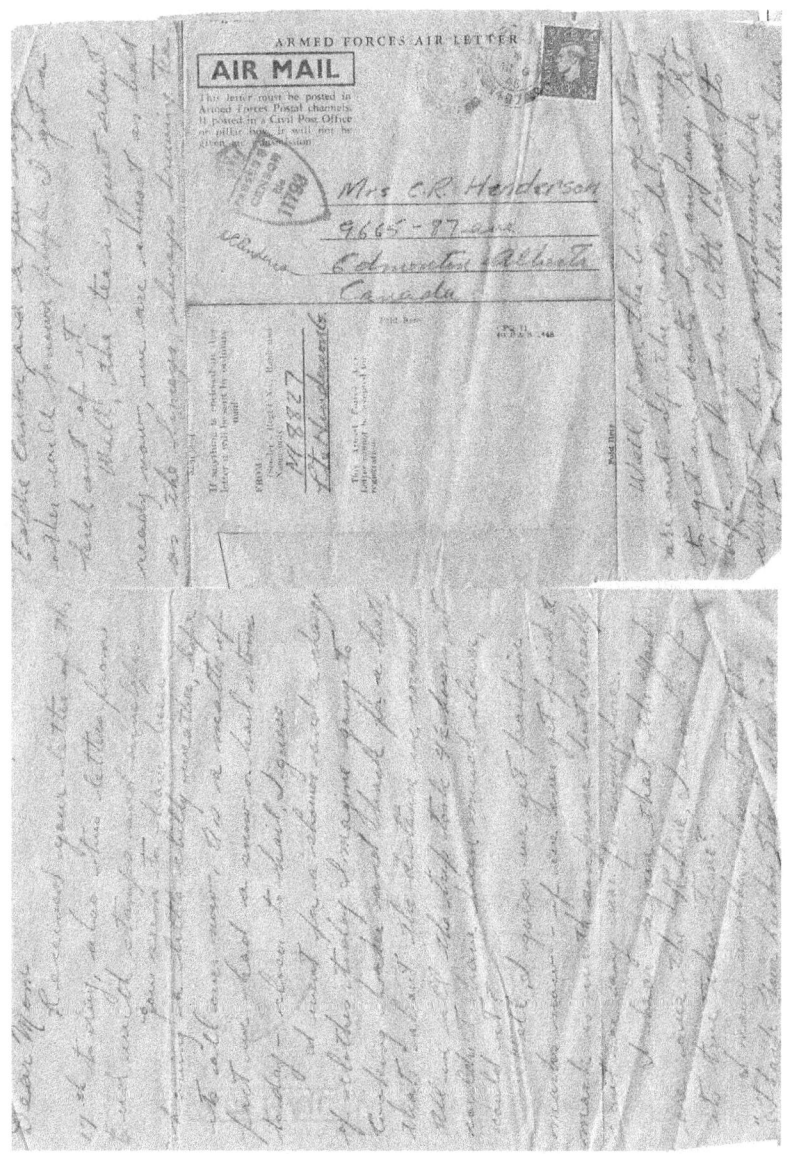
ARMED FORCES AIR LETTER

AIR MAIL

This letter must be posted in Armed Forces Postal channels. If posted in a Civil Post Office or pillar box it will not be given air transmission

Mrs C.R. Henderson
9665 - 97 ave
Edmonton Alberta
Canada

M 8827
F. Henderson

March 2, 1945

Dear Mom:

Received your letter of the 17th today, also two letters from Bud with stamps and envelopes.

You seem to have been having a little chilly weather, I hope it's over now, As a matter of fact we had a snow or hail storm today – closer to hail, I guess.

I went for a shower and a change of clothes today. Imagine going to cooking lake and back for a bath, that's about the distance we covered. All in all, the trip took 4 ½ hours, it couldn't have been much slower, could it?

Well I guess we get paid in Marks now – if we ever get paid. A Mark is worth sixpence but I really can't see any use for money here.

I hear again that the Yanks are over the Rhine, I wonder if it's true this time?

I saw another show tonight "Thank Your Lucky Stars" starring Eddie Cantor and a few dozen other well known people. I got a kick out of it.

Well, the tea is just about ready now; we are almost as bad as the limeys, always brewing tea.

Well, from the looks of it we are out of the water long enough to get our boots dry anyway. Let's hope it lasts a little longer. It's alright to have a nickname like "Water Rats" but no hell having to live up to it.

Love

Grant

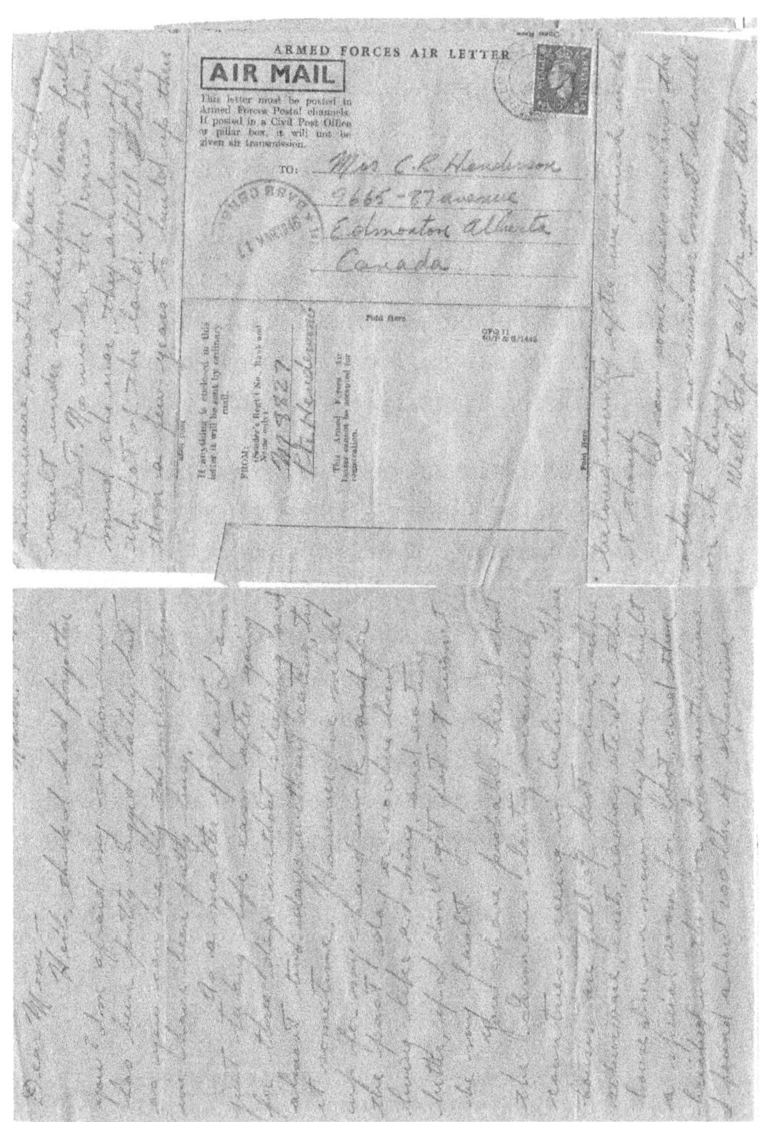

ARMED FORCES AIR LETTER

AIR MAIL

This letter must be posted in Armed Forces Postal channels. If posted in a Civil Post Office or pillar box, it will not be given air transmission.

TO: Mrs C.R. Henderson
9665 - 87 avenue
Edmonton Alberta
Canada

If anything is enclosed in this letter it will be sent by ordinary mail.

FROM: Sender's Regt'l No., Rank and Name only:
M 43827
Pte Henderson

This Armed Forces Air Letter cannot be accepted for registration.

March 8, 1945

Dear Mom:

Hello, think I had forgotten you? I'm afraid my correspondence has been pretty ragged lately but as you can see by the newspapers we have been pretty busy.

As a matter of fact, I am just taking life easy after going for three days without sleeping and almost two days without eating, try it sometime. However, I've made up for my hard work and for the past day or so I've been living like a king and eating better, if I don't get fat it won't be my fault.

You have probably heard about the Germans looting occupied countries – seeing is believing. These houses are full of loot – linen, silks, silverware, suits, radios, etc. In this house I'm in now they even built a special room for the loot and they bricked in the door. In another house I found about 100 lbs of expensive silverware, another place had a vault under a chicken house full of loot. No wonder the Jerries don't mind the war, they are living off the fat of the land. It'll take them a few years to build up their beloved country after we finish with it, though.

I saw some pussy willows the other day so summer must be well on its way.

Well that's all for now lady,

Love Grant

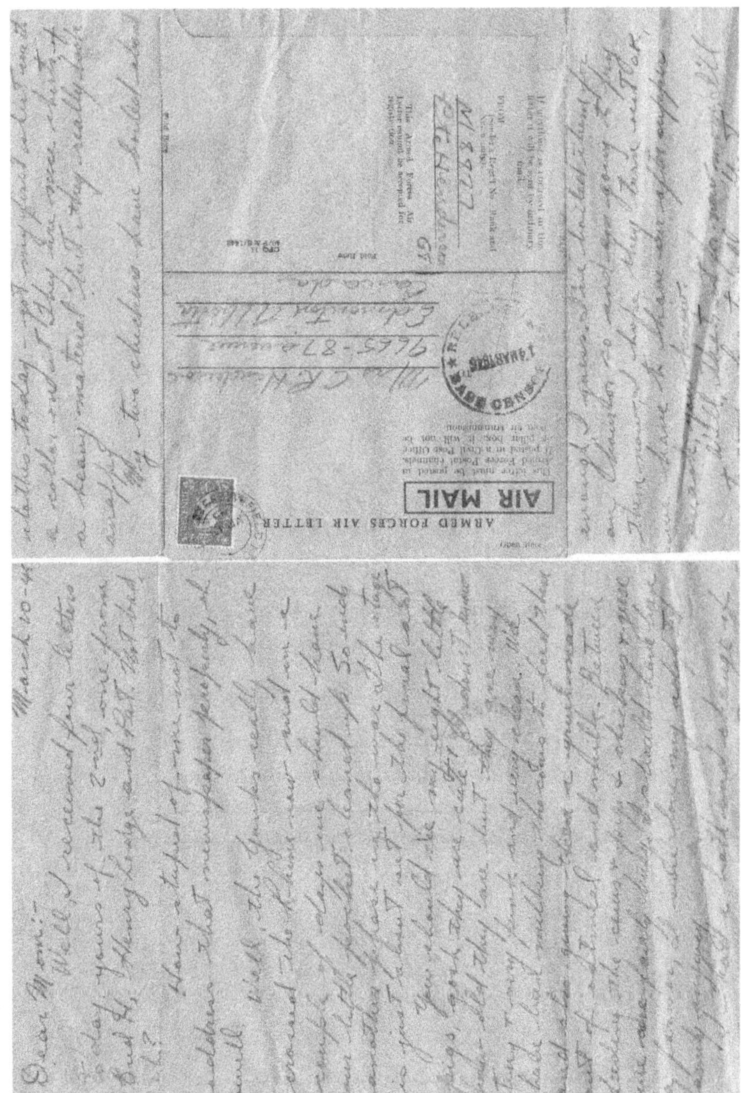

March 10, 1945

Dear Mom:

Well, I received four letters today, yours of the 2nd, one from Bud H, Henry Lodge and Pat, Not bad, eh?

How stupid of me not to address that newspaper properly, oh well.

Well, the Yanks really have crossed the Rhine now and in a couple of days we should have our little pocket cleaned up. So ends another phase in the war. The stage is just about set for the final act.

You should see my eight little pigs, gosh they are cute! I don't know how old they are but they are very tiny & very pink and very clean. We have been milking the cows to feed them and also giving them a gruel made out of oatmeal and milk. Between feed the cows & pigs & chickens & geese we are fairly busy! I should have been a farmer; I sure love my adopted family anyway.

I had a bath and a change of clothes today – got my first shirt with a collar on it. They are nice shirts of a heavy material but they really look snappy.

My two chickens have boiled about enough, I guess, I've boiled them for an hour or so and am going to fry them now, I hope they turn out o.k. we have to have our after supper snack you know.

Well that's all for now. I'll write soon.

Love to all

Grant.

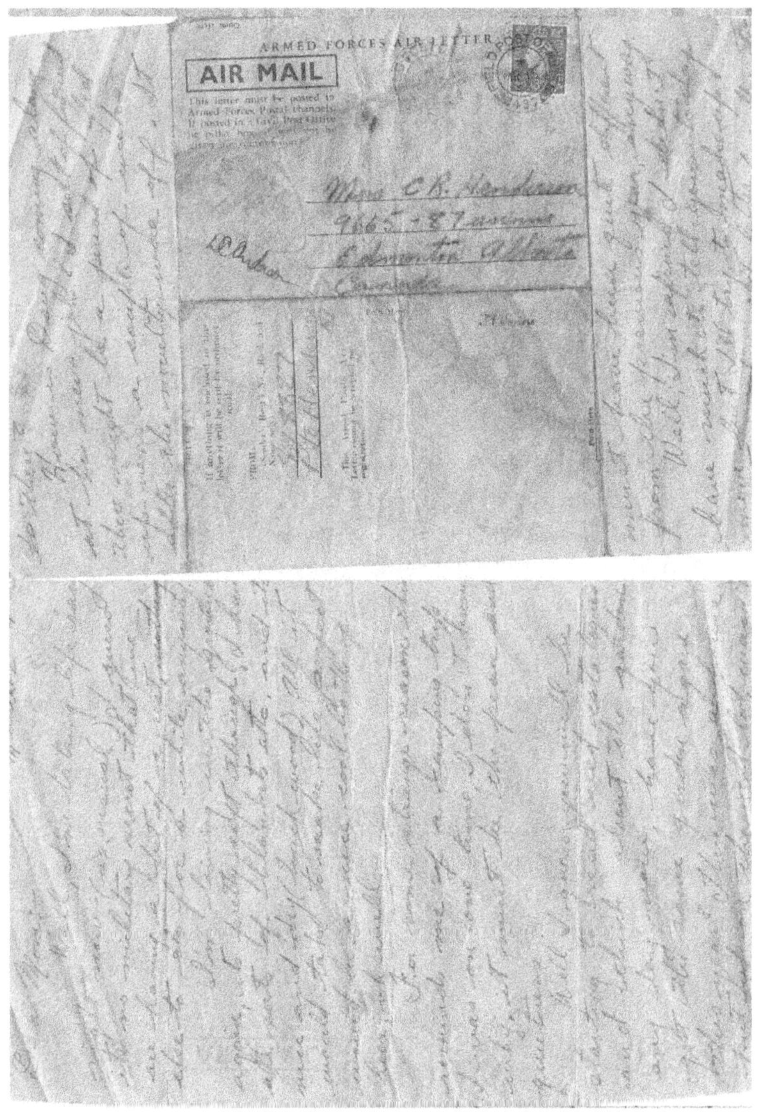
ARMED FORCES AIR LETTER

AIR MAIL

This letter must be posted to Armed Forces Postal channels.

Miss C.R. Henderson
9665 - 87 avenue
Edmonton Alberta
Canada

March 12, 1945

Dear Mom:

Well, I'm taking life easy right now (as usual). I guess it's no military secret that we are having a bit of rest, nothing else to do for a while, anyway.

I'm living in the ground again, it's pretty soft though, I have all sorts of blankets etc, and it's nice and dry (touch wood). All it would take to make life perfect would be a nice cool bottle of beer, oh well.

For some strange reason this reminds me of a camping trip I was on one time, I don't know why, it must be the peace and quietness.

Well I guess you will be starting to read the seed catalogues and think about the garden any day now. Have you got the same garden again this year? There was a house put up on the next lot, wasn't there?

How is Doug coming along at his new job? I sort of figured there might be a period of fed upness a couple of weeks after the novelty wore off. It must have been quite different from the previous year, anyways.

Well I'm afraid I didn't have much to tell you today mom but I'll try to make up for it in the next letter.

Love

Grant

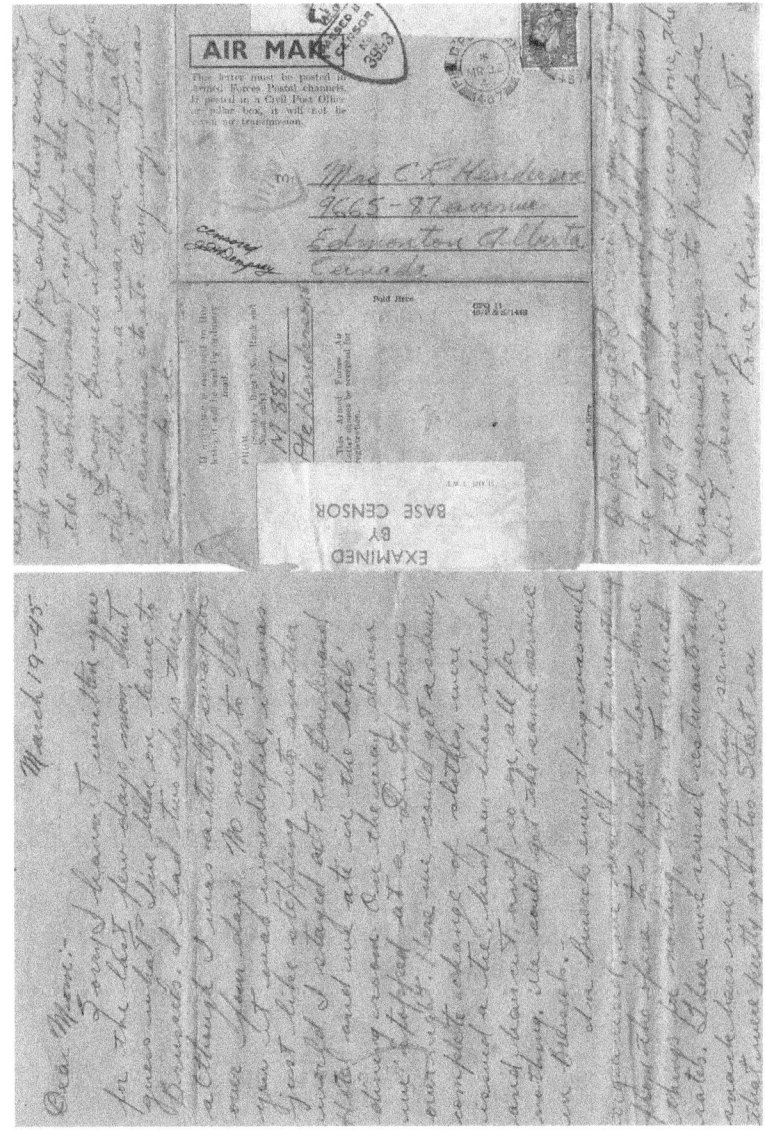

AIR MAIL

This letter must be posted in Armed Forces Postal channels. If posted in a Civil Post Office or pillar box, it will not be given air transmission.

TO: Mrs C.R. Henderson
9665 - 87 avenue
Edmonton Alberta
Canada

EXAMINED BY BASE CENSOR

March 19-45

Dear Mom:-

March 19, 1945

Dear Mom:

Sorry I haven't written you for the last few days, mom, but guess what? I've been on leave to Brussels. I had two days there although I was actually away for over four days. No need to tell you it was wonderful; it was just like stepping into another world. I stayed at the Boulevard Hotel and we ate in the hotel's dining room. On the way down we stopped at a Dutch town over night. Here we could get a shower, complete change of clothes, were issued a tie, had our shoes shined and hair cut and so all for nothing. We could get the same service in Brussels.

In Brussels everything was well organized, we could go to everything from the opera to a picture show, some things for nothing, others at reduced rates. There were several restaurants and snack bars run by auxiliary services that were pretty good too. Street car service was free. As you can see the army paid for everything except the amusement end of the deal.

From Brussels it is hard to realize that there is a war on, with all its civilians etc, etc. Anyway it was a nice break.

Before I forget, I received your letter of the 7th in 7 days, not bad eh? Yours of the 9th came while I was gone; the mail service seems to picked up a bit, doesn't it.

Love and Kisses

Grant

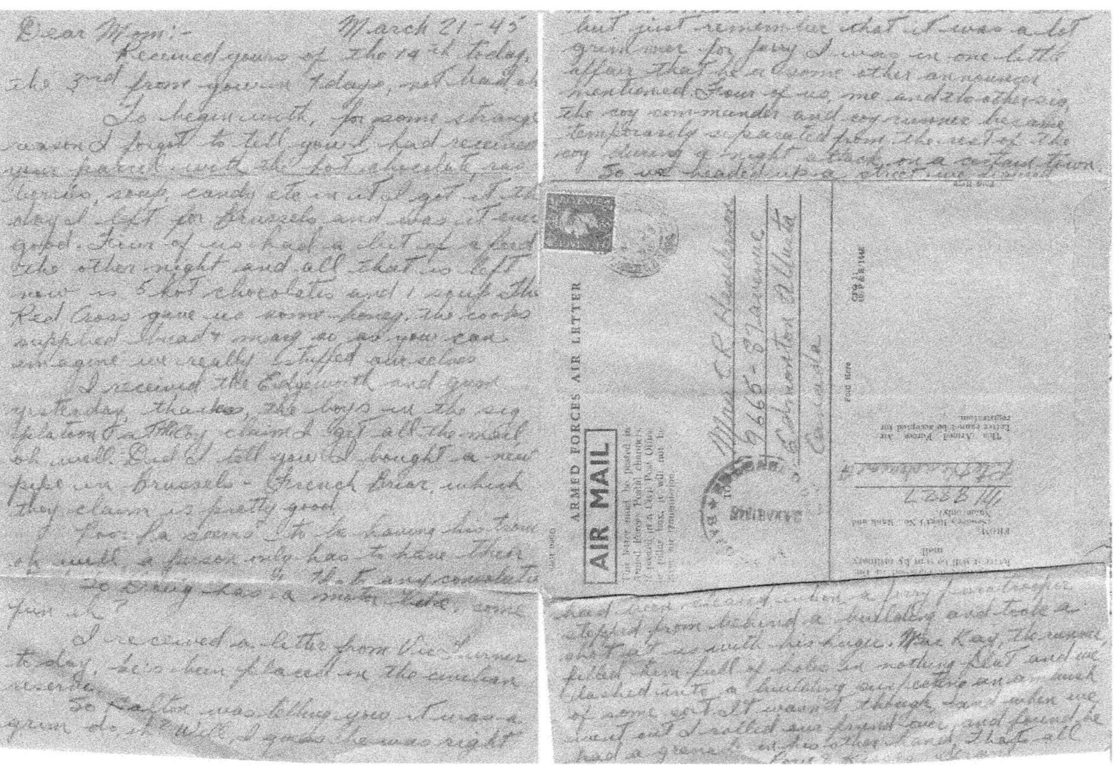

Dear Mom:- March 21-45

Received yours of the 14th today, the 3rd from you in 7 days, not bad [illegible]

To begin with, for some strange reason I forgot to tell you I had received your parcel with the hot chocolate, [illegible], soap, candy etc in it. I got it the day I left for Brussels and was it ever good. Four of us had a [illegible] of a [illegible] the other night and all that is left now is 5 hot chocolates and 1 [illegible]. The Red Cross gave us some honey, the cooks supplied bread & [illegible] so as you can imagine we really stuffed our selves.

I received the Edgeworth and [illegible] yesterday, thanks, the boys in the sig platoon & [illegible] claim I get all the mail, oh well. Did I tell you I bought a new pipe in Brussels - French Briar, which they claim is pretty good.

[illegible] seems to be having his [illegible] of [illegible] a person only has to have them [illegible] that any [illegible]

So Doug has a [illegible], some fun eh?

I received a letter from Vic [illegible] today, he's been placed in the civilian reserve.

So [illegible] was telling you it was a grim do, eh. Well, I guess he was right but just remember that it was a lot grimmer for [illegible]. I was in one little affair that he & some other announcer mentioned. Four of us, me and 2 other sig, the coy commander and coy runner became temporarily separated from the rest of the coy during a night attack on a certain town. So we headed up a street [illegible]

[illegible] when a [illegible] paratrooper stepped from behind a building and took a shot at us with his Luger. Mac Kay, the runner, [illegible] and we filled him full of holes [illegible] and we dashed into a building suspecting an ambush of some sort. It wasn't though and when we went out I rolled our friend over, and found he had a grenade in his other hand. That's all [illegible]

ARMED FORCES AIR LETTER

AIR MAIL

Mrs C.R. [illegible]
9665-87 Avenue
Edmonton Alberta
Canada

FROM: (Sender's Regt'l No., Rank and Name only)
M 8827
Pte [illegible]

This Armed Forces Air Letter cannot be accepted for registration.

Fold Here

March 21, 1945

Dear Mom:

Received yours of the 14th today, the 3rd from you in 7 days, not bad eh?

To begin with for some strange reason I forgot to tell you I had received your parcel with the hot chocolate, raspberries, soup, candy etc in it. I got it the day I left for Brussels and was it ever good. Four of us had a bit of a feed the other night and all that is left now is 5 hot chocolates and 1 soup. The Red Cross gave us some honey, the cooks supplied bread & marg so as you can imagine, we really stuffed ourselves.

I received the Edgeworth and gum yesterday, thanks, the boys in the sig platoon at HQCoy claim I get all the mail, oh well. Did I tell you I bought a new pipe in Brussels – French Briar, which they claim is pretty good.

Poor Pa seems to be having his troubles, oh well; a person only has to have their teeth pulled once, if that's any consolation.

So Doug has a motor bike, some fun eh?

I received a letter from Vic Turner today; he's been placed in the civilian reserve.

So Halton was telling you it was a grim do, eh? Well, I guess he was right but just remember that it was a lot grimmer for Jerry. I was in one little affair that he or some other announcer mentioned. Four of us, me and the other sig, the coy commander and coy runner became temporarily separated from the rest of the coy during a night attack on a certain town.

So we headed up a street we figured had been cleared when a Jerry paratrooper stepped from behind a building and took a shot at us with his Lugar. Mac Kay, the runner, filled him full of holes in nothing flat and we dashed into a building suspecting an ambush of some sort. It wasn't though and when we went out I rolled our friend over and found he had a grenade in his other hand. That's all.

Love & Kisses

Grant

ARMED FORCES AIR LETTER

AIR MAIL

This letter must be posted in Armed Forces Postal channels. If posted in a Civil Post Office or pillar box, it will not be given air transmission.

TO: Mrs C R [illegible]
9665-87 ave.
Edmonton
Alberta
Canada

Fold Here

If anything is enclosed in this letter it will be sent by ordinary mail

FROM: (Sender's Regt'l No. Rank and Name only)

This Armed Forces Air Letter cannot be accepted for registration.

March 23, 1945

Dear Mom:

Hi, lady, what's new? Not a heck of a lot from this end anyway.

I am sending you some so called pictures of myself by ordinary mail today. Frankly, I didn't like any of them but I thought they might be of some interest to you.

The weather is truly wonderfuly. I have been walking around without my tunic for days now. After the miserable winter we had I never thought it could be so nice in the spring. It is as warm as July right now, I imagined I should have quite a tan in a couple of weeks.

By the way, I had my hair cut pretty short before I left Brusssels not as you see it in the pictures. It's much more comfortable this way easier to keep clean, a real problem when one is living in the ground.

Two friends of mine from the Grande Prairie days called on me last night. It was really swell to see them one of which I hadn't seen since I left Canada. Its funny how I run across the old boys, a person would never imagine that he would meet them again in a place so large as the Army.

Well for once lady, I've run out of words, so good bye for now.

Love & Kisses

Grant.

March 27-45

Dear Mom:-

Hi, lady, how's she go? I received yours of the 20th tonight and received the parcel of nuts yesterday, so you can see that the mail is perking along. Many thanks for the nuts, the other boys thank you too.

Well, I imagine you know where I am right now. I had the honour of being in the first company of the first regt in the Can Army, in fact, I guess I can lay claim to be the first infantry reg in the Can. army to cross the Rhine. How's that?

I have my troubles too, I wrenched my ankle a couple of days ago and so I am taking life easy at Battalion HQ right now. It's not very bad though, I had it taped up and hobbled around with a cane until last night. Today I graduated and am going about without one. I imagine I'll be out to [illegible]

returned [illegible] they threatened me with imprisonment and a heavy fine if I didn't fill their form? Gosh, isn't it awful? If they bother you too much though, tell them that if they come and speak to me about it I'll [illegible]

[illegible] so that my secretary gives them the necessary info.

Well, we've got them beat lady, they sure didn't stop us at the Rhine I think we can start to count the days now, it's nice to be winning, isn't it?

Love & kisses [illegible]

ARMED FORCES AIR LETTER

AIR MAIL

This letter must be posted in Armed Forces Postal channels. If posted in a Civil Post Office or pillar box it will not be given [illegible] transmission

Mrs C. R. Henderson
9555 - 87 avenue
Edmonton, Alberta
Canada.

If anything is enclosed in this letter it will be sent by ordinary mail

FROM
(Sender's Rank, Name, Unit and Army only)

[illegible]

The Armed Forces Air Letter cannot be accepted for registration.

Fold Here

March 27, 1945

Dear Mom:

Hi, lady, how's she go? I received your s of the 20th tonight and received the parcel of nuts yesterday, so you can see that the mail is perking along. Many thanks for the nuts, the other boys thankyou too.

Well, I imagine you know where I am right now. I had the honour of being in the first company of the first regt. In the Can. Army, in fact, I guess I can lay claim to the first infantry sig. in the Can. Army to cross the Rhine. Thrilling what?

I have my troubles too, I wrenched my ankle a coupleof days ago and so I am taking life easy at Battalion H.Q. right now. It's not very bad though, I had it taped up and hobbled around with a cane until last night. Today I graduated and am going about without said cane. I imagine I'll be out to good old C coy again in a few days.

So they want my income tax return. Did they threaten me with inprisionment and a heavy fine if I didn't fill their form? Gosh, isn't awful? If they bother you too much though, tell them that if they come and speak to me about it, I'll see that my secretary gives him the necessary info.

Well, we've got them beat lady, they sure didn't stop us at the Rhine. I think we can start to count the days now, it's nice to be winning isn't it?

Love & Kisses Grant

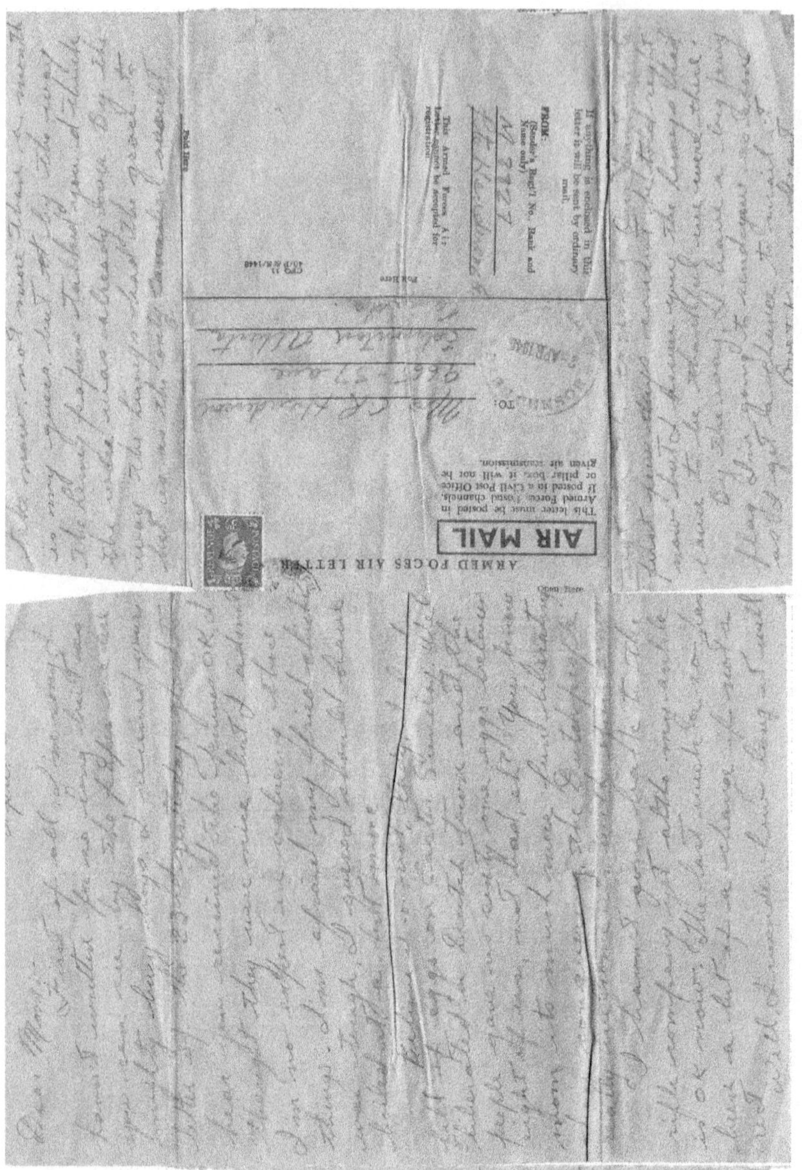

ARMED FORCES AIR LETTER

AIR MAIL

This letter must be posted in Armed Forces Postal channels. If posted in a Civil Post Office or pillar box, it will not be given air transmission.

If anything is enclosed in this letter it will be sent by ordinary mail.

FROM: (Sender's Regt'l No. Rank and Name only)

This Armed Forces Air Letter cannot be accepted for registration.

April 4, 1945

Dear Mom:

First of all, I'm sorry I haven't written for so long but as you can see by the papers we are mighty busy boys. I received your letter of the 23rd yesterday, glad to hear you received the knives o.k. I thought they were nice but admit I'm no expert in valueing those things. I'm afraid my fried chicken was tough, I guess I should have boiled it a bit more.

Believe it or not lady, I had my fill of eggs on Easter Sunday. We liberated a Dutch town and the people gave us sixty one eggs between eight of us, not bad eh? You know mom its much more fun liberating than conquering. The Dutch peoplereally welcome us with open arms.

I haven't gone back to the rifle company yet although my ankle is o.k. now. The last week or so has been a bit of a change if not a rest.

Well I wonder how long it will take now, not more than a month is my guess but by the way the Limey papers talked you'd think the war was already over. By the way the Limeys had the grace to list us as the only Canadian assult regt in the crossing. Our part in the first few days cannot be told right now but I assure you the Limeys had cause to be thankful we were there.

By the way, I have a big Jerry flag I'm going to send you as soon as I get a chance to mail it.

Love and Kisses

Grant

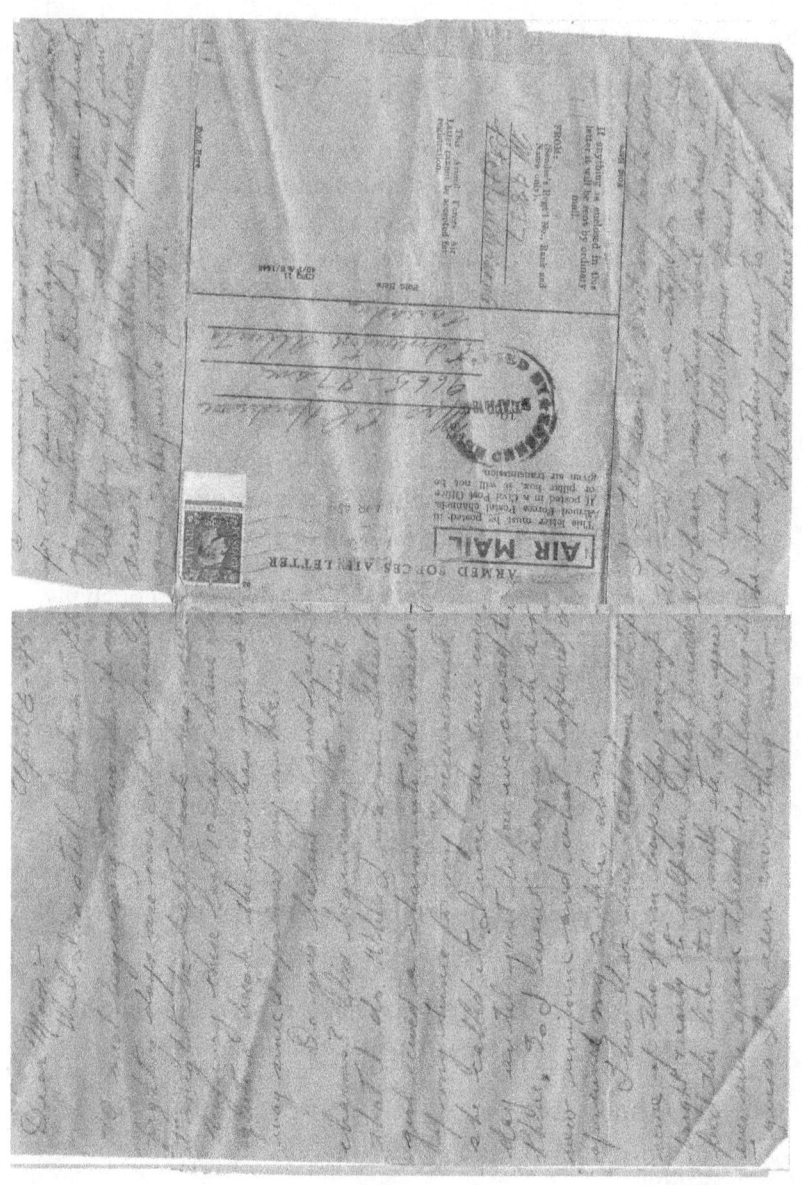

ARMED FORCES AIR LETTER

AIR MAIL

This letter must be posted in Armed Forces Postal channels. If posted in a Civil Post Office or pillar box, it will not be given air transmission.

If anything is enclosed in this letter it will be sent by ordinary mail.

FROM: (Sender's Regt'l No., Rank and Name only).

This Armed Forces Air Letter cannot be accepted for registration.

April 6, 1945

Dear Mom:

Well, I'm still back at btn H.Q. and beginning to wonder if my fighting days are over. It is possible.I might be kept back here now. Anyway these last 10 days have been quite a break, the war has gone a long way since I sprained my ankle.

Do you believe in good luck charms? I'm beginning to think that I do. When I was in Ghent a girl sewed a charm into the inside of my tunic for my "presevement" as she called it . I wore the tunic everyday until just before we crossed the Rhine. So I went across with a nice new uniform and what happened, I sprained my ankle, ah me.

This has been "old home Week" for some of the farm boys. They are up bright & early to help out Dutch friends feed the livestock, milk, etc. Have you ever seen grain threshed by flailing it ? I guess I've seen everything now.

The weather hasn't been so hot for the past few days, it rained most of yesterday. Did I tell you about the big field of gladiolas I saw? Acres and acres of them in full bloom, gosh they were pretty.

I still havn't had my tooth fixed, the next time we stop for a while I'll have something done about it.

I had a letter from Bud yesterday, he has nothing new to report.

That's all for now.

Love & Kisses Grant

AIR MAIL

If anything is enclosed in this letter it will be sent by ordinary mail.

TO:

FROM:
(Sender's full name and address)

April 9, 1945

Dear Mom:

I received you parcel with the marshmallows , soup mixes, etc in it yesterday. Needless to say it was very welcome, the cheese & the mlik formed the main part of a nice snack yesterday afternoon. I still have the soup mixes (amazing isn't it?) I am espescially interested in the tomato one, if I can get some fresh or powered milk from the cooks, I will have cream of tomato soup, o.k. eh? I also received a carton of gum from Ma, also very much appreciated, I am going to write her this evening.

We havn't had any mail for a few days now, too busy to sort it, I guess, so I should receive a heap of mail tomorrow or the next day.

I see by the "Maple Leaf" that only those who volunteer for Pacific fighting will be sent there. That most definetly won't include me. The way things now look, I have every hope of being a civvy again before Christmas.

It's really nice out this evening, hardly a cloud in the sky. It has been foggy and fairly cool for the past couple of mornings but has warmed up by noon.

I see the Limeys are getting all excited about their so called "V" day too. London is one place I wouldn't want to be when peace is declared, apparently it will cost a person his life savings for standing room on the side walk that day.

Well, Lady, the war looks very good, it's not raining, and I getting plenty to eat.

P.S. Thanks a million for the picture, one lad asked if you were Doug's girl friend, thrilling eh?

Grant

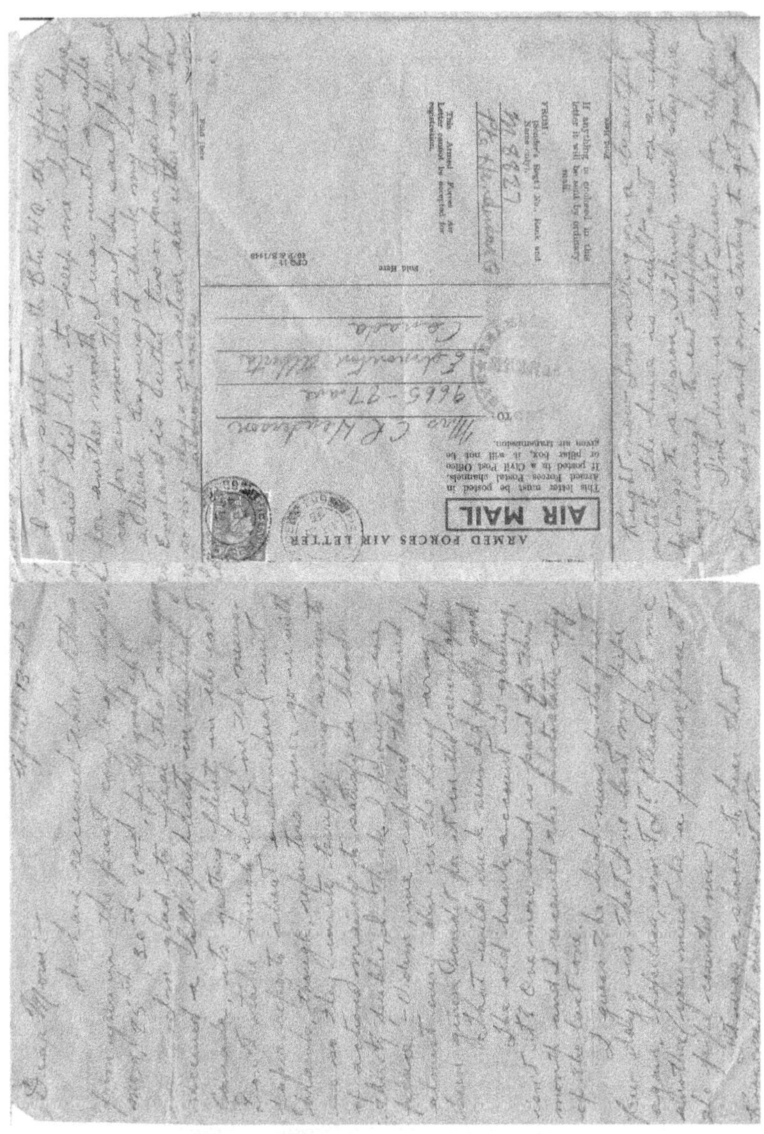

ARMED FORCES AIR LETTER

AIR MAIL

This letter must be posted in Armed Forces Postal channels. If posted in a Civil Post Office or pillar box, it will not be given air transmission.

TO:
9665-97 Ave
Edmonton Alberta
Canada

Fold Here

If anything is enclosed in this letter it will be sent by ordinary mail.

FROM: Sender's Regt'l No., Rank and Name only.

This Armed Forces Air Letter cannot be accepted for registration.

Fold Here

April 13, 1945

Dear Mom:

I have received three letters from you in the past couple of days, 25th, 30th & 2nd , pretty good eh?

I'm glad to hear that our gang received a little publicity in Western Canada, its getting plenty in the east. Don't take much stock in the newspaper reports about individual unit brawls, though, reporters never go in with us so they write terriffying accounts of actions mainly to satisfy a blood thirsty public, I think I know of one place – Udem, we captured that and almost every div. in the Limey army has been given credit for it in the newspapers.

That wild duck sounded pretty good.

The old bank account is growing isn't it? One more bond is paid for this month and I received the photostatic copy of the last one.

I guess the bad news of the past few days is that I've lost my pipe again, hopeless, aren't I? Please get me another (you must be a familiar face at the pipe counter now).

It was a shock to hear that Roseveldt died, wasn't it?

I am still with Btn H.Q., the officer said he'd like to keep me back here for another month. I was with a rifle coy for six months and he said I deserve a break. Anyway I think my leave to England is either two or four weeks off so my days in action either over or almost over.

Right now I'm sitting on a beautiful estate. The house is built out on an island, belongs to a baron. I think we'll stay here long enough to eat supper.

I've been in shirt sleeves for the past few days and am starting to get quite a tan.

Love & Kisses

Grant

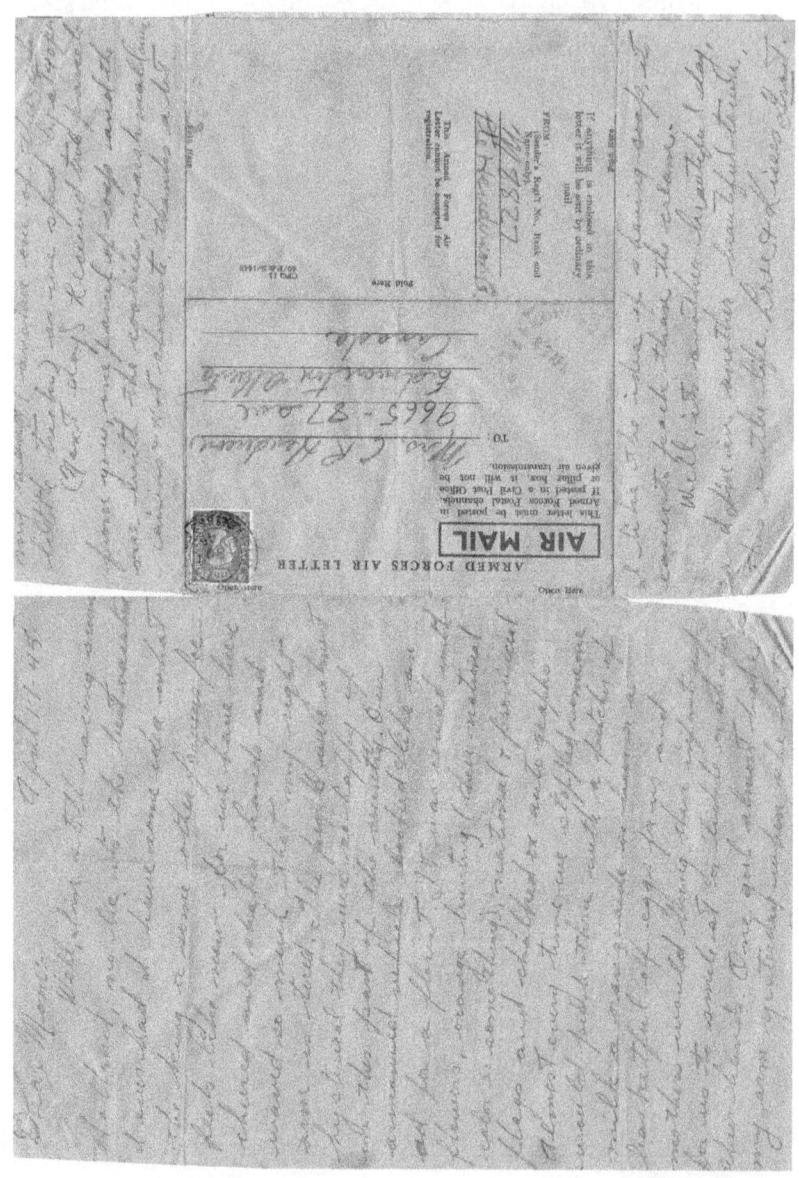

April 17, 1945

Dear Mom:

Well, I'm still racing around Holland, no lie it's the best vacation I ever had. I have some idea what the king or some other famous Joe feels like now for we have been cheered and shaken hands and waved so much that my right arm is tired. The people were almost hysterical, they were so happy up in this part of the country. Our armoured vehicle looked like an ad for a florist. It was covered with flowers, orange bunting (their national color or something), national & provincial flags and chalked on autographs. Almost everytime we stopped someone would push thru with a pitcher of milk or orange aide or beer or a basketful of eggs for us and mothers would bring thir infants up for us to smile at or tickle or shake their hands. One girl almost broke my arm yesterday when she hit my hand (another one of their cute little tricks) as we sped by at 40 per.
(next day) Received two parcels from you, one parcel of soap and one with the cookies, marshmallows, raisens & hot choclate, thanks a lot.
I like the idea of shaving soap, its easier to pack than the cream.

Well, it's another beautiful day and I'm in another beautiful town, this is the life.

Love & Kisses

Grant

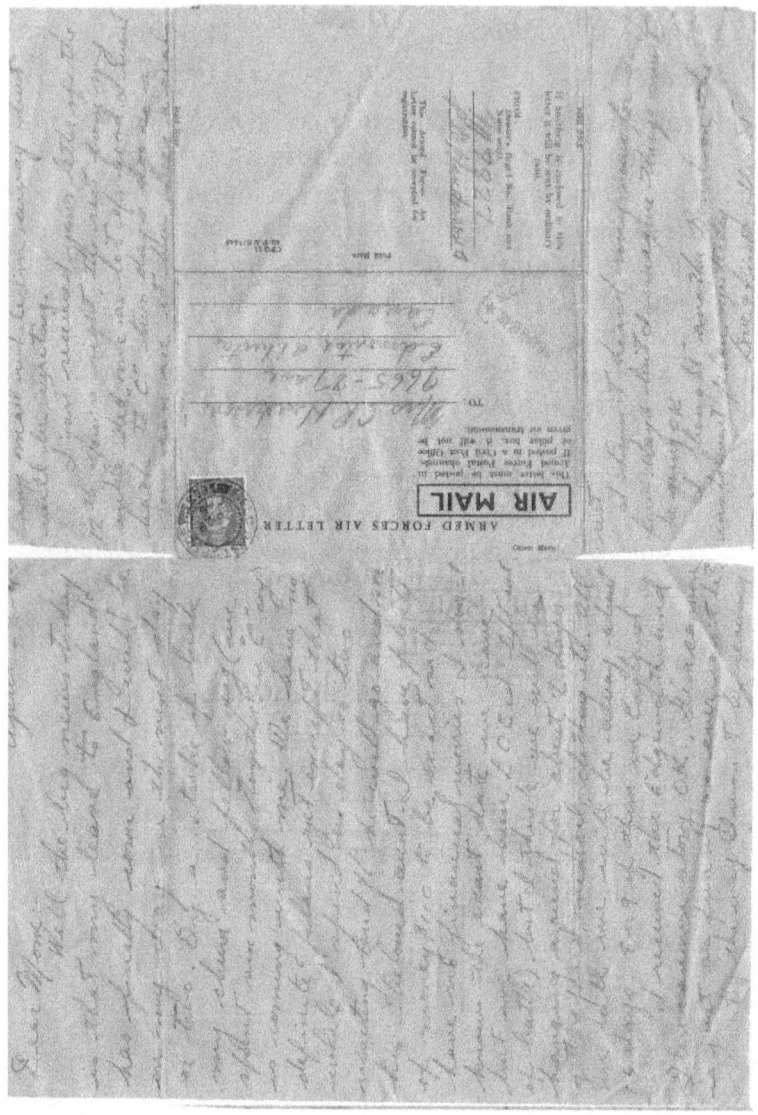

ARMED FORCES AIR LETTER

AIR MAIL

April 22, 1945

Dear Mom:

Well, the big news today is that my leave to England has finally come and I will be on my way in the next day or two. By a stroke of luck my chum and fellow sig (we spent six months together in "C" coy) is coming with me. We have not definite plans yet except that while I spend a day or two visiting Bud H.he will go see his beloved aunt. I have plenty of money $110 to be exact so I have no financial worries. I don't know the exact date we leave but we have been LOBed (left out of battle)but I think we will be hanging around for about 2 days getting paid, medical, clothing etc. All in all we will be away about 16 days, 8 or 9 of them in England.

I received the Edgewoth and Glen Cannon story o.k. Glen Cannon is just as funny as ever isn't he?

By the way, I won't be receiving any mail while I'm away but will be writing.

Just received your letter of the 12th. You're right, the rest from my ankel did me a lot of good. I went bact to "C" two days ago so as you can see it has been a real rest.

I havn't heard any news for a few days but I imagine things must be going o.k.

Bought another bond on the installment plan yesterday.

Love and Kisses

Grant

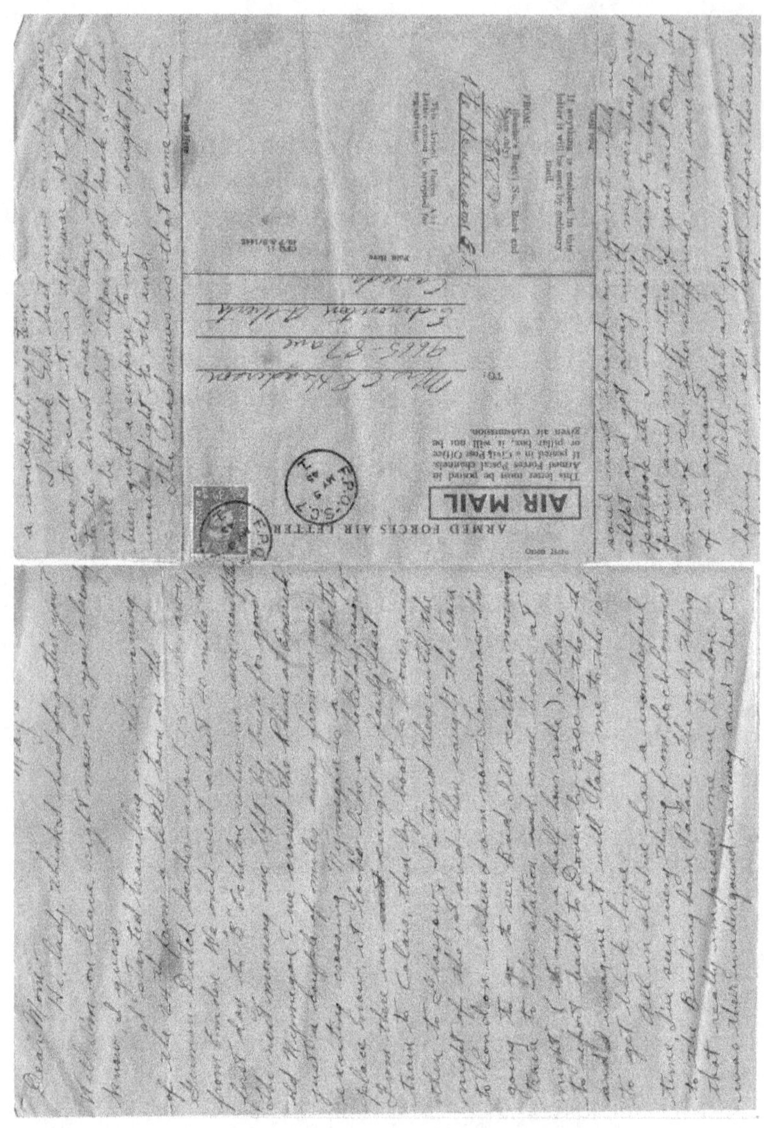

May 5

Dear Mom:-

He lady, thinks I had forgotten you? Well I'm on leave right now as you already know, I guess.

I started travelling on the morning of the 24th from a little town on the German-Dutch border about 13 miles away from Emden. We only went about 40 miles the first day to "B" Echelon where we were reoutfitted. The next morning we left by truck for good old Nymegan & we crossed the Rhine at Emmerich just a couple of miles away from our more exciting crossing. Nymegan is a very pretty place now, it looks like a holiday resort. From there we ~~went~~ caught a fairly fast train to Calais, then by boat to Dover, and then to Glasgow. I stayed there until the night of the 1st and then caught the train to London where I am now. Tomorrow I'm going to go to see Bud. I'll catch a morning train to his station and come back at night. (It's only a half hour ride) I have to report back to Dover by 2300 of the 6th and I imagine it will take me to the 10th to get back home.

All in all I've had a wonderful time. I've seen everything from Loch Lomond to the Buckingham Palace. The only thing that really impressed me in London was their underground railway and that is a wonderful system.

I think the best news or what you care to call it, is the war. It appears to be almost over. I have hopes that all will be finished before I get back. It has been quite a surprise to me. I thought Jerry would fight to the end.

The bad news is that some brave soul went through our pockets while we slept and got away with my eversharp and paybook etc. I was really sorry to lose the pencil and my picture of you and Doug but most of the other stuff was army issue and of no account.

Well that's all for now, mom. Here's hoping that all is kaput before this reaches

ARMED FORCES AIR LETTER

AIR MAIL

This letter must be posted in Armed Forces Postal channels. If posted in a Civil Post Office or pillar box, it will not be given air transmission.

TO: Mrs C. E. Henderson
9665-87 Ave
Edmonton Alberta
Canada

If anything is enclosed in this letter it will be sent by ordinary mail.

FROM: (Sender's Regt'l No., Rank and Name only)
Pte Henderson E.T.

This Armed Forces Air Letter cannot be accepted for registration.

May 3, 1945

Dear Mom:

Hi, lady, think I had forgotten you? Well, I'm on leave right now as you already know, I guess.

I started travelling on the morning of the 24th from a little town on the German-Dutch border – about 15 miles away from Emden. We only went about 40 miles the first day to "B" Echelore where we were reoutfitted. The next morning we left by truck for good old Nymegan and we crossed the Rhine at Emerick, just a couple of miles away from our more exciting crossing. Nymegan is a very pretty place now, it looks like a holiday resort. From there we caught a fairly fast train to Calais, then by boat to Dover and then to Glasgow. I stayed there until the night of the 1st and then caught the train to London – where I am now. Tomorrow I'm going to see Bud, I'll catch a morning train to his station and come back at night. (it's only a half hour ride) I have to report back to Dover by 2300 of the 6th and I imagine it will take me to the 10th to get back home.

All in all, I've had a wonderful time, I've seen every thing from Lock Lomond to Buchingham Palace. The only thing that impressed me in London was their underground railway and that is a wonderful system.

I think the best news or what you care to call it, is the war. It appears to be almost over. I have hopes that all will be finished before I get back. It has been quite a surprise to me. I thought Jerry would fight to the end.

The bad news is that some brave soul went through our pockets while we slept and got away with my eversharp and paybook etc. I was really sorry to lose the pencil and my picture of you and Doug but most of the other stuff was army issue and of no account.

Well that's all for now mom. Here's hoping that all is Kaput before this reaches you.

Love and Kisses

Grant.

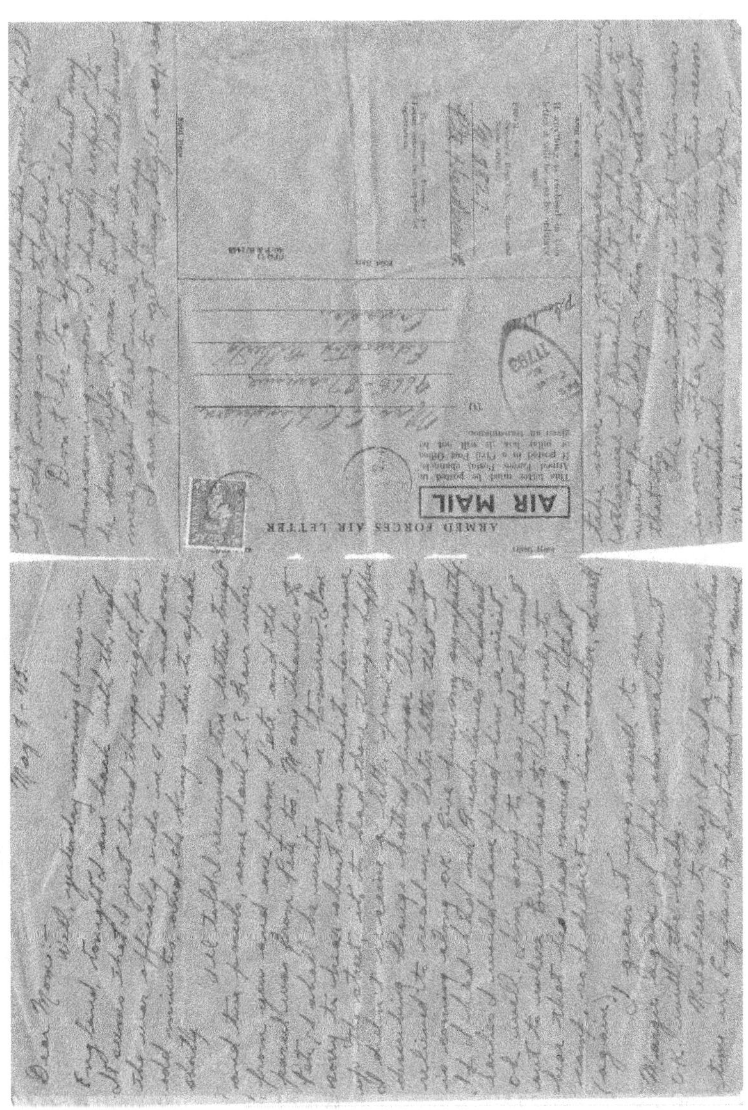

May 8, 1945

Dear Mom:

Well, yesterday morning I was in England, tonight I am back with the regt. It seems that I just timed things right for the war officially ends in 4 hours and some odd minutes and the King is due to speak shortly.

All told I received ten letters tonight and two parcels, some haul eh? Four were from you and one from Pete, and the parcel from Pete, too. Many thanks to Pete, I shall be writing him tomorrow. I'm sorry to hear about Mrs. Whats-here name up the street, its too bad those things happen. I didn't receive a letter from you describing Dougs battered finger but I am relieved to read in a later letter that it is coming along o.k. Give him my sympathy . If I had had Mr. Aucherloimes address earlier, I would have paid him a visit, oh well. Im sorry to say that I went out to where Bud used to live only to hear that hehad moved out of the camp, so I didn't see him either, Oh well.(again)

I guess it was swell to see Margie again. I hope she makes out o.k. with the baby.

Needless to say, I had a marvelous time in England & Scotland but of course that is overshadowed by the new. (Hold it, the king is going to speak)

Don't be to optomistic about my home coming, mom. I hardly expect to be home before Xmas. But we shall know more about that in a few days.

I am going to get busy right away and take some course, corespondence or otherwise, (other wise if possible) but I shall have to wait for a day or two to find out about that too.

The main thing is this war is over, other things at this time seem immaterial.

With all my love

Grant.

Dear Mom:- May 10-45.

Well, what new, lady?

Holy cow, this is a soft life, nothing to do and no hope of ever having to do anything. All I sit at a desk every day or every other day and look smart. But it's better than dodging bullets, isn't it?

We had a kit check-up today. I feel sorry for the army, it's going to cost them a lot to re-outfit me. All I have is a battledress, a small pack with my shaving kit, mess tins and soap and towel, a leather jerkin and a sten gun with several magazines. Everything else, blankets, groundsheet, gas cape, overcoat, brushes, shirts, underwear, extra battledress and countless small items were disposed of back in those days when a person wore what he wanted and carried just what he wanted and nothing else. I don't know what I'm going to do with all this junk when I do get it. I traded my machine gun for a rifle today, it's easier to keep clean.

The latest official news on our going home is that we will all be home before the new year. The volunteers for Japan go first, then the married men with five years service, one in Canada and four overseas. Then the rest of us go home by regiments. Probably we will go in order […]

[…] and so on.

So far they aren't bothering us about volunteering for the other show. My officer officially explained it to me today but didn't ask me to go or not to go.

The weather is beautiful. It must [be] warmer than May at home.

I have no complaints at all now except that this life is going to become awfully dull after a while.

I'm glad to hear Wilf Labine is O.K. Still bet it hurt his pride to be taken prisoner though.

Love & kisses Stuart

ARMED FORCES AIR LETTER

AIR MAIL

This letter must be posted in Armed Forces Postal channels. If posted in a Civil Post Office or pillar box, it will not be given air transmission.

TO: Mrs. C.L. Henderson, 9615 - 79 Avenue, Edmonton, Alberta, Canada.

If anything is enclosed in this letter it will be sent by ordinary mail.

FROM: M 8827 Pte Henderson

May 10, 1945

Dear Mom:

Well, what's new lady?

Holy cow this is a soft life, nothing to do and no hope of ever having to do anything. Oh, I sit at a desk every day or every other day and look smart. But it's better than dodging bullets, isnt it?

We had a kit check up today. I feel sorry for the army, it's going to cost them a lot to reoutfit me. All I have is a battle dress, a small pack with my shaving kit, mess tins and soap and towel, a leather jerkin and a sten gun with several magazines. Everything else, blankets, ground sheet, gas cape, overcoat, brushes, shirts, underwear, extra battle dress and countless small items were disposed of back in those days when a person wore what he wanted and carried just what he wanted and nothing else. I don't know what I'm going to do with all this junk when I do get it. I traded my machine gun for a rifle today. It's easier to keep clean.

The latest official news in about going home is that we will all be home before the new year. The volunteers for Japan go first, then the married men with five years service, one in Canada and four over here. Then the rest of us go home by regiments. Probably we will go in order of forming up (First Div. first, then second and so on)

So far they aren't bothering us about volunteering fot the other show. My officer offically explained it to me today but didn't ask me to go or not to go.

The weather is beautiful. It's much warmer than May at home.

I have no complaints at all now except that this life is going to become awfully dull after while.

I'm glad to hear the Wilf Galimore is o.k. I'll bet it hurt his pride to be taken prisoner though.

Love & Kisses

Grant.

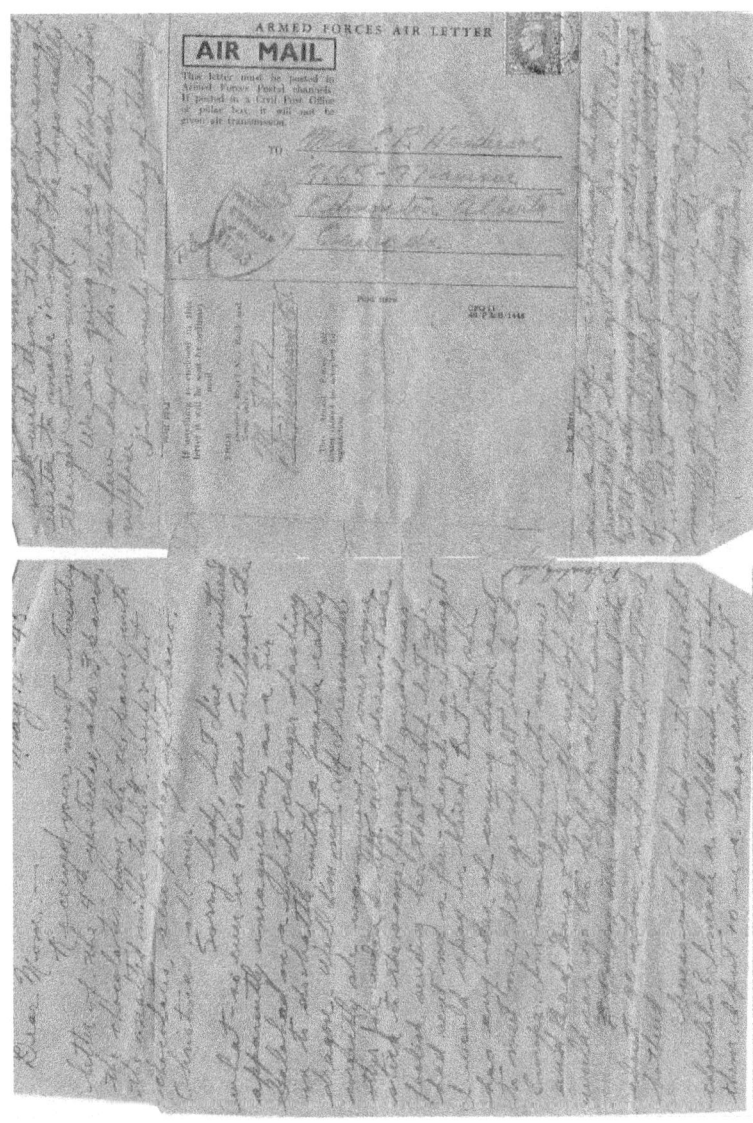
ARMED FORCES AIR LETTER

AIR MAIL

This letter must be posted in Armed Forces Postal channels. If posted in a Civil Post Office or pillar box, it will not be given air transmission.

TO:

May 12, 1945

Dear Mom:

Received your most interesting letter of the 4th yesterday, also 3 parcels: the choclates from Pete, the parcel with the malted milk tablets, soup & hot choclates, also packages of tobacco. Christmas all over!

Sorry lady, but I've no interest what so ever in dear Miss Sullivan. She apparently imagines me as a Sir Galahad on a white charger dashing in to do battle with a smoke eating dragon. Well I'm not. If I remember correctly she was swooning over some other Joe when I left. Why doesn't she stick to the same person. I guess I was foolish sending her that scarf but she had sent me a few parcels so I thought I would repay in kind. But if she has any idea of coming down east to meet me, I'll go straight back to Europe. I'm coming home to see you and Dad, Doug and Pete. The rest of the world can go to hell for all I care.

Pardon the temper mom, but its about 90 above and I am all hot and bothered.

Guess what I did with those hot chocolates? I made a cold drink out of them. I put 10 in a large coffee pot and mixed 5 small cans of condensed milk with them, then put in enough water to make 10 cups. The boys really thought It was swell.

We are going back to Holland in a few days – for Victory Parades I suppose.

I'm seriously thinking of taking on a bit of occupational duties provided I can get home leave first. I'm still pretty young and another year or two of this wouldn't hurt me would it? In that time, I could save a little money and I think in the long run I would be farther ahead.

With all my Love

Grant.

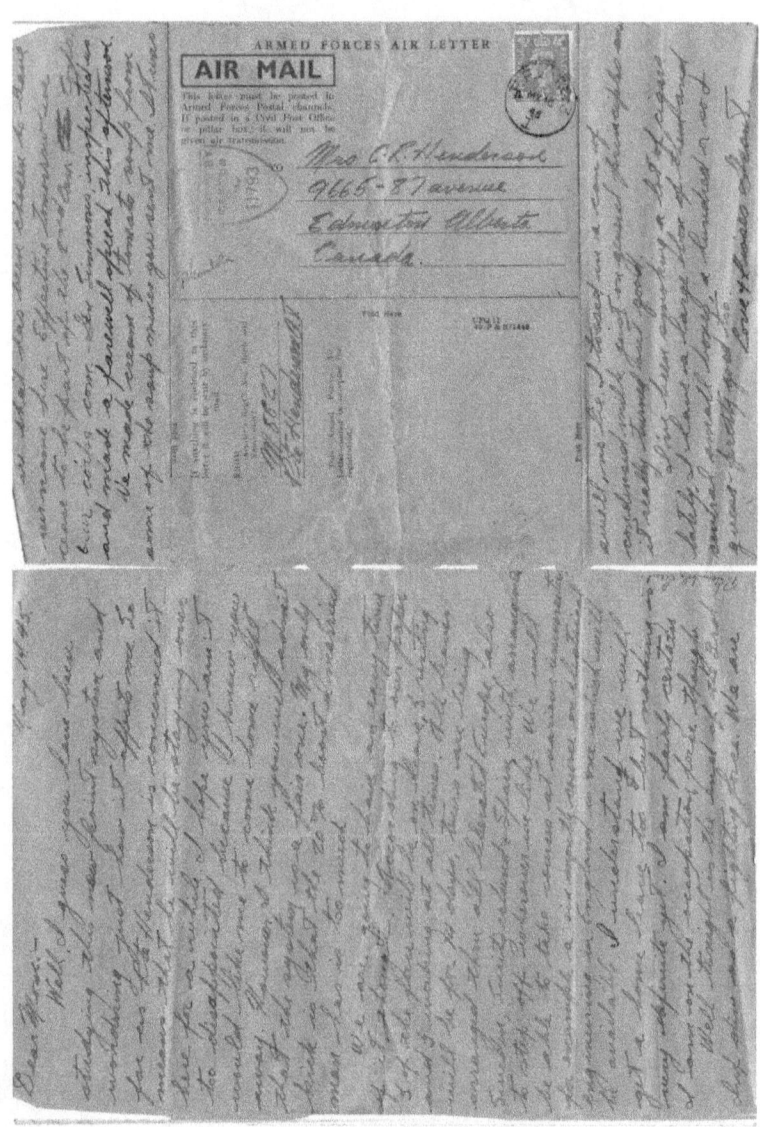

ARMED FORCES AIR LETTER

AIR MAIL

This letter must be posted in Armed Forces Postal channels. If posted in a Civil Post Office or pillar box, it will not be given air transmission.

Mrs C.R. Henderson
9665-87 avenue
Edmonton Alberta
Canada

May 14, 2010

Dear Mom:

Well, I guess you have been studying this new point system and wondering just how it affects me. So far as Pte Henderson is concerned it means that he will be staying over here for a while. I hope you aren't too disappointed because I know you would like me to come home right away. However, I think you will admit that the system is a fair one. My only kick is that the 20% boost a married man has is too much.

We are going to have an easy time of it though. According to our paper 1/3 of the force will be on leave, 1/3 resting and 1/3 working at all times. All leaves will be for 14 days, tours are being arranged thru all liberated Europe also Sweden, Switzerland & Spain with arrangements to stop off whereever we like. We will be able to take courses at various universities for example a six month course on electrical engineering in England is one which will be available. I understand we will get a home leave too but nothing very definite yet. I am fairly certain I am on the occupation force though.

Well tonight is the end of the 3rd Inf. Div as a fighting force. We are the div. that has been chosen to leave their name here. Effective tomorrow we cease to be part of the 2nd Can. Corps. Our corps com – Gen Simmons, inspected us and made a farewell speech this afternoon.

We made cream of tomato soup from some of the soup mixes you sent me. It was swell, no lie. I tossed in a can of condensed milk just on general principles and it really turned out good.

I've been smoking a lot of cigars lately, I have a large box of them and several small boxes, a hundred or so I guess – pretty good too.

Love & Kisses

Grant

ARMED FORCES AIR LETTER

AIR MAIL

This letter must be posted in Armed Forces Postal channels. If posted in a Civil Post Office or pillar box it will not be given air transmission.

TO: Mrs C.C. Henderson,
9665-97 ave
Edmonton Alberta
Canada.

May 17, 1945

Dear Mom:

Well, I'm back in Holland again, about 15 miles north of Arhnew to be exact. I expect we will stay in this area for another day and then we will make another short move. Then the reorganization starts. I expect it will take about a month. I'm not sure just how they will work it but the Burma bound and the old timers will be leaving shortly.

You would be surprized at the number of volunteers for Burma and for the A of O. The first day over three times the required number volunteered for the Far East. The Chaudieres had 65% of their men volunteer for army of occupation. All in all forty per cent of the brigade volunteered for army of occupation (I'm in the 9th Highland Lt Inf. Brigade) As you can see by that, the fighting men figure its going to be o.k. over here.

I caught a rather miserable cold a couple of days ago but I've just about got it beat now.

In a way, I feel sorry for the Dutch, their soldiering days are just starting. Apparently they are going to send quite a force to the far East.

The weather has turned nice again after one miserable day. There are inches of dust on the dirt roads, most of the roads are paved though.

We could take a lesson from these people and plant trees along our highways. I rode around two hundred miles yesterday and I never saw a stretlch of bare and ugly highway like our roads in Canada.

I have a kit bag again and the Q M has started to reissue equipment. It's going to be funny to have all this stuff again.

I haven't written Pete yet. I hope he doesn't think I am ungrateful or something. The truth is I am running low on stamps but I'm going to buy a bunch in a day or so.

Hope this isn't too dull.

Love & Kisses

Grant.

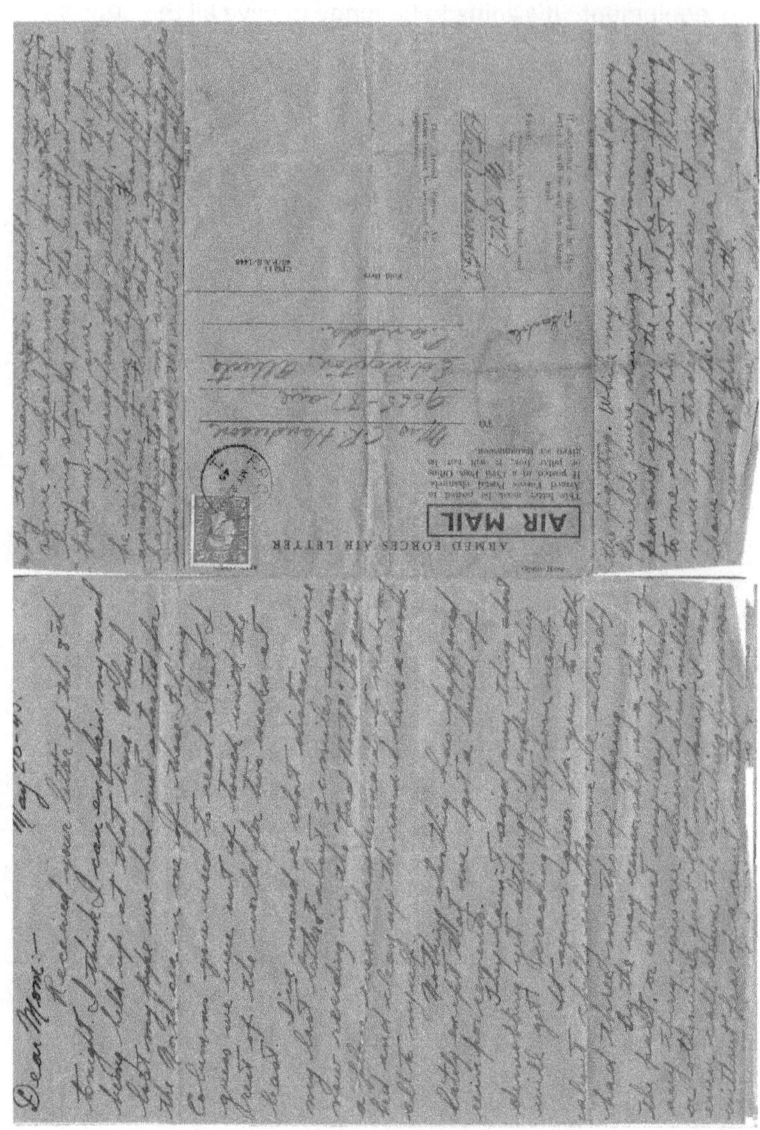

May 20, 1945

Dear Mom:

Received your letter of the 8th tonight. I think I can explain my mail being held up at that time. When I lost my pipe we had just started for the North sea in one of these Flying Columns you used to read about. I guess we were out of touch with the rest of the world for two weeks at least.

I've moved a short distance since my last letter, about 30 miles and am now residing in the "Bad Hotel". It's quite a place even chambermaids to make my bed and clean up the room. I have a room all to myself.

Nothing startling had happened lately except that we got a bunch of reinforcements.

They havn't said anything about demobbing yet although I expect they will get cracking pretty soon now.

It seems queer for you to talk about chilly weather we've already had three months of spring.

By the way censorship is a thing of the past or almost anyway. If there's anything you are curious about military or other wise just let me know. I can even call down the stinking Limeys now with out fear of court martial.

By the way mom, would you send me some airmail forms? I'm going to start buying stamps from the unit post master but am not so sure about getting the forms.

I heard from Bud yesterday, he figures he will be home before me. Frankly, it annoys me to think that he and his kind have priority on me and the other infantry Joes who took all the risks and did all the fighting. While my wounded and dying friends were shivering and moaning from fear and cold and the wet, he was yapping to me about his sore chest. But I would never have traded him places. It would have hurt my pride to wear a battledress and never go thru a battle.

Love & Kisses

Grant

May 21 or 22, 1945

Dear Mom:

Thanks a million for the chocolates, mom, they are elegant. I also received a carton of cigarettes from Henry Lodge, pretty nice of him, I thought.

I'm still living at the same place, which is o.k. by me and have heard no more about getting out of the army except a rumor saying that all men with at least six months combat duty go home first after the old timers regardless of the length of service. But rumors are a dime a dozen in the army.

We have had our first electrical storm of the year, a humdinger it was. It rained and thundered for 24 hours.

We have a little dog now, as cute as can be. He looks like a little Teddy bear; he can't be more than two or three weeks old.

By the way, I got a bunch of stamps and airmail forms today, so there isn't any rush about sending me those forms.

We were told on parade yesterday morning that we have to stop addressing our officers and sergeants-majors by nickname, first name, etc. Ah me, the discipline is getting awful.

We had another beer issue last night.

Our food has been wonderful since the war ended, almost as good as the time Montgomery told us we would have to live off the land. Our average meal is better than any meal served in restaurants. We eat away better than we ever did in camps in England.

You should see this hotel mom. It's built in the style of a Chinese pagoda and the grounds around it are really wonderful.

Love Grant

ARMED FORCES AIR LETTER

AIR MAIL

This letter must be posted in Armed Forces Postal channels. If posted in a Civil Post Office or pillar box, it will not be given air transmission.

TO: Mrs C.R. Henderson
9665 - 87 avenue
Edmonton Alberta
Canada.

May 25, 1945

Dear Mom:

Received the swell pipe and Glen Cannon story yesterday, Thanks. I really got a kick out of the way that Glen Cannon got the money for those darned alligators. Only he could think of that.

We can buy cigarettes from the Q M now (Canadian ones) at the rate of $1.00 for 300 to a limit of 900. I ordered 600 yesterday. Perhaps I should start sending you smokes.

I'm going to go to Amsterdam tomorrow to have a look at the place. It's not very far away and they have started to run trucks up there for us who would like to sight see.

I see by the papers that the Churchill govt. has resigned. I wonder how our election will turn out? I have a vote this time for the first time in my long life and I sure can't figure who to vote for, oh well.

My new pay book is gradually being assembled. I have 140 or 150 dollars in it and as soon as it is properly straightened out I'm going to send you 100 to put in the bank. The money might as well be drawing interest.

This money situation is really funny. I have the equivalent of about seventy five Canadian dollars in Dutch money. So long as I'm in Holland I'm o.k. from the money angle but as soon as I get back to Germany my cash is useless. The paymaster will only change guilders into marks to the equivalent of that drawn from my pay book. Since I've never drawn Dutch money from my pay book I can't exchange it for marks. Anyway there isn't anything to buy here except beer and nothing to buy in Germany so money doesn't mean very much to us.

I think we are going to move pretty soon – to Arnhem, in a way I hope so because then we could get into Nijmegen occasionally. But it wouldn't be such an easy life there.

Well, I've run out of words so I guess I'll stop now.

Love& Kisses

Grant

May 27, 1945

Dear Mom:

Well, I spent all day yesterday sightseeing in Amsterdam. It's a very nice city, but quite different from the average. The heart of the town is as old fashioned as can be, with narrow streets and lanes and towering buildings. But the rest of the city is very modern. Some of the new buildings were almost like what we picture buildings in the two thousands to look like. You know, the ones with walls of glass, stream lined etc. As usual there are the canals; they are pretty too with their rows of trees along either side.

It was really very lucky to have seen Amsterdam yesterday for it was put out of bounds this morning.

We had a large draft of reinforcements today; most of them had been in the regt before and were wounded. Among them were four fellow sigs who were all hurt in the same battle. That had been a bad day for us, of the 8 that went in with the four rifle coys we suffered five casualties, one killed and four wounded. My partner was the unlucky Joe who got killed that day.

The weather hasn't been up to scratch for the past few days. Rain seems to be in style right now and when it rains here it pours.

We will be moving any day now. I guess the first bunch for home will be picked out then and with luck we will be back in Germany in a couple of weeks. This breaking up of the regt is going to be a hectic affair and the sooner it's finished the quicker we will settle down to normal again.

I hear that Himmler committed suicide. It's funny isn't it five years ago Germany was the most powerful nation in the world, now she is nothing, and from what I've seen I don't think she could ever be an industrial nation again.

By the way, lady, I'm willing to lay you odds that dear Mr. King gets elected again. Why didn't some party with a decent platform come out to oppose him?

Love

Grant

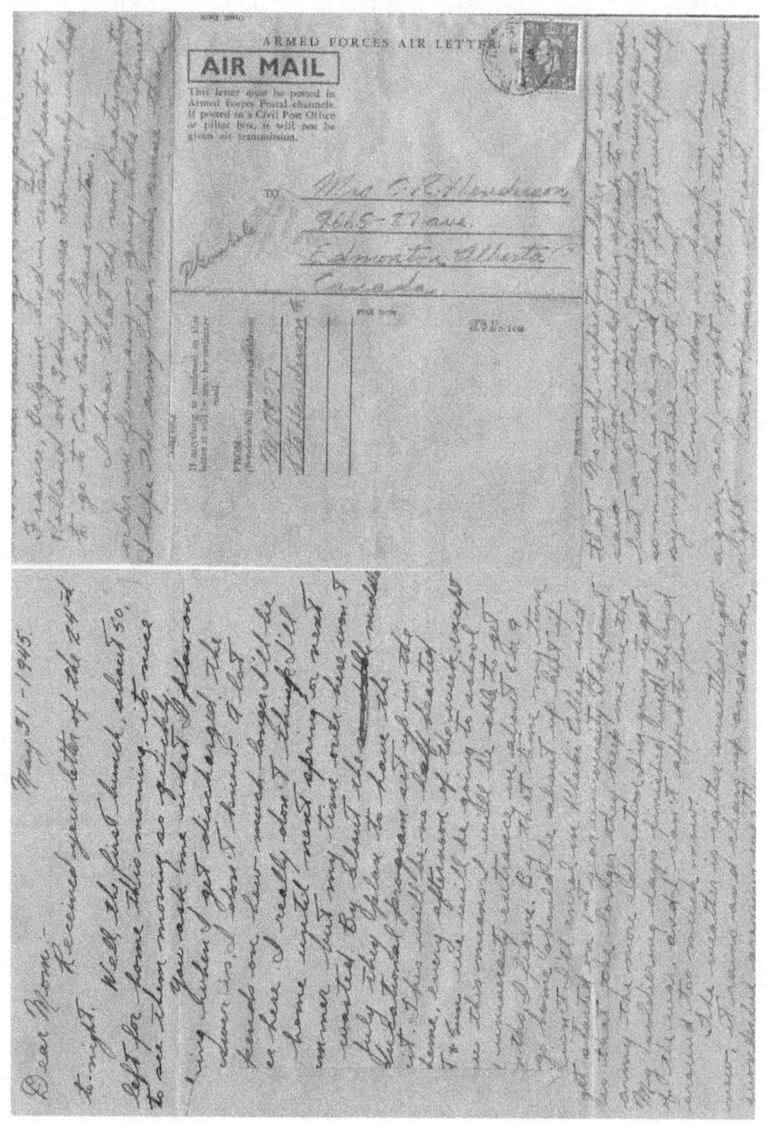

ARMED FORCES AIR LETTER

AIR MAIL

This letter must be posted in Armed Forces Postal channels. If posted in a Civil Post Office or pillar box, it will not be given air transmission.

TO: Mrs C. R. Henderson
9665 - 87 ave.
Edmonton Alberta
Canada

May 31, 1945

Dear Mom:

Received your letter of the 24th tonight.

Well, the first bunch, about 50 left for home this morning, it's nice to see them moving so quickly.

You ask me what I plan on doing when I get discharged; the answer is I don't know. A lot depends on how much long I'll be over here. I really don't think I'll be home until next spring or next summer but my time over here won't be wasted. By about the middle of July they plan to have the educational program set up in the unit. This will be no half hearted scheme, every afternoon of the week, except Sat & Sun we will be going to school. Thru this means I will be able to get my university entrance in about 6 or 9 months, I figure. By that time my turn to go home should be about up but if it isn't I'll enroll in Khaki College and get started on 1st year university. The point is that the longer they keep me in the army, the more education I'm going to get. My soldiering days finished with the end of the war and I can't afford to fool around too much now.

The weather is rather unsettled right now, it rains and clears up and so on, wonderful growing weather.

We can now go to any place in France, Belgium and in certain parts of Holland on 3 day leaves. Formally we had to go to Can. Army leave centres.

I hear that the non fraternization order in Germany is going to be loosened. I hope the army has more sense than that. No self respecting soldier who ever saw action would ever speak to a German but a lot of these Zombies who never saw so much as a good fist fight will probably sympathize with them.

Amsterdam is back in bounds again so I might go back there tomorrow night.

Love & Kisses

Grant

ARMED FORCES AIR LETTER

AIR MAIL

This letter must be posted in Armed Forces Postal channels. If posted in a Civil Post Office or pillar box, it will not be given air transmission.

TO: Mr. P. Henderson
9665-87 ave
Edmonton Alberta
Canada

Dear Pete—

June 5-43

I received your letter of the 27 ...

June 5, 1945

Dear Pete:

I received your letter of the 29th tonite, old boy, very glad to hear from you and all that.

I see you are interested in our part in the Rhine crossing, so here goes. I'll start from the beginning. The general plan was that the 51st Highland div with the HLI of C attached and under their command should make the assault. The Argyle Highlanders were to take a small town called Bienne and we were to pass thru them to do our job. It was planned that we would attack about 7 or 8 in the morning. Well after a 15 mile march we reached the Rhine and crossed it in small 10 man storm boats. For about the last 5 miles of the march and during the crossing we were under a pretty heavy barrage of shells, rockets etc but never met any small arms. We were supposed to land in a cleared area but the first thing we met was 40 or 50 Jerries in good positions, however there wasn't much fight in them so they didn't cause any harm. Then we dug in and waited for word to pass thru the Argyles. In the mean time the 7th Black Watch was supposed to take a place called Speldrop over to the left of Bienne. They got into town without opposition but were counter attached so they retreated leaving their wounded.

So the Limeys sent us in to take out Speldrop. We did although it took us till about 2 in the morning. By this time the Argyles had retreated out of Bienne so first thing in the morning we with the North Novas (who had since landed) recaptured Bienne and took our original objectives.

It took us about 27 hours to recapture Bienne and do our original part in the plan. The Reginas, Winnipegs and Can Scots landed while that battle was on and captured Emerrick. We went thru them and cleared up to the Dutch border and liberated the town of Herenburg. By that time all organized resistance had ceased, we had done all the fighting and the Limeys just came across for the ride and took the credit.

Love

Grant

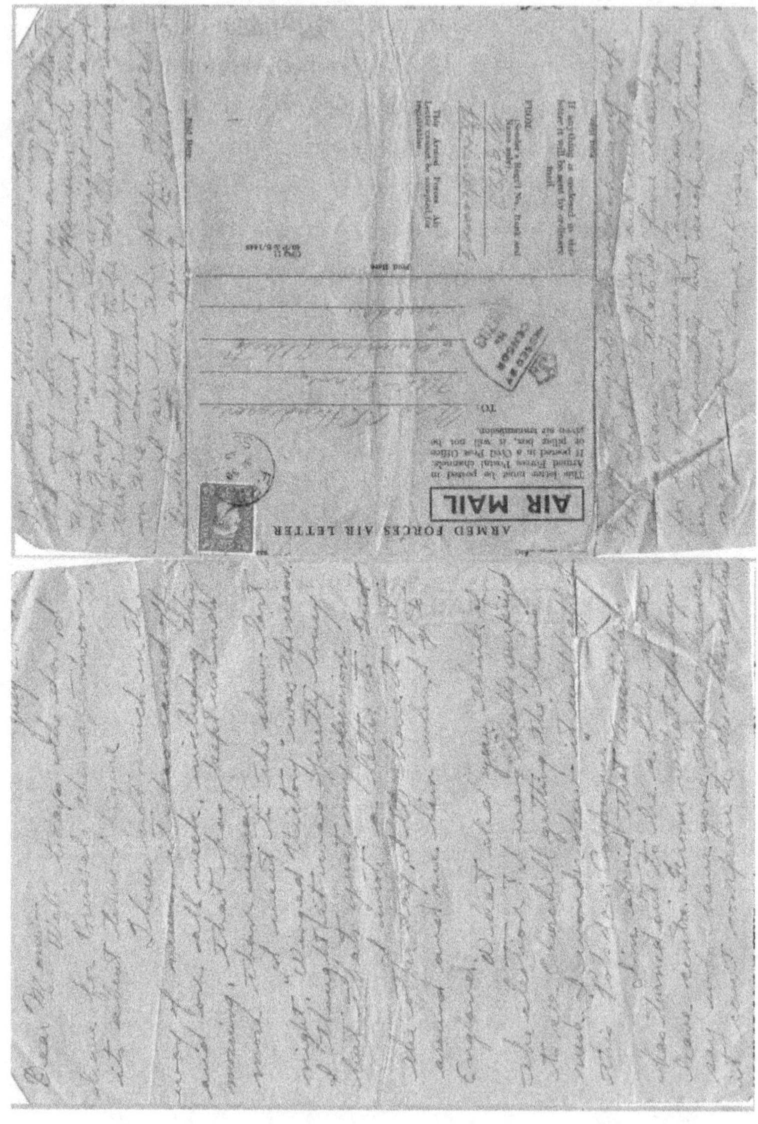

ARMED FORCES AIR LETTER

AIR MAIL

This letter must be posted in Armed Forces Postal channels. If posted in a Civil Post Office or pillar box, it will not be given air transmission.

TO

FROM

Sender's Name, Regtl No., Rank and Unit only

If anything is enclosed in this letter it will be sent by ordinary mail.

This Armed Forces Air Letter cannot be accepted for registration.

July 28, 1945

Dear Mom:

Well, today's the day I leave for Brussels this afternoon; it's about time I figure.

There's not much in the way of news. It has rained off and on all week, including this morning, that has kept us indoors more than usual.

I went to the show last night; "Winged Victory" was the name. I thought it was pretty lousy but that is just my opinion.

I wrote a letter to Bud the other day. I'll have to get around and see him when I go to England.

What did you think of the election? I was really surprised to see Churchill getting the bums rush. I wonder how it will effect this Potsdam Conference.

I am afraid that Amsterdam has turned out to be a flop as a leave centre. From what the boys say who have gone there on leaves it can't compare to the other centres.

I have been there a few times but only for evenings and I didn't think much of it. However the "Meet the Nave" show is there right now and that is supposed to be the best stage show in the continent.

I see by the paper that the Dutch are going to start giving the girls the old haircut if they don't stop going out with Canadians – that's a fine thank you for the five thousand

Canadian graves in this country but such is human nature, I guess.

Love & Kisses

Grant

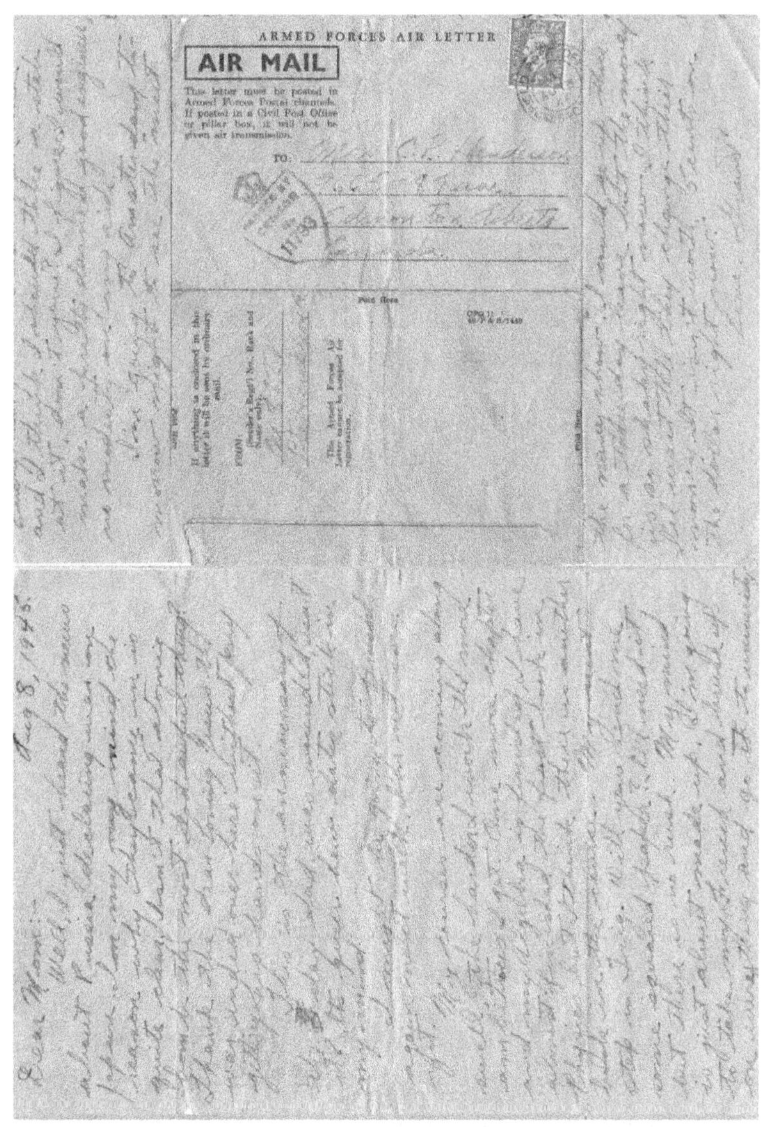

ARMED FORCES AIR LETTER

AIR MAIL

This letter must be posted in Armed Forces Postal channels. If posted in a Civil Post Office or pillar box, it will not be given air transmission.

TO:

Aug 8, 1945

Dear Mom:

Well, I just heard the news about Russia declaring war on Japan. In my mind the reason why they came in is quite clear. Isn't that atomic bomb the most God awful thing? Thank the dear loving Jesus the war ended over here without Jerry getting his hands on it.

This is the anniversary of the day dad was wounded isn't it? It's queer how dates stick in my mind.

I might be going to Brussels again next week. I'm not sure yet.

My courses are coming along swell, the harder I work the more ambitious I get. One more chapter and my Algebra is finished. I have almost finished the first book in Physics but I think there is another book in the course. My next step is Trig. Will you send me some squared paper? I'll need it but there is no rush. My mind is just about made up; I'm going to take my French and brush up on everything and go to university.

Everything is waiting for me and I think I should take a stab at it, don't you? I figure I would make a pretty darned good engineer, no modesty on my side.

I am going to Amsterdam tomorrow night to see the "Meet the Navy Show". I could go up there for a three day leave but the money is so shaky right now, I think I'll wait till they change their money. It isn't worth 5 cents on the dollar right now.

Love Gran

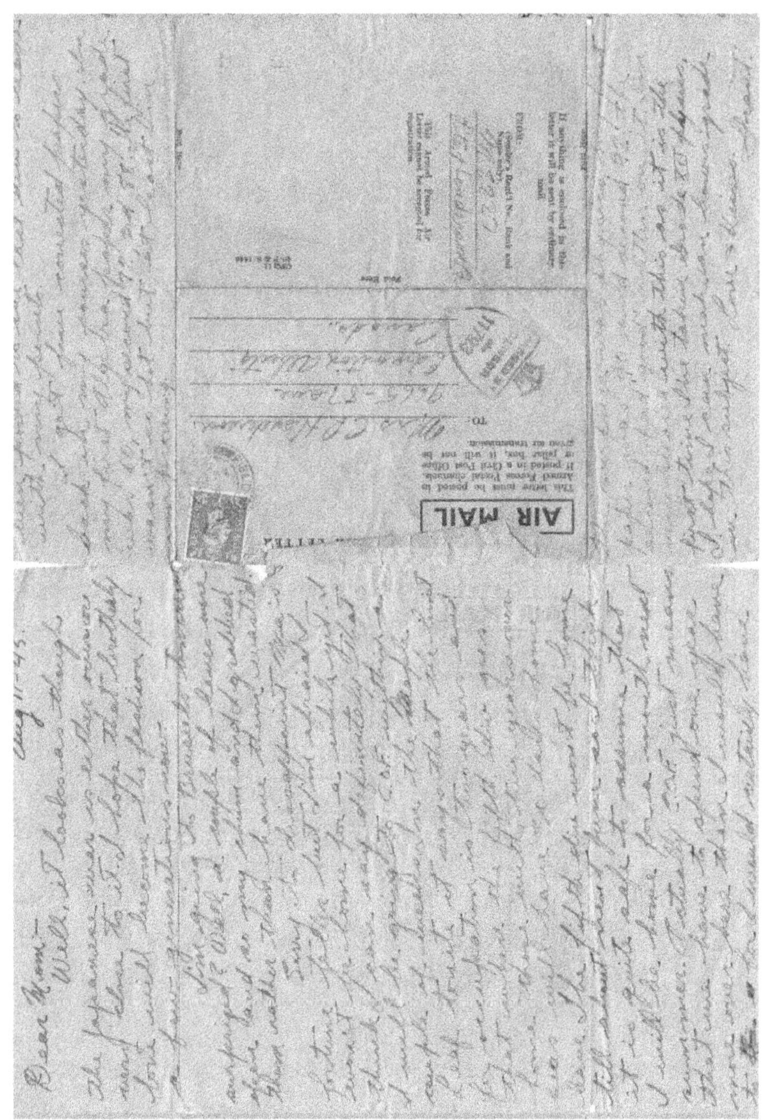

Aug 11, 1945

Dear Mom:

Well it looks as though the Japanese war is either over or very close to it. I hope that brotherly love will become the fashion for a few generations now.

I'm going to Brussels tomorrow, surprised? Well a couple of leaves were open and so my chum and I grabbed them rather than have them wasted.

Sorry to disappoint Ma's fortune teller but I'm afraid I won't be home for a while yet. I think I can say definitely that I will be going to C.O.F. within a couple of weeks. In the Maple Leaf tonight it says that the limit for occupation is two years and that when the fifth division goes home those with two years overseas will have 30 days home leave. The fifth div. won't be home till about next June so I think it is quite safe to assume that I will be home for a month next summer. Actually C.O.F just means that we have to spend one year more over here than I would have to as I would certainly have been posted to the last div to leave with my points.

I got five corrected papers back in my courses yesterday. In my first Algebra paper my grade was 60, my second 72, and 3rd 88. The first wasn't so hot but at least I'm improving.

The surprise was physics, my first paper was 90 and second 92, the second had "good" written on it. I'm very pleased with this as it is the first time I've taken Grade XII physics; I hope I can make an honors grade in this subject.

Love & Kisses

Grant.

Aug 30 - 45.

Dear Mom:—
Well, the date for my England leave has finally been decided. I'm going on the 4th will be in England on the 5th and leave on the 17th 18th. The leaves were increased from 8 to days last week so I'm not sorry that I had to wait for a little.

I'll write Bud and let him know when to expect me, he said he might be able to wangle a 48 which would be swell.

Has Junior changed his plans about going to Varsity?

The Dutch are really celebrating their Queens birthday. It isn't till tomorrow but there are parades, street dances etc in full swing today — I suppose tomorrow is to them as the 24th of May is to us.

It is alternately pouring and shining — what a country!!

There is a show on at the club to-nite "The Affairs of Susan", I think I'll trip and see it. We can buy all the Coca Colas we can drink at a service canteen now — there's also a chocolate ration up there once or twice a week. They will only sell these things to Canadians, it makes the Limeys sore but they can buy anything else that's for sale.

Well, the Japanese landings seem to be going ahead according to plan — it looks as though they have decided to be very friendly.

Love & Kisses

Aug 30, 1945

Dear Mom:

The date for my England leave has finally been decided. I'm going on the 4th, will be in England on the 5th and leave on the 17th or 18th. The leaves were increased from 8 to 12 days last week so I'm not sorry that I had to wait for a while.

I'll write Bud and let him know when to expect me. He said he might be able to wangle 48 which would be swell.

Has junior changed his plans about going to Varsity?

The Dutch are really celebrating their Queens birthday. It isn't till tomorrow but there are parades, street dances etc in full swing today – I suppose tomorrow is to them what the 24th of May is to us.

It is alternately pouring and shining – what a country.

There is a show on at the club tonight "The Affairs of Susan", I think I'll go up and see it. We can buy all the Coca colas we can drink at a service canteen now – there is also a chocolate ration up there once or twice a week. They will only sell these things to Canadians, it makes the Limeys sore but they can buy anything else that's for sale.

Well the Japanese landings seem to be going ahead according to plan – it looks as though they have decided to be very friendly.

Love & Kisses

Grant

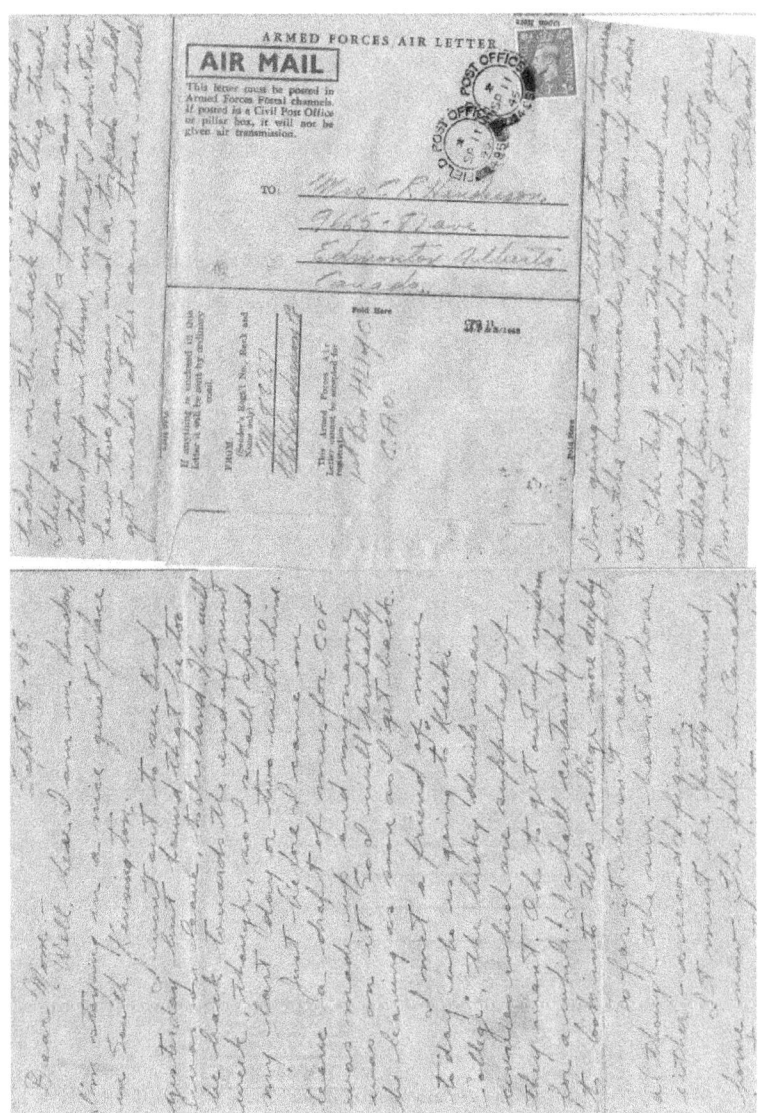

ARMED FORCES AIR LETTER

AIR MAIL

This letter must be posted in Armed Forces Postal channels. If posted in a Civil Post Office or pillar box, it will not be given air transmission.

TO:

Sept 8, 1945

Dear Mom:

Well, here I am in London. I'm staying in a nice quiet place in South Kensington.

I went out to see Bud yesterday but found that he too was on leave, to Ireland. He will be back towards the end of next week, though, so I shall spend my last day or two with him.

Just before I came on leave a draft of men for COF was made up and my name was on it. So I will probably be leaving as soon as I get back.

I met a friend of mine today who is going to "Khaki College". The lucky devil wears civvies which are supplied if they want. Oh to get out of uniform for a while. I shall certainly have to look into this college more deeply.

So far it hasn't rained although the sun hasn't shone either – a record I figure.

I must be pretty around home now. The fall, in Canada is to me the nicest season of all.

I saw one of those midget subs today, on the back of a big truck. They are so small a person can't even stand up in them; in fact I don't see how two persons and a torpedo could get inside at the same time- oh well.

I am going to do a little touring tomorrow to see the waxworks, the Tower of London etc.

The trip across the channel was very rough. The old tub I was on rolled something awful – but I guess I am not a sailor.

Love & Kisses

Grant

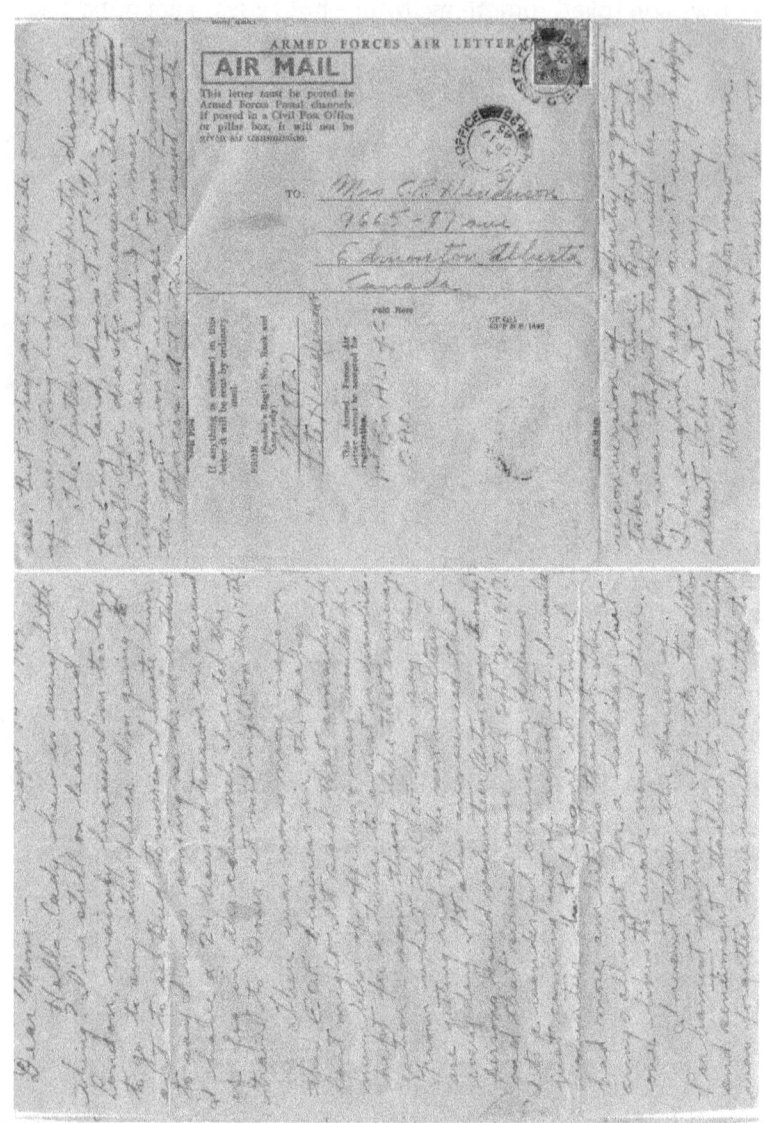

ARMED FORCES AIR LETTER

AIR MAIL

This letter must be posted in Armed Forces Postal channels. If posted in a Civil Post Office or pillar box, it will not be given air transmission.

TO: Mrs C.E. Henderson
9665-87 ave
Edmonton Alberta
Canada

Sept 14, 1945

Dear Mom:

Hello Lady, how is every little thing? I'm still on leave and in London mainly because I'm too lazy to go to any other place. I'm going out to see Bud tomorrow, I wrote him to say I was coming so he'll be there. I have 24 hour extension on account of fog in the channel. I catch the train to Dover at midnight on the 17th.

There was some more info on this COF business in the paper last night. It said that considerable numbers of officers & men would be kept for a time to assist in demobilization – something like that anyway. From what the COF boys say they are getting rid of the non volunteers every day. It also announced that persons could volunteer (Active army only) and that service was till Sept 30, 1947. It's a wonderful chance for fellows just coming out of school etc. I would volunteer but I figure its time I had more ambitious thoughts. The army is alright for a holiday but one likes to work now and then.

I went thru the Houses of Parliament yesterday. If the tradition and sentiment attached to these buildings was forgotten there would be little to see. But they are the pride and joy of every Englishman.

The future looks pretty dismal for England, doesn't it? The situation calls for drastic measures. The industries are howling for men but the govt won't release them from the forces. At the present rate reconversion of industry is going to take a long time. By that time her pre-war trade will be lost.

The English papers aren't very happy about the set up anyway.

Well that's all for now mom

Love & Kisses

Grant

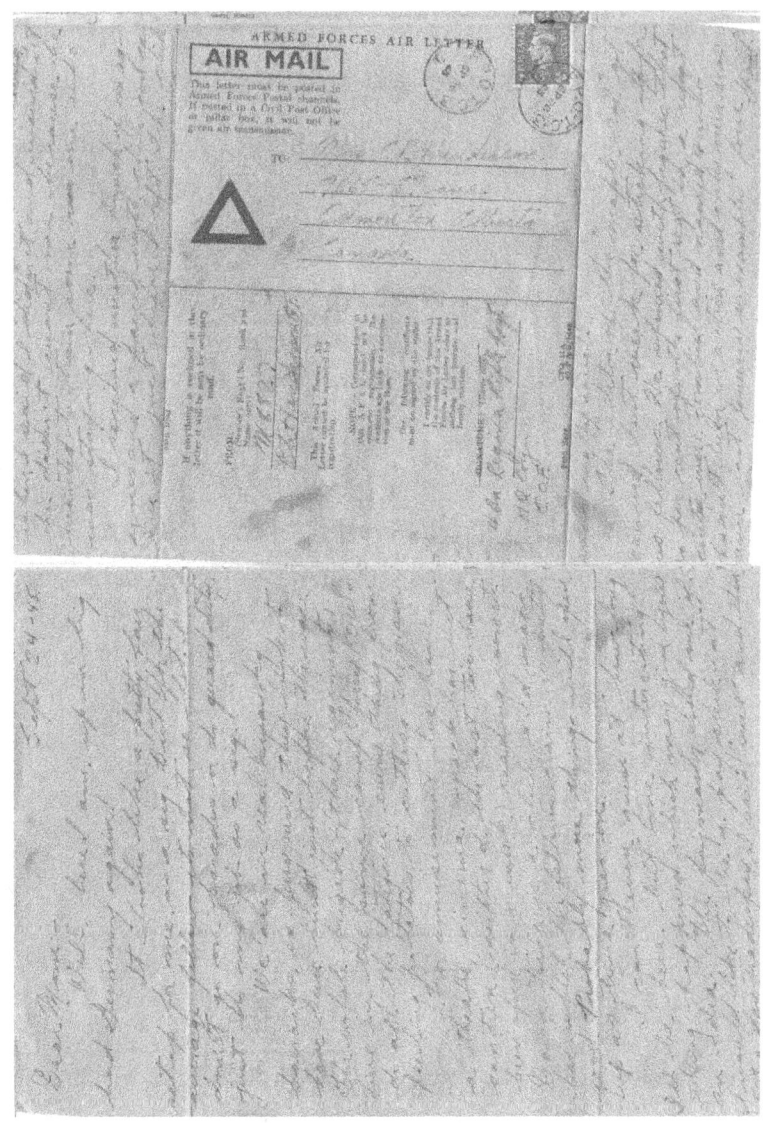

ARMED FORCES AIR LETTER

AIR MAIL

This letter must be posted in Armed Forces Postal channels. If posted in a Civil Post Office or pillar box, it will not be given air transmission.

TO:

Sept 24, 1945

Dear Mom:

Well, here I am up in big bad Germany again!

It looks like a pretty fair set up for me, as a sig. But for the average fellow it's not so hot. I don't go on parade or do guard duty, just do my job as a sig.

We are in real swanky barracks, ex-Jerry and they look to have been built just before the war. The whole brigade – (three regiments) live in the same camp. Jerry POW's do all the fatigues, everything from peeling potatoes to cutting the grass.

For amusement we have a theatre, cinema, snack bar, wet canteen (neither of the last two have been open in a week) reading room etc. Down Town is a club and snack bar which the fellows claim is pretty good. Probably more things will open up as time goes on.

I can't even guess at how long I'll be here but one interesting thing happened which may give you an idea. The paymaster asked me if I would like to be a pay clerk – at 50cents a day trades pay, I said "sure" and then he asked me if I had volunteered when I said I didn't and wouldn't he didn't want me because he wanted to train someone who was staying here.

I received another bunch of magazines and a parcel with chili con carne in it just before I left. The chili was really swell.

The editor of the maple leaf got canned last week for sticking up for us fellows. He showed figures that 30 percent of the first regt in a report center were Zombies and named 4 who hadn't been in action and only had been overseas since last January as examples.

Love

Grant

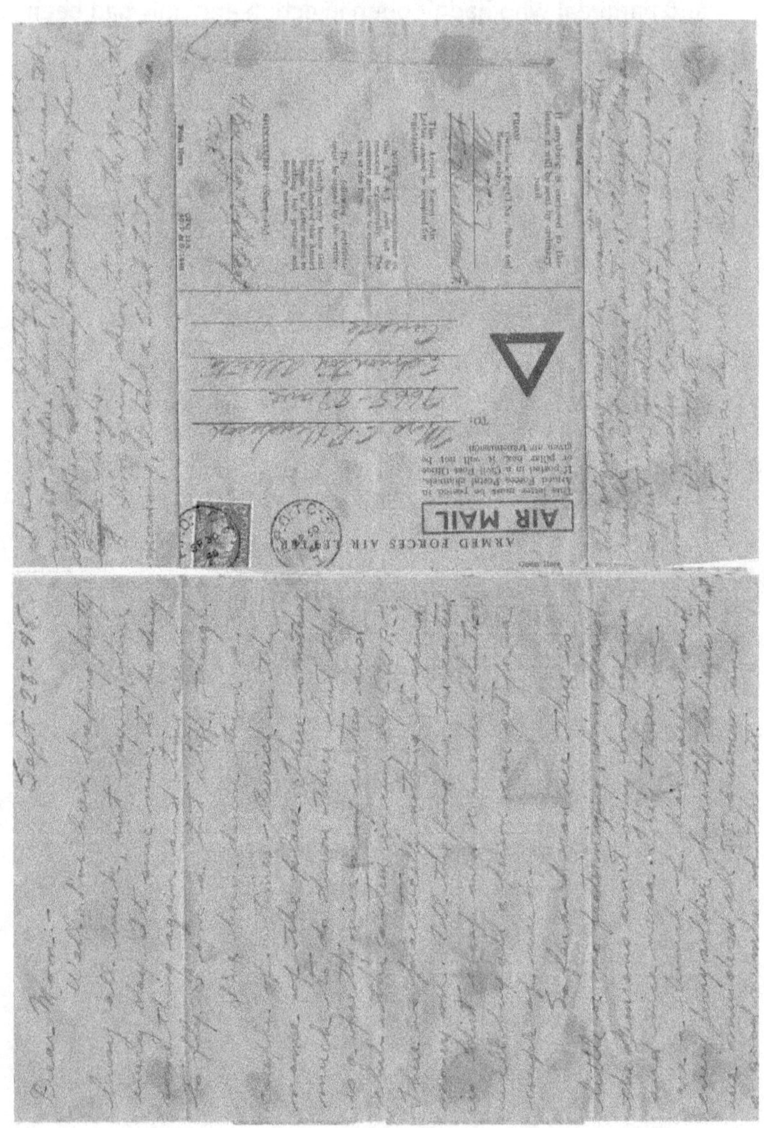

Sept 28, 1945

Dear Mom:

Well, I have been keeping pretty busy all week, out laying line every day. It's sure nice to be doing something again and time seems to fly . I am a bit stiff though.

I've been down town a couple of times – Aurich is the name of the place. There is nothing much to do down there but there is a pretty nice army canteen and club. The canteen is run by CWAC's. There is practically nothing to spend money on. All the food in the canteen is dirt cheap and 10 marks (about 1.00) will buy al a person can get for a couple of weeks.

So far as I can see there is little or no fraternizing, I'm afraid the Germans aren't very fond of us and vice versa. They think we are a bunch of barbarians and every Jerry Soldier honestly believes that we murdered all S.S. prisoners and a good number of the rest.
I saw a pretty good show the night before last, "Jack Oakie" was the Star. He's always good for a few laughs.
I'm going down to see the MO in the morning, I took a shick test for diphtheria the other day and he wants to see the results. It turned out o.k. though (I'm an expert on needles) so I won't need any more needles for that for a while.

Well that's all for now, mom. I'll write in a day or so.

Love

Grant

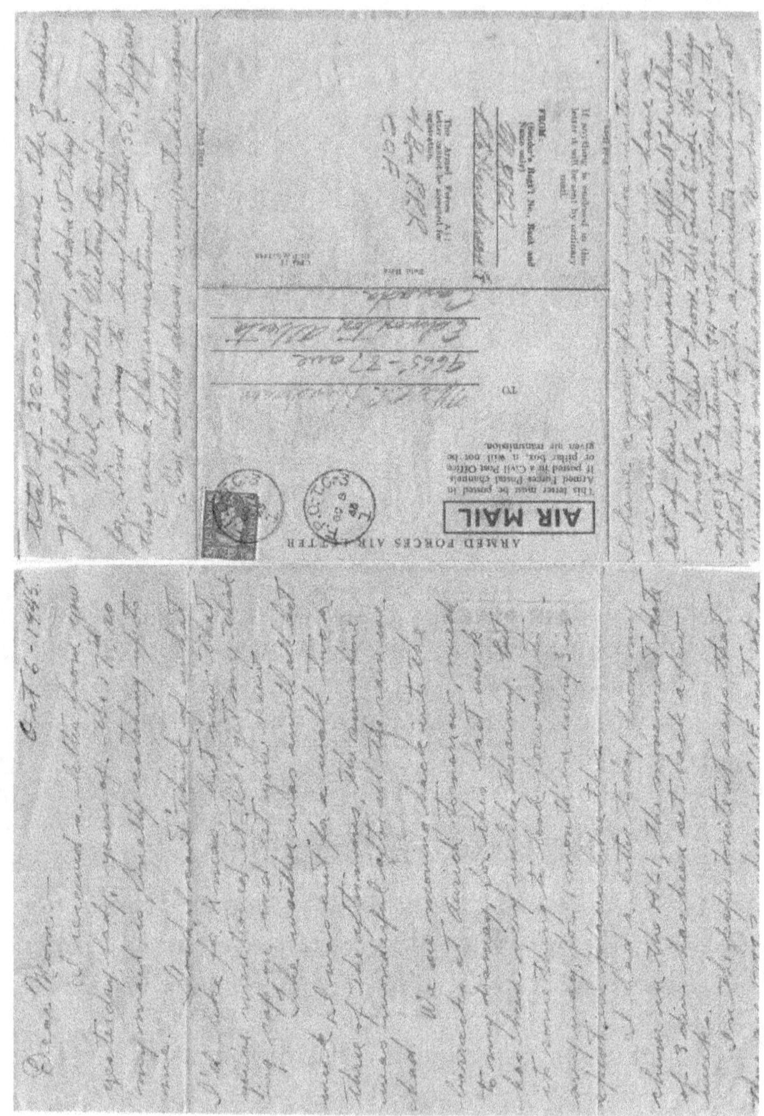

Oct 6, 1945

Dear Mom:

I received a letter from you yesterday lady, yours of the 17th, so my mail is finally catching up to me.

Gosh, I can't think of what I'd like for Xmas, but now that you've mentioned it I'll get my thinking cap on and let you know.

The weather was swell all last week, I was out for a walk two or three of the afternoons, the sunshine was wonderful after all the rain we had.

We are moving back into the barracks at Aurich tomorrow, much to my dismay for this last week had been very unlike the army. But it's something to look forward to anyway, for 1 month in every 3 is spent in places like this.

I had a letter today from my chum in the HL1, the movement date of 3 div has been set back a few weeks.

In the papers tonite it says that there are 1778 Zombies in COF out of a total of 22000 odd men. The zombies got off pretty easy, didn't they?

Well, another Victory Bond is paid for, I'm going to buy another 50, I figure they are a fair investment.

I'm settled down in my studies again. I have a new friend whose interests are similar to mine so we have a lot of fun figuring out the difficult problems.

I met a lieut. From the south side. He lives on 105 street between 84 & 85 avenue – west side of the street. He used to be a furniture salesman at Woodwards and his name is Newburt.

Love and Kisses

Grant.

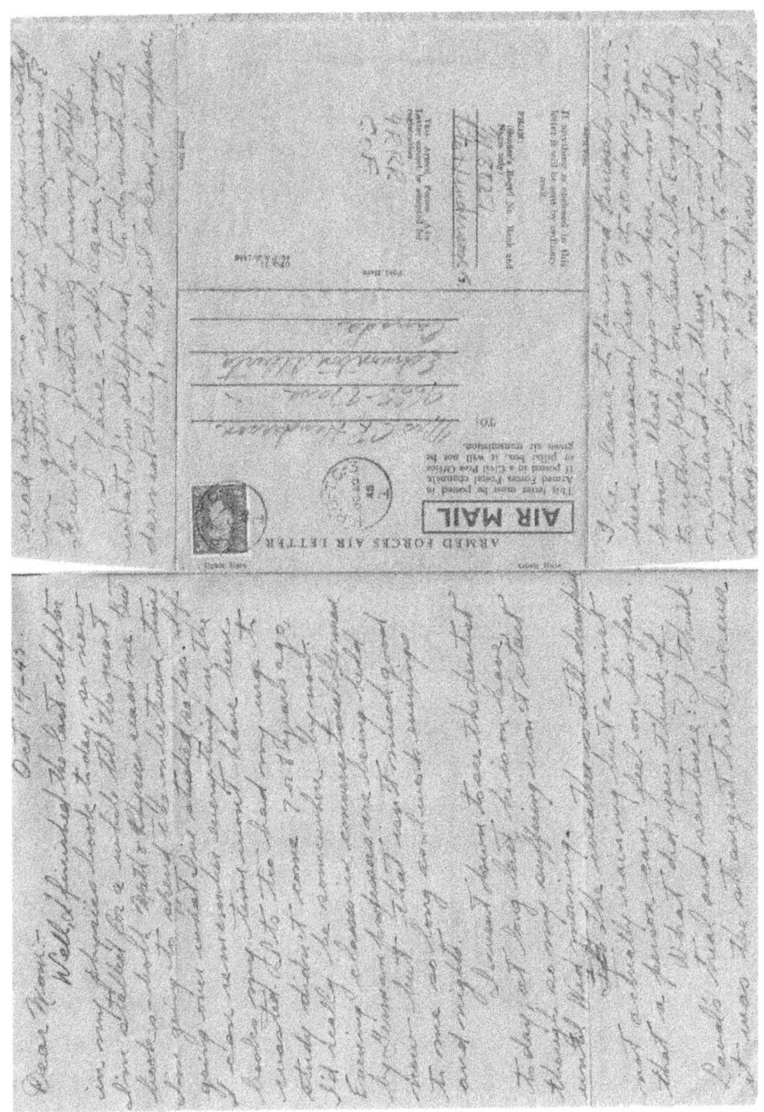

Oct 19, 1945

Dear Mom:

Well, I finished the last chapter in my physics book today, so now I'm stalled for a while till the next books – both math & physics reach me. But I'm going to spend the in between time going over what I've studied so far. If I can remember everything in the books my time won't have been wasted. It's too bad my urge to study didn't come 7 or 8 years ago, I'd really be somewhere by now. Evening classes in conversational German by German professors are being held now but that isn't much good to me so long as I work evenings and nights.

I went down to see the dentist today, at long last, he is on leave though, so my suffering won't start until Wed. morning.

The weather is still dampish, not actually raining but a mist that a person can feel on his face.

What did you think of Laval's trial and sentence? I think it was the strangest trial I've ever read about, no time was wasted in getting rid of him, was it? French justice is funny stuff.

I have a rifle again. I wonder what I'm supposed to do with the darned thing, keep it clean, I suppose.

The leave to Paris and Brussels have been increased from 9 to 10 days, you know these guys up here won't go to either place on leave? It's England or Ireland for them, but not for this Chicken, I'm not going to England for a long time.

Love & Kisses

Grant.

Oct 22, 1945

Dear Mom:

Hi, lady, what's new?

I bought $150 worth of bonds on the installment plan – spread out over 12 months but I decided to leave my gratuities alone. After the plan I decided that it wasn't worth it. Besides I might want the cash when I get discharged and I want to hold on to my bonds if possible.

According to the "Maple Leaf" we are to be released anytime after March 31, depending on how quickly the P.F. can be formed. If that is fact and not some writers pipe dream I think I can pretty well count on starting university next fall, I hope so anyway. I picked up a book on trig the other day so I'm studying up on that while I'm waiting for my next books on algebra & physics. I noticed a store downtown yesterday that sells school equipment so I think I'll invest in a ruler, compass etc. I'm pretty well off when it comes to studying because I do most of my work between supper time & breakfast and I can use the writing room almost every afternoon when it isn't crowded and noisy.

The weather is still wet.

This letter should get to you about Halloween. Remember the Halloween night two years ago? Dad and I went out shooting in the afternoon and got caught in a snow storm on the way back. The old Model "A" was out of timing that day too. Well, I hope we're doing the same thing next fall.

That's all for now.

Love & Kisses

Grant.

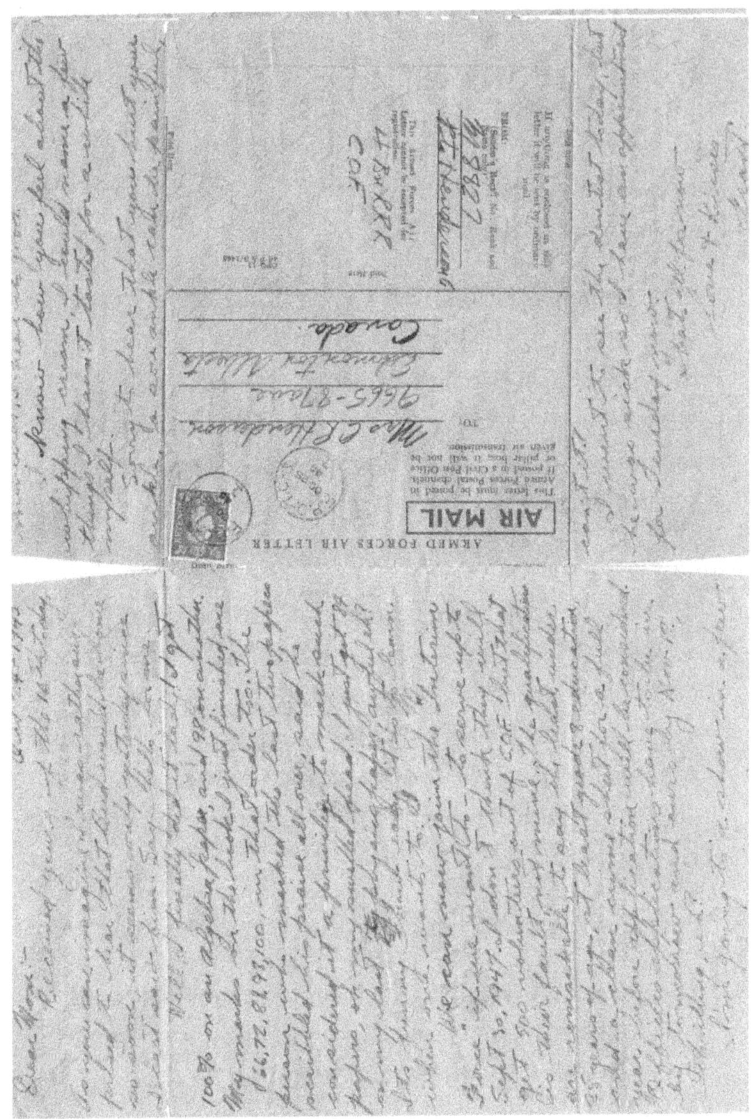

Oct 24, 1945

Dear Mom:

Received yours of the 16th today.

As you can imagine I was rather surprised to hear that Bud would be home so soon, it seems only yesterday since I last saw him. Say hello for me.

Well, I finally did it lady! I got 100% on an Algebra paper and 98 on another. My marks on the book I just finished are 66,72, 88, 98, 100 in that order too. The person who marked the last two papers scribbled his praises all over, said he considered a privilege to mark such papers, oh my swelled head. I just got 84 on my last physics paper, awful eh? It's funny how easy it is to learn when one wants to.

We can now join the" Interim Force" if we want to – to serve up of C.O.F. but that is their fault, not mine. The qualifications are remarkable to say the least, under 25 years of age, at least a grade 8 education and a clean crime sheet for a full year before application will be considered. Officers applications have to be in by tomorrow and ours by Nov 12, thrilling eh?

I'm going to a show in a few minutes, I hear it's good.

I know how you feel about the whipping cream, I could name a few things I haven't tasted for a while myself.

Sorry to hear that you hurt your ankle, a sore ankle can be painful, can't it?

I went to see the dentist today, but he is sick so I have an appointment for Tuesday now.

That's all for now.

Love & Kisses

Grant.

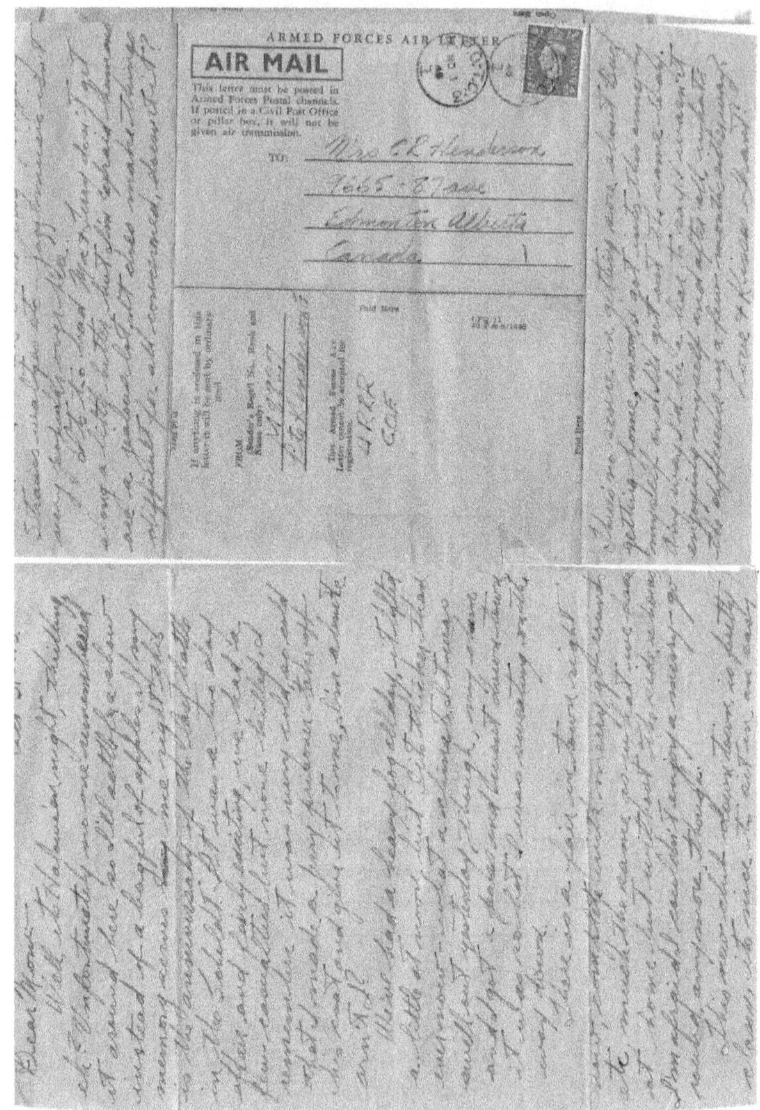

ARMED FORCES AIR LETTER

AIR MAIL

This letter must be posted in Armed Forces Postal channels. If posted in a Civil Post Office or pillar box, it will not be given air transmission.

TO: Mrs C.R. Henderson
7665 - 87 ave
Edmonton Alberta
Canada

Oct 31, 1945

Dear Mom:

Well, it's Halloween night, thrilling eh?" Unfortunately no one remembered it around here so I'll settle for a show instead of a bagful of apples. If my memory serves me right this is the anniversary of our last battle in the Scheldt. It was a two day affair and fairly exciting, we had a few casualties but none killed. I remember it was very cold, so cold that I made a Jerry prisoner take off his coat and give it to me, I'm a brute aren't I?

We've had heavy fog all day, it lifted a little at noon but it's thicker than ever now – what a climate. It was swell out yesterday, though, my chum and I got a pass and went downtown. It was so hot I was sweating on the way down.

There is a fair in town right now, complete with merry go rounds etc, much the same as we have at home but without the side shows. I'm afraid I couldn't enjoy a merry-go-round, anymore, though.

This new club down town is pretty classy, its nice to sit in an easy chair and listen to the Jerrys playing Strauss waltzes etc, jazz music isn't very popular over hear.

It's too bad Ma & Terry don't get along a little better, but I'm afraid humans are a jealous lot, It does make things difficult for all concerned, doesn't it?

There's no sense in getting sore about Bud getting home, mom, I got into this army by myself and I'll get out the same way. Anyway I'd be a liar to say I wasn't enjoying myself and after all what's the difference in a few months either way?

Love & Kisses

Grant

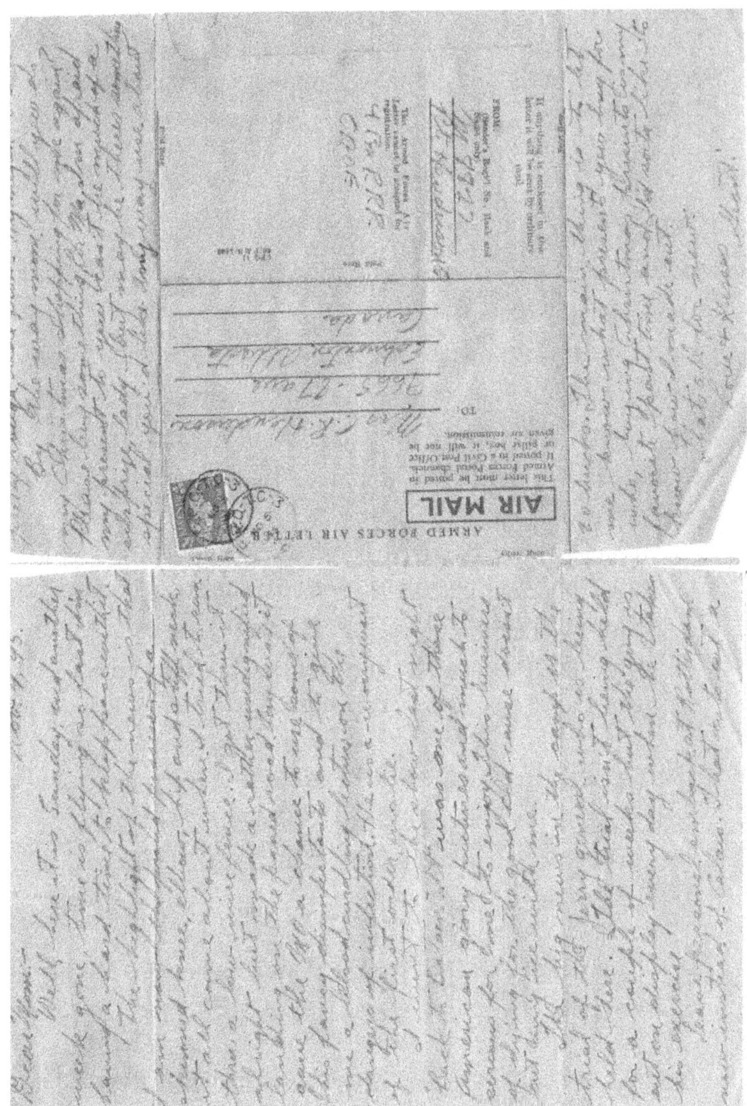

Nov 4, 1945

Dear Mom:

Well, here it is Sunday and another week gone, time is flying so fast I'm having a hard time to keep pace with it.

The highlight of the news is that I am now the proud possessor of a skinned knee, elbow, hip and stiff neck. It all came about when I tried to run thru a low wire fence. I got thru it alright but made a rather undignified landing on the paved road. Anyway it gave the M.O. a chance to use some of his fancy disinfectants and to give me a blood curdling lecture on the dangers of infection. He is a worry wart of the first order, no lie.

I went to the show last night "Back to Batoon" It was one of those American glory pictures and much to serious for me to enjoy. This business of dying for the good old cause doesn't cut any ice with me.

The big news in the camp is the trial of the Jerry general who is being held here. The trial isn't being held for a couple of weeks but the guy is out on display everyday when he takes exercise.

Leave personel embark at Rotterdam now instead of Calais. That cuts out a pretty rough ride from Nymegan to Calais.

By the way mom, will you do my Christmas shopping for me again? Please buy something for Ma. I'm afraid my present to you can't be much of a surprise, lady but may be there's something special you'd like. Anyway use about 20 bucks. The main thing is to let me know what presents you buy for who, buying Christmas presents is my favorite past time and I'd sorta like to know how I made out.

That's all for now.

Love & Kisses

Grant.

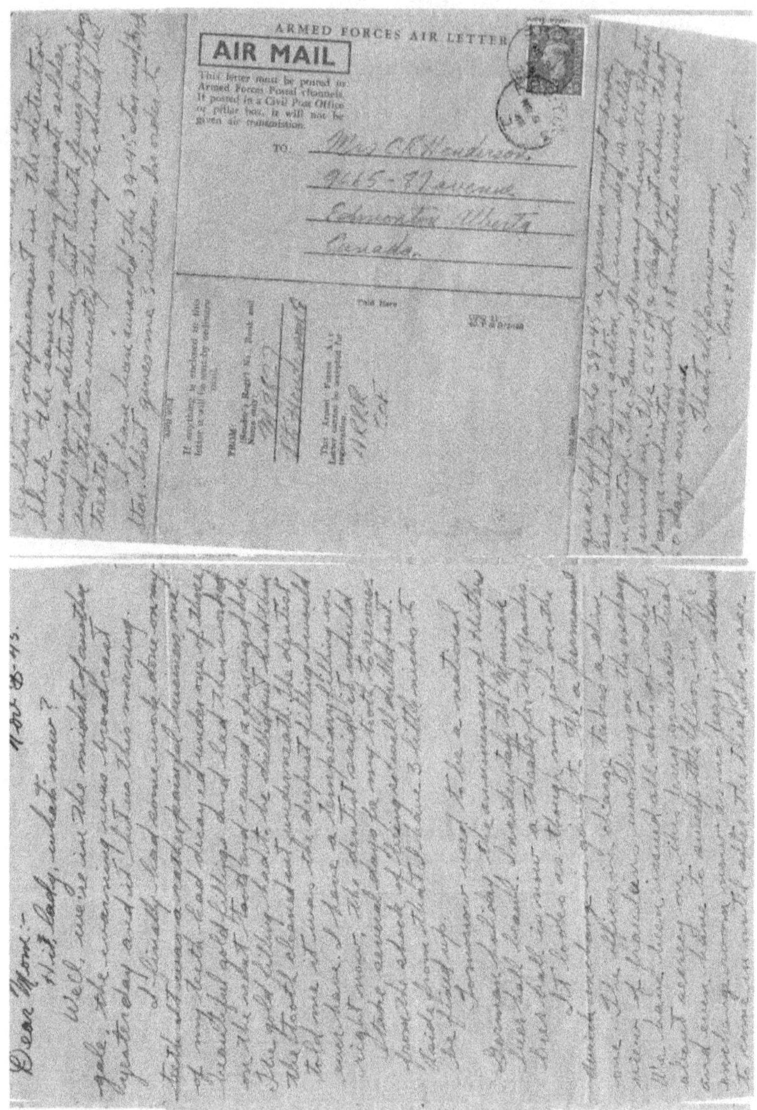

ARMED FORCES AIR LETTER

AIR MAIL

This letter must be posted in Armed Forces Postal Channels. If posted in a Civil Post Office or pillar box, it will not be given air transmission.

TO: Mrs. C.K. Henderson.
9645-87 avenue
Edmonton Alberta
Canada.

If anything is enclosed in this letter it will be sent by ordinary mail.

FROM: (Sender's Regt'l No., Rank and Name only):
M3627(?)
[illegible] Henderson(?)

Dear Mom:- Nov 8-45.

Hi, lady, what's new?

Well, we're in the midst of another gale, the warning was broadcast yesterday and it hit us this morning.

I finally had some work done on my teeth. It was a rather painful business, one of my teeth had decayed under one of those beautiful gold fillings and had then worked on the next tooth and caused a fair sized hole. The gold filling had to be drilled out and then the tooth cleaned out underneath. The dentist told me it was the deepest filling I would ever have. I have a temporary filling in right now. The dentist said it would take several days for my tooth to recover from the shock of being so well drilled out. Aside from that I have 3 little ones to be fixed up.

Tomorrow used to be a national German holiday, the anniversary of Hitler's beer hall brawl. Incidentally the Munich beer hall is now a theatre for the Yanks.

It looks as though my job on the Munich exchange is going to be a permanent one. The officer in charge takes a dim view of [illegible] working on the exchange. We have been issued all sorts of orders about secrecy on this [illegible] trial and even have to sweep the floor in the exchange room now as no [illegible] is allowed to come in until after the trial is over.

[illegible] solitary confinement in the detention block the same as any private soldier undergoing detention but with fewer privileges and that is exactly the way he should be treated.

I have been awarded the 39-45 star with the [illegible] star. That gives me 3 ribbons. In order to qualify for the 39-45 a person must have been [illegible] in action, be wounded, or killed in action. The France, Germany shows the theatre I served in. The CVSM & clasp just shows that I am a volunteer with 18 months service and [illegible] days overseas.

That's all for now mom,
Love & kisses
Grant.

Nov 8, 1945

Dear Mom:

Hi, lady, what's new?

Well, we're in the midst of another gale, the warning was broadcast yesterday and it bit us this morning.

I finally had some work done on my teeth. It was a rather painful business, one of my teeth had decayed under one of those beautiful gold fillings and had then worked on the next tooth and caused a fair sized hole. The gold filling had to be drilled out and then the tooth cleaned out underneath. The dentist told me it was the deepest filling I would ever have. I have a temporary filling in right now, the dentist said it would take several days for my tooth to recover from the shock of being so well drilled out. Aside from that I have 3 little nicks to be fixed up.

Tomorrow used to be a national German holiday the anniversary of the Hitler beer hall brawl. Incidentaly the Munich beer hall is now a theatre for the Yanks.

It looks as though my job on the Aurich exchange is going to be a permanent one. The officer in charge takes a dim view of frauleins working on the exchange. We have been issued all sorts of orders about secrecy on this Jerry general's trial and even have to sweep the floor in the exchange room now as no Jerry is allowed to come in until after the trial. In case you're interested the General is in solitary confinement in the detention block the same as any private soldier undergoing detention but with fewer privileges and that is exactly the way he should be treated.

I have been "awarded" the 39-45 star and Fr/Germ Star. That gives me 3 ribbons. In order to qualify for the 39-45 a person must have six months in action, be wounded or killed in action.
The France, Germany shows the theatre I served in. The CVSM & Clasp just shows that I am a volunteer with 18 months service and 60 days overseas.

That's all for now mom.

Love & Kisses

Grant

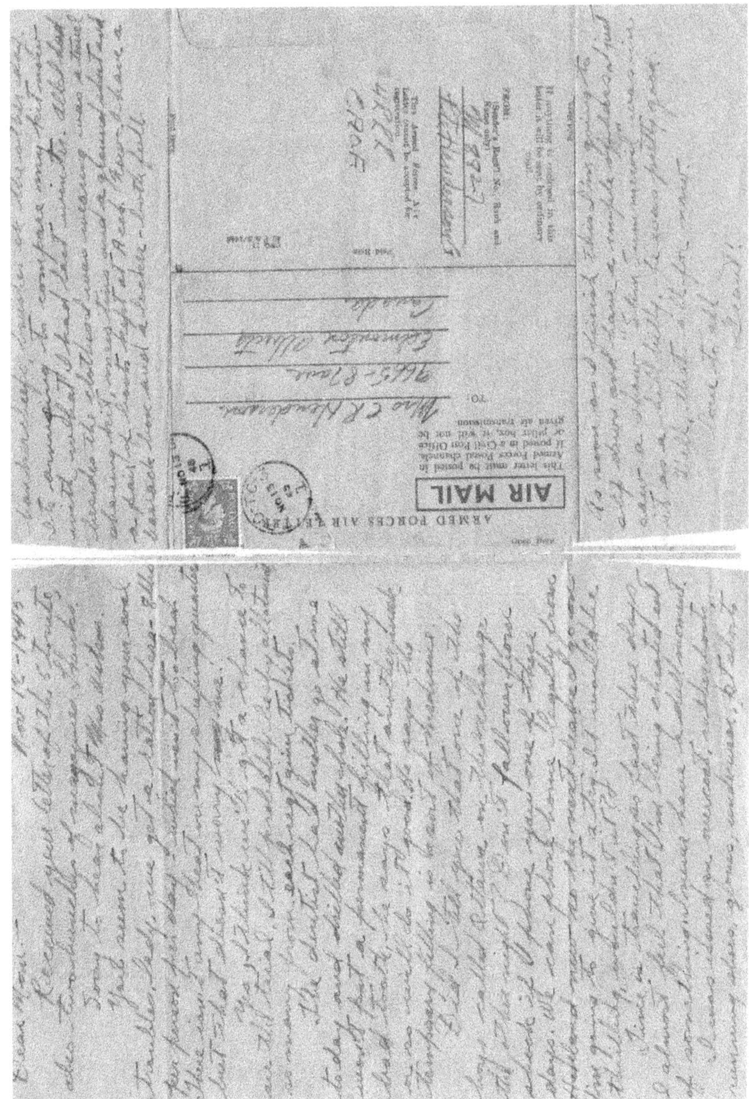

Nov 12, 1945

Dear Mom:

Received you letter of the 5th tonight, also two bunches of magazines. Thanks.

Sorry to hear about Mrs. Wilson.

You seem to be having your coal troubles, lady we get a ration here – 8lbs per person per day – which isn't too bad.

There isn't any heat in my sleeping quarters but that doesn't worry me.

Yes, I think we'll get a chance to see the trial. It'll probably be by allotment, so many from each regt given tickets.

The dentist had another go at me today and drilled another hole. He still won't put a permanent filling in my bad tooth, he says that another week or so will do it good. He says the temporary filling is sort of medicine.

Did I tell you that one of the boys called Ottawa on the exchange the other night? Don't fall over from shock if phone you one of these days. We can phone home legally from Holland now so the next leave I go on I'm going to give it a try. It would be thrilling wouldn't it?

Time is travelling so fast these days, I almost feel that I'm being cheated out of something, I never have a dull moment.

I was issued an overcoat, rubber boots, running shoes, gloves, underwear, pt shorts, handkerchiefs, brushes etc the other day. It's amusing to compare my kit now with what I had last winter. All I had besides the clothes I was wearing was a towel, shaving kit, mess tins and a ground sheet and a pair of boots kept at Aech. Now I have a barrack box and locker – both full.

As soon as I finish this I'm going to slip down and have a couple of beers. I just saw a show "Slim Summervil" was in it as a hill billy, he was pretty good.

Well, that's all for now.

Love to all

Grant

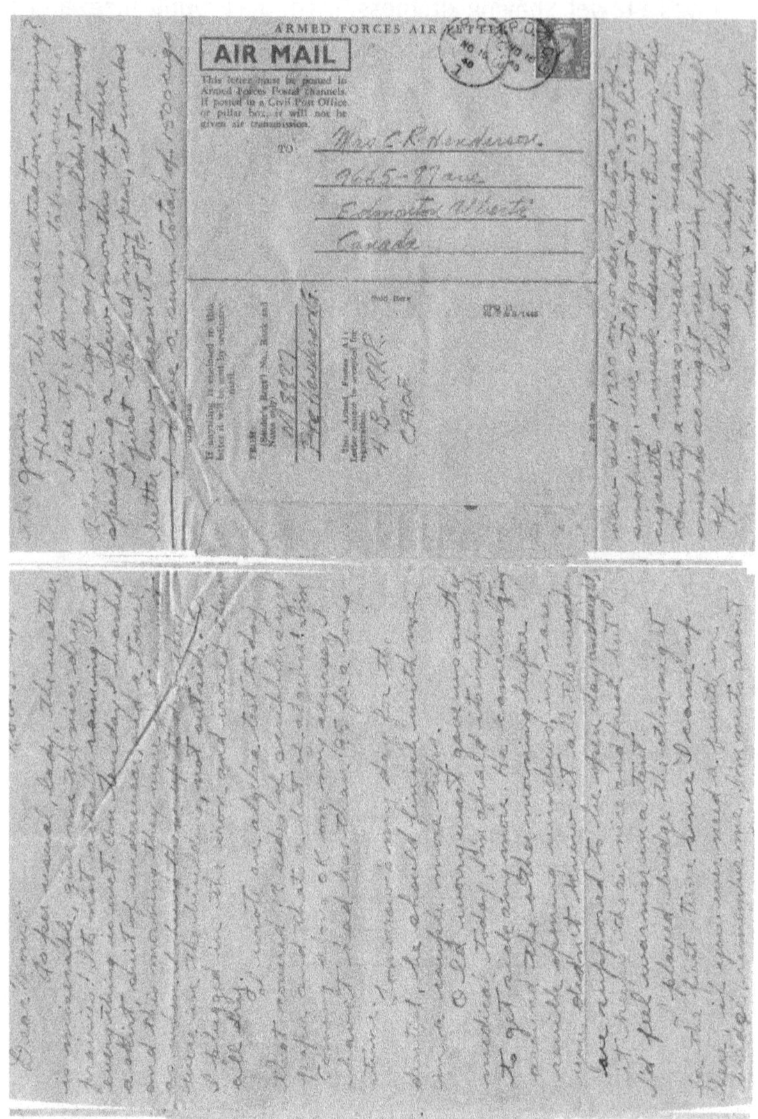

ARMED FORCES AIR LETTER

AIR MAIL

This letter must be posted in Armed Forces Postal channels. If posted in a Civil Post Office or pillar box, it will not be given air transmission.

TO: Mrs C.R. Henderson.
9665-87 ave.
Edmonton Alberta
Canada

Nov 15, 1945

Dear Mom:

As per usual, lady, the weather is miserable, give me the nice dry prairies! It's not actually raining but everything is wet. On Tuesday I washed a shirt, suit of underwear and a towel and this morning they were just as wet as when I hung them up to dry, they were in the building, not outside. So I plugged in the iron and iron them all dry.

I wrote an algebra test today that covered 12 sides of scribbler size paper and that's a lot of algebra! I'm coming along ok on my courses. I haven't had less than 95 for a long time.

Tomorrow's my day for the dentist, he should finish with me in a couple more trips.

Old worry wart gave us another medical today, I'm afraid it's impossible to get sick any more. He came waltzing around the other morning before revile opening windows, in case you didn't know it all the windows are supposed to be open day and night, it keeps the air nice and fresh but I'd feel warmer in a tent.

I played bridge the other night for the first time since I came up here, if you ever need a fourth in bridge, remember me, I'm nuts about the game.

How's the coal situation coming?

I see the army is taking over the Alaska highway, I wouldn't mind spending a few months up there.

I just cleaned my pen, it works better now, doesn't it?

I have a sum total of 1500 cigs now and 1200 on order, that is a lot of smoking, we still get about 150 Limey cigarettes a week issued to us. But in this country a man's wealth is measured in smokes so right now I'm fairly well off.

That all lady

Love & Kisses

Grant

Nov 25-45

Dear Mom—

Received the parcel with the lobster, chile con carne and graph paper many thanks a million. We had the lobster last night, it was swell.

Sorry to hear that Mr Edwards died he was a fine man.

Montgomery paid us a visit this morning, I didn't have the ambition to get out of bed (this is Sunday) so I didn't see him. I've seen him before though and he's just a little fellow.

Some radical changes are going to take place in the next few days. The infantry and in the three regiment of the brigade are all coming under one command. Just how much that is going to affect me individually is hard to say right now.

[illegible] in the recent day, we've had nice weather, there was a white frost last night and the sun is really shining to day, just like a day in September back home. However the weather forecast says snow and rain tomorrow.

I made application for my leave yesterday — to Paris or Copenhagen. I'd just as soon go to Denmark right [illegible] out there. Travelling the army way in cold weather is no [illegible].

I haven't decided what to do about a language opt. I think I'll let it slide for the time being till I get a little more time.

Incidentally our food is much better now, our old cooks were given rifles and put on the parade square and the replacements know a little about cooking.

That's all for now.

Love Grant.

ARMED FORCES AIR LETTER

AIR MAIL

This letter must be posted in Armed Forces Postal channels. If posted in a Civil Post Office or pillar box it will not be given air transmission.

TO: [illegible]
Edmonton Alberta
Canada

If anything is enclosed in this letter it will be sent by ordinary mail.

FROM: (Sender's Regt'l No. Rank and Name only) [illegible]

This Armed Forces Air Letter cannot be accepted for registration.

Nov 25, 1945

Dear Mom:

Received the parcel with the lobster, chili con carne and graph paper mom thanks a million. We had the lobster last night, it was swell.

Sorry to hear that Mr. Edwards died, he was a fine man.

Montgomery paid us a visit this morning, I didn't have the ambition to get out of bed (this is Sunday) so I didn't see him. I've seen him before though he's just a little fellow.

Some radical changes are going to take place in the next few days. The infantry sigs in the three regiments of the brigade are all coming under one command. Just how much that is going to affect us as individual, is hard to say right now.

This is the nicest day we've had in weeks, there was a frost last night and the sun is really shinning today, just like a day in September back home. However the weather forecast says snow and rain tomorrow.

I made an application for my leave yesterday – to Paris or Copenhagen. I'd just as soon go to Denmark right now, there's a lot less travelling to get there. Travelling the army way in cold weather is no hell.

I haven't decided what to do about a language yet. I think I'll let it slide for the time being till I get a little more time.

Incidentally our food is much better now, our old cooks were given rifles and put on the parade square and the replacements know a little cooking.

That's all for now

Love

Grant

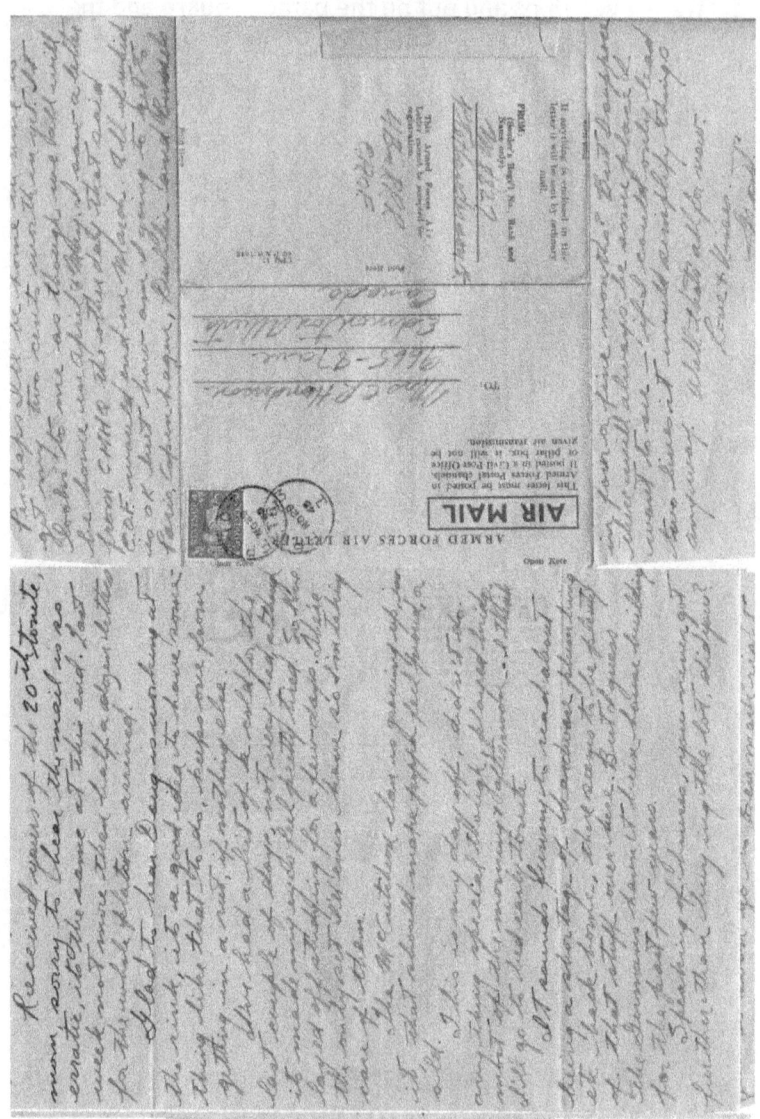

Received yours of the 20th tonite, mom, sorry to hear the mail is so erratic, its the same at this end. Last week not more than half a dozen letters for the whole platoon arrived.

Glad to hear Doug is working at the rink, its a good idea to have something like that to do, keeps one from getting in a rut, if nothing else.

We've had a bit of a cold for the last couple of days, not very bad, altho it made my eyes feel pretty tired. So I've layed off studying for a few days. These the only set I'll ever have so I'm taking care of them.

The McCutcheon clan is growing up, isn't it. That should make pappa feel proud, & old.

This is my day off, didn't do anything special though, played bridge most of the morning & afternoon – I think I'll go to bed early tonite.

It sounds funny to read about there being a shortage of hardware, plumbing etc. back home, there seems to be plenty of that stuff over here. But I guess the Germans haven't been house building for the past few years.

Speaking of houses, you never got further than buying the lot, did you?

Perhaps I'll be home in time to get my two cents worth in yet. It looks to me as though we'll still be home in April & May. I saw a letter from CMHQ the other day that said C.O.F. would end in March. All of which is ok but how am I going to get to Paris, Copenhagen, Berlin and Brussels in four or five months? But I suppose there will always be some place I want to see – if I could only lead two lives it would simplify things anyway.

Well that's all for now.

Love & kisses.

[signature]

ARMED FORCES AIR LETTER

AIR MAIL

This letter must be posted in Armed Forces Postal channels. If posted in a Civil Post Office or pillar box, it will not be given air transmission.

TO: Mrs. C. P. Henderson
9665-87 Ave.
Edmonton Alberta
Canada

If anything is enclosed in this letter it will be sent by ordinary mail.

FROM: (Sender's Regt'l No. Rank and Name only)
M 8827 [illegible]

The Armed Forces Air Letter cannot be accepted for registration.

Nov 28, 1945

Dear Mom:

Received yours if the 20th tonight, mom, sorry to hear the mail is so erratic, it's the same at this end. Last week not more than half a dozen letters for the whole platoon arrived.

Glad to hear Doug is working at the rink, it's a good idea to have something like that to do, keeps one from getting in a rut, if nothing else.

I've had a bit of a cold for the last couple of days, not very bad, although it made my eyes feel pretty tired. So I've layed off studying for a few days. The're the only set I'll ever have so I'm taking care of them.

The McCutcheron clan is growing up, isn't it that should make poppa feel proud or old.

This is my day off, didn't do anything special though, played bridge most of the morning & afternoon. I think I'll go to bed early tonite.

It sounds funny to read about there being a shortage of hardware plumbing etc back home, there seems to be plenty of that stuff over here. But I guess the Germans haven't been house building for the past few years.

Speaking of houses, you never got further than buying the lot, did you? Perhaps I'll be home in time to get my two cents worth in yet. It looks to me as though we all will be home in April & May. I saw a letter from CMHQ the other day that said C.O.F would end in March. All of which is ok but how am I going to get to Paris, Copenhagen, Dublin and

Brussels in four or five months? But I suppose there will always be some place I want to see – if I could only lead two lives it would simplify things anyway.

Well that's all for now.

Love & Kisses

Grant.

Grandfathers have a unique role in our lives and Grant Henderson has fulfilled that role in a unique way. He is, to me, the archetypal proud grandfather, I could not imagine how our lives would have developed without him there.

My Aunt Barbara has done an extraordinary service to our family in collecting and publishing my grandfather's letters home from the front of World Ward II. Reading them has been a delight and have imparted on me two lessons that I will carry forth and hopefully pass along to those that come after me.

All my life, I have only known Grant Henderson in his role as my grandfather. I know that might seem like an obvious thing to say, but these letters have, for one, revealed a depth to my grandfather that I previously haven't been privy to.

He is a quiet, intelligent and cheerful man. Despite his unassuming demeanor, has been an eminently important presence in the lives of his grandchildren. The resilient impression of him that I retain from my childhood was of him as an intent and dutiful listener, delivering sparing but insightful wisdom, teaching us about our own history and the history that surrounds us. Photos from the same time show a man exceedingly proud of both his children and grandchildren.

That's why I value this collection of letters so much. Since my grandfather has fulfilled such a distinct and important role in my life, one that no one else could fill, it wasn't until I read these letters that I came to realize, as odd as it might sound, that my grandfather was once a young man who was still trying to understand the world around him and how he fit into it. To me, my grandfather has always been someone whom I depended on to help me understand the world, my place in the context of history and how my actions would affect others. These letters show a young man of vulnerable intelligence reassuring his mother despite being obviously worried about his own fate, as anyone would be. To see my grandfather as someone in need of mentorship rather than someone who dispenses it humanizes him in the best way; it lets us know that we grow into the indispensable mentor in the lives of those that come after us, that no one is born with it. That we all feel the uncertainty of the future and that we all must work before we are equipped to serve the generations that follow us is a wonderful lesson from my grandfather.

The second lesson is somewhat more obvious, but still vitally important. Reading these letters, written by a living figure in my life, is a stark reminder of the selfless sacrifice that my grandfather and the rest of his generation, both at home and on the front, made so that we could live the lives we do.

My grandfather is clearly proud of his time as a soldier in one of the most important events of human history. That is, he is quietly proud of it. He has kept his medals and a dress uniform and attends the odd ceremony when he has the opportunity, or so my grandmother tells me. If you bring it up in discussion with him, he will calmly relay a memory or two from World War II, but he never had us gather around to hear war stories or tales of glory from the Great War. In fact, my grandfather has, more than any book or film ever could, helped us understand that what his generation did in World War II should be treated with thoughtful reflection and a mind to honour what those who fought have given us.

None of us as grandchildren have had to fight for our country. We have been able to travel abroad, have our own children, educate ourselves and pursue our passions, sometimes on the very lands that my grandfather was stationed on. As clichéd as it may sound, we owe that to our grandfather and the brave men and women that made up the war effort.

These letters are not the dramatized depictions of war that we see on TV, read in books or celebrate in films. More than anything, they describe a young man happily doing his part for his country, but concerned, as anyone might be, that he won't make it home from the fighting. They are the words of a young man that doesn't know that what he is doing will ultimately be one of the most important things anyone in his family would ever do.

Despite pouring over these letters, I can't imagine what it would feel like to walk through a war-torn continent every day. Thankfully, because of my grandfather and those who fought along with him, I never will.

So, from your grandchildren, we offer a heartfelt thank you that only a grandfather could earn.

Sincerely,

Chris Henderson

www.ingramcontent.com/pod-product-compliance
Lightning Source LLC
Chambersburg PA
CBHW032032150426
43194CB00006B/242

* 9 7 8 0 9 8 6 7 6 2 4 0 6 *